Occidentalism

Edinburgh Studies in Modern Arabic Literature
Series Editor: Rasheed El-Enany

Writing Beirut: Mappings of the City in the Modern Arabic Novel
Samira Aghacy

Autobiographical Identities in Contemporary Arab Literature
Valerie Anishchenkova

The Iraqi Novel: Key Writers, Key Texts
Fabio Caiani and Catherine Cobham

Sufism in the Contemporary Arabic Novel
Ziad Elmarsafy

Gender, Nation, and the Arabic Novel: Egypt 1892–2008
Hoda Elsadda

The Unmaking of the Arab Intellectual: Prophecy, Exile and the Nation
Zeina G. Halabi

Post-War Anglophone Lebanese Fiction: Home Matters in the Diaspora
Syrine Hout

Prophetic Translation: the Making of Modern Egyptian Literature
Maya I. Kesrouany

Nasser in the Egyptian Imaginary
Omar Khalifah

Conspiracy in Modern Egyptian Literature
Benjamin Koerber

War and Occupation in Iraqi Fiction
Ikram Masmoudi

Literary Autobiography and Arab National Struggles
Tahia Abdel Nasser

The Arab Nahdah*: The Making of the Intellectual and Humanist Movement*
Abdulrazzak Patel

Blogging from Egypt: Digital Literature, 2005–2016
Teresa Pepe

Occidentalism: Literary Representations of the Maghrebi Experience of the East–West Encounter
Zahia Smail Salhi

Sonallah Ibrahim: Rebel with a Pen
Paul Starkey

Minorities in the Contemporary Egyptian Novel
Mary Youssef

edinburghuniversitypress.com/series/smal

Occidentalism

Literary Representations of the Maghrebi Experience of the East–West Encounter

Zahia Smail Salhi

EDINBURGH
University Press

Edinburgh University Press is one of the leading university presses in the UK. We publish academic books and journals in our selected subject areas across the humanities and social sciences, combining cutting-edge scholarship with high editorial and production values to produce academic works of lasting importance. For more information visit our website: edinburghuniversitypress.com

© Zahia Smail Salhi, 2019, 2021

First published in hardback by Edinburgh University Press 2019

Edinburgh University Press Ltd
The Tun – Holyrood Road
12 (2f) Jackson's Entry
Edinburgh EH8 8PJ

Typeset in 11/15 Adobe Garamond by
Servis Filmsetting Ltd, Stockport, Cheshire

A CIP record for this book is available from the British Library

ISBN 978 0 7486 4580 0 (hardback)
ISBN 978 1 4744 5322 6 (paperback)
ISBN 978 0 7486 4581 7 (webready PDF)
ISBN 978 1 4744 5323 3 (epub)

The right of Zahia Smail Salhi to be identified as author of this work has been asserted in accordance with the Copyright, Designs and Patents Act 1988 and the Copyright and Related Rights Regulations 2003 (SI No. 2498).

Contents

Series Editor's Foreword	vi
Acknowledgements	ix
Introduction	1
1 The Maghreb and the Occident: Towards the Construction of an Occidentalist Discourse	10
2 From the Faraway Orient to the Reclaimed Occident: French Civilisation, Religious Conversion and Cultural Assimilation	37
3 The Occident and the Barbary Corsairs: Pre-colonial Maghrebi Encounters with the Occident	71
4 'La France, c'est moi': Love and Infatuation with the Occident	93
5 The Occident and the Oriental Woman: Rescuing the Oriental Man's Victim?	125
6 The New Maghrebi Woman and the Occident: From Occidentophilia to Ambivalence	154
7 The End of the Chimera: Disillusion, Alienation and Ambivalence	188
Afterword	216
Notes	220
Bibliography	252
Index	265

Series Editor's Foreword

Edinburgh Studies in Modern Arabic Literature is a new and unique series that will, it is hoped, fill in a glaring gap in scholarship in the field of modern Arabic literature. Its dedication to Arabic literature in the modern period, that is, from the nineteenth century onwards, is what makes it unique among series undertaken by academic publishers in the English-speaking world. Individual books on modern Arabic literature in general or aspects of it have been and continue to be published sporadically. Series on Islamic studies and Arab/Islamic thought and civilisation are not in short supply either in the academic world, but these are far removed from the study of Arabic literature qua literature, that is, imaginative, creative literature as we understand the term when, for instance, we speak of English literature or French literature. Even series labelled 'Arabic/Middle Eastern Literature' make no period distinction, extending their purview from the sixth century to the present, and often including non-Arabic literatures of the region. This series aims to redress the situation by focusing on the Arabic literature and criticism of today, stretching its interest to the earliest beginnings of Arab modernity in the nineteenth century.

The need for such a dedicated series, and generally for the redoubling of scholarly endeavour in researching and introducing modern Arabic literature to the Western reader, has never been stronger. Among activities and events heightening public, let alone academic, interest in all things Arab, and not least Arabic literature, are the significant growth in the last decades of the translation of contemporary Arab authors from all genres, especially fiction, into English; the higher profile of Arabic literature internationally since the award of the Nobel Prize in Literature to Naguib Mahfouz in 1988; the growing number of Arab authors living in the Western diaspora and writing both in English and Arabic; the adoption of such authors and others by mainstream, high-circulation publishers, as opposed to the academic publishers of the past; the establishment of prestigious prizes, such as the International Prize for Arabic Fiction (IPAF) (the Arabic Booker), run by the Man Booker Foundation, which brings huge publicity to the shortlist and winner every year, as well as translation contracts into English and other languages; and, very recently, the events of the Arab Spring. It is therefore part of the ambition of this series that it will increasingly address a wider reading public beyond its natural territory of students and researchers in Arabic and world literature. Nor indeed is the academic readership of the series expected to be confined to specialists in literature in the light of the growing trend for interdisciplinarity, which increasingly sees scholars crossing field boundaries in their research tools and coming up with findings that equally cross discipline borders in their appeal.

This monograph fills a glaring gap in studies of modern literature of North Africa. The theme of the East–West encounter in Arabic literature, important as it is and dating back in Arabic writing to the early nineteenth century (specifically from 1798, the year of Napoleon's invasion of Egypt) and continuing with unabated interest until today – this theme has remarkably remained until recently little studied, except in the odd journal article or incidental treatment in a literary history or general genre study. My own monograph, *Arab Representations of the Occident: East–West Encounters in Arabic Fiction* (2006), went some way towards redressing this deficiency in scholarship. I recall while researching the subject how I gradually discovered the massiveness of the field. Despite stringent and restrictive criteria of selection, I ended up studying fifty-four authors from across the Arab world and hundreds of works spanning a two-century period. I am giving this detail in order to come to the point most relevant to the monograph in hand. The vastness of the subject and immensity of primary sources meant that I had to make a difficult decision, namely, to limit myself to the Arab east or *mashriq* and exclude the *maghrib* or North Africa. While my exclusion was dictated by practical considerations, it was certainly aided by other substantial factors, particularly the historical and cultural specificity of the North African experience that distinguishes it from that of the *mashriq*, as well as the de facto disciplinary division that exists in academia between studies of the Middle East on the one hand, and North Africa on the other. The current volume does exactly what my own study has fallen short of: to extend the investigation of representations of the theme of East–West encounters to North African literature, and particularly that of Algeria as a case study. The relevance of this book acquires more immediacy in view of the dramatic political changes that have been taking place on the ground in North Africa since the Tunisian revolution of 2010 and its widespread regional repercussions. Those events make the need even more pressing today for such studies as this, which trace back the historical and cultural encounter to its origins and seek to represent the region's view of the western other by reversing, so to speak, the Orientalist coin which normally only showed the colonialist European view of the Arab.

Professor Rasheed El-Enany, Series Editor,
Emeritus Professor of Modern Arabic Literature,
University of Exeter

Acknowledgements

I would like to extend my thanks to everyone who supported me through the writing of this book. I am especially grateful for the support of my family and I hope they will understand why I could not be among them for the last few summers.

My gratitude goes to Professor Rasheed El-Enany, the series editor, for his patience and understanding and for his invaluable comments on the first draft of this book. I hope my Maghrebi voice will succeed in joining his Mashriqi voice in his inspirational *Arab Representations of Occident*, to draw a fuller picture of the encounter between the Arab world and the Occident.

To my late father, Smail Si Idir N'Bouassem I dedicate this book

Introduction

From Orientalism to Occidentalism

Edward Said defines Orientalism as 'a style of thought based upon an ontological and epistemological distinction made between "the Orient" and "the Occident"'.[1] The literature thus produced takes the distinction between East and West/Orient and Occident as the dividing line between Orientalism and Occidentalism. While in Said's view 'Orientalism derives from a particular closeness experienced between Britain and France and the Orient,'[2] Occidentalism derives from this same closeness. He elucidates, 'Out of that closeness whose dynamic is enormously productive even if it always demonstrates the comparatively greater strength of the Occident . . . comes the large body of texts I call Orientalist.'[3] The same relationship also produced, and continues to so produce, a considerable amount of writings by Arab authors, whom I call here 'the Orientals', on their encounter with the Occident, which I term 'Occidentalist literature'. This same literature is also called 'colonial' or 'post-colonial', but what I would specifically call Occidentalist literature is that corpus of works whose main concern is the portrayal of the Occident and the experience of the East–West encounter from the Orientals' perspective. The authors of these works engage with the occident by speaking to it in a direct or an indirect manner. Such encounters may have taken place in the 'Orient' during the colonial period or in the Occident, both during the colonial and the post-colonial periods.

It is, in fact, this part of the relationship which Said's *Orientalism* did not engage with. His focus was solely on the hegemonic Western popular and academic discourse of the Orient, providing an analysis of the relationship between European colonialism and the intertwined discursive formations constructing the European experience of the Orient. The corpus of literature and other output which the Orientals created in response to these discursive formations did not receive Said's attention, and while he scrutinised European portrayals of the Orient as meaning the Middle East, consisting of Egypt and the Arab and Muslim countries East of Egypt, the Maghreb was totally overlooked by Said in *Orientalism*.

This view is shared by Robert Irwin in his book, *For Lust of Knowing: the Orientalists and their Enemies*, which he wrote as a criticism of Said's *Orientalism*. Irwin argues that Said used the word 'Orientalism' in a very restrictive sense as referring to those who travelled, studied or wrote about the Arab world, while in reality the term should be extended to include Persia, India, Indonesia and the Far East as A. J. Arberry did in his book on *British Orientalists* in 1943.

Irwin's view, however, reveals that there are many Orientalisms. Since Said's critique is an Arab's response to the Orientalists, covering other regions outside of the Arab world would therefore be beyond his area of interest. I do, however, agree with Irwin's observation concerning Said's exclusion of the Maghreb: 'he [Said] excluded consideration of North Africa west of Egypt. I cannot guess why he excluded North Africa.'[4] Edward Said was not the first scholar to exclude the Maghreb from the study of the Arab world or the Middle East. In most studies conducted on the so-called 'Arab world' as one uniform region, be they in the humanities or the social sciences, the Maghreb is often excluded. In literary studies for example, very few would include one or two authors from the Maghreb and even so these authors would be approached in a somehow cautionary manner not totally engaging them in the general study of the literature of the Arab world.

This, indeed, is symptomatic of the sidelining of this region, which is not a novel phenomenon, but one which goes back to the Golden ages of the Islamic civilisation when this region was defined as the 'Maghrib' meaning the West/Occident, as a separate part from the 'Mashriq' meaning the East/Orient, which was considered the mainland Arab and Muslim world.

But then again, I would not necessarily see this as a fundamental methodological fault. On the contrary, grouping the study of the Maghreb as part of the study of the Mashriq/ the Middle East would be erroneous due to the fundamental differences which exist between these two parts of what we know as 'the Arab world' – a term Rasheed El-Enany persuasively describes as loose and unscientific. He explains that while the 'Arab world is made up of Arabic-speaking communities that indeed share a common enough culture to justify the use of such a term . . . significant distinctions exist, particularly in terms of socio-political and intellectual development',[5] for instance an Arab from Egypt enjoys a distinctively different culture from a Moroccan Arab who, most of the time while they declare their belonging to the Arab world they certainly practice their culture in a different manner and oftentimes may speak Berber/ Thamazighth as their mother tongue while at the same time being part of the Arabic speaking world. Therefore, focusing on the study of the Maghreb as a separate entity is a means of averting this tradition of overlooking the fundamental differences which exist between the Maghreb and the Mashriq. In consequence, the experience of the East–West encounter is shown to be very different from the perspective of the Maghreb from that of the Mashriq, as will be demonstrated throughout the pages of this book.

The study of the encounter with the Occident from the perspective of the Maghreb preceded Said's *Orientalism* by decades. The complex method of Orientalising the Maghreb received the attention of Albert Memmi who, in his seminal study *The Coloniser and the Colonized*, first published in 1957, pondered the psychological effects of colonialism on both the coloniser and the colonised. His attention was also given to the mechanisms deployed by each party to portray the other, with the colonising Occidental as the powerful party often imposing their own portrayals of both Orientals and Occidentals to the point of resulting in a process of self-Orientalisation from the part of the colonised. Deeply infatuated with the superiority and power of the Occident, the colonised end up not only believing in the images and discourses created by the former to orientalise the Maghreb and its native people, but also engaged in a process of seeing their own people through the lens of the Occident, as will be seen in the literature produced in the first half of the twentieth century by the first generation of native Maghrebi intellectuals. While this phenomenon is in effect not surprising, due to the colonial condition, it is hardly comprehensible to see post-colonial authors engaging in self-Orientalism.

Occidentalism and Self-Orientalism

The way the image of the 'Other' is constructed and depicted often betrays part of the 'Self', for the 'Other' is often imagined as the reverse image of the 'Self' and the exploration of the Other and of the Self are convolutedly bound together. While Nicholas Thomas explains how 'the capacities of populations to impose and act upon their constructions of others has been highly variable throughout history',[6] Carrier, who agrees with this view, rightly argues that 'Westerners have been more powerful and hence better able than people elsewhere to construct and impose images of alien societies as they see fit'.[7] Not only so, but Western power can often also shape self-conceptions and make the Orientals believe that the constructed stereotypes of the Orient and the Orientals are true. This is especially the case when the Oriental is under colonial domination. Jean Amrouche, an Algerian poet, author and critic whose parents converted to Christianity and whose upbringing was shaped by Catholicism and French education, confirms that: 'the colonised sees himself primarily as he would be seen by his coloniser.'[8] A good example of this is the way colonised intellectuals not only strive to adopt European looks and manners but also saw their own people through the colonial lens, thus reproducing the images expected of them by the Occident in its very language. The colonised intellectual not only shapes him/herself to fit the expected prototype but goes further to reach the phase of seeing through the eyes of the coloniser and producing images and discourse which could be part of the mainstream cultural production of the colonial order. Looking back at the early Maghrebi novels written at the beginning of the twentieth century mainly by Algerian authors who paved the way to this tradition for their neighbours, one is struck by their faithful imitation of the Colonial French novel, both in style and content. This tendency was especially cultivated through the collaborative novels written by French Orientalist authors along with their native Algerian disciples. Examples include *Khadra, danseuse des Ouled Nail* (*Khadra, the Ouled Nail danser*), by Étienne Dinet and Slimane Ben Brahim Baamer (1926),[9] *La tente noire, roman saharien* (*The Black Tent, a Saharan Novel*) by Saad Ben Ali and René Pottier (1933),[10] and many others.

These French authors, who subscribed to a new literary current known as Les Algérianistes, were keen to launch a francophone literature in Algeria, a literature which would confirm the country's total assimilation of French language and culture while at the same time contributing to and endorsing the flow of exotic images created and propagated by the French Orientalists. In this, the native authors internalised the Orientalist representations of the Maghreb and its people, and portrayed them in terms very similar to French European accounts of the region and its native inhabitants, as enthralling, exotic and mystical, but at the same time outmoded, dangerous, crippled by severe and barbaric customs and therefore in need of being saved from their barbarity.

For this reason this literature has been ignored, largely marginalised and therefore severely understudied. For French critics, it is seen as an odd literature which does not deserve critical attention. For Maghrebi critics, it is perceived as a literature that does not deserve to be classified as Maghrebi because it did not oppose colonialism. They considered its authors as traitors and 'domestic animals of colonialism' on account of their subservient attitude towards French colonial administration, but also for seeing their own people through colonial eyes and therefore contributing to the construction of the colonial's misleading representations of the Maghreb and its people.

All the same, these works constitute an invaluable heritage, and one emblematic of the circumstances that gave birth to it. Therefore, it is an important task to rehabilitate them regardless of the way they were received at their time of production, especially when a radically anticolonial literature was born in the 1950s across the Maghreb and accompanied the liberation project of its countries all the way to their political independence.

In the post-colonial era, however, while this early literature continues to be rejected and largely disregarded as exotic, didactic and lacking in political correctness, self-Orientalisation became endemic in some Maghrebi and Middle Eastern countries, where tourism strived to respond to and satisfy Western phantasms and the thirst for exotica.

While Edward Said's work reflected on the mechanisms used by the Orientalists to exoticise the Orient and everything it contains, he did not engage with the possibility of the Orientals to believe in the images created by the Occident about themselves to the point of adopting them as truth.

In the post-colonial Maghrebi fashion industry, Orientalist paintings and photographs have become a source and reference for recreating 'Oriental' Maghrebi costumes and interior decors both in private homes and hospitality establishments.

The same is true in the case of post-colonial Maghrebi literature. The works of Moroccan novelist Tahar Ben Jelloun (1944–), for instance, and more specifically his two novels *The Sand Child* (1985)[11] and its sequel *The Sacred Night* (1987),[12] confirm the possibility of the Orientals being trapped in a process of self-Orientalisation and self-Exoticisation. While such authors portray their country and people in a manner that pleases the Occidental reader who continues to believe in the enchanting Orient, such works also either totally disfigure and alienate the Orientals whom they depict or encourage a whole process of working towards the replication of these Orientalist clichés to attract the Occidental reader and tourist. In the case of Ben Jelloun it is revealing that it was not until the publication of *The Sand Child*, immediately followed by *The Sacred Night* which together present a searing allegorical portrait of the Maghreb that he was accorded extensive praise and appreciation, with the second text being awarded the prestigious French literary prize *Prix Goncourt* in 1993.

Furthermore, unlike his other works, which mainly focus on the problems experienced by the Maghrebi migrant community in France, these two novels were translated into forty languages. This is also indicative that the Occidental thirst for the exotic continues to shape the created images of the Orient, this time not by Orientalist authors, artists and photographers but by the Orientals themselves in order to satiate their Occidental consumers.

In his prolific oeuvre, Moroccan novelist and philosopher Abdelkebir Khatibi (1938–2009) insists on the Maghreb as a plural space that is complex both culturally and linguistically due to its similarly complex history and geographical location. By virtue of its location at the nexus of the Orient and the Occident, making it at one time in its history the Occident of the Orient and at another the Orient of the Occident, the Maghreb was, and continues to be, a space of crossing over rather than one for grounding!

A Contribution to Maghrebi Studies

Although the initial aim of this book was to cover the whole Maghreb (Morocco, Algeria, Tunisia), from colonial to post-colonial times, it subsequently engaged in more depth with the works written by Algerian authors who dominated the Maghrebi literary scene in the first four decades of the twentieth century. In addition to works written by Algerian authors, the book also explored works written by European authors who began writing about their newly found African Orient as soon as they took possession of it. On the one hand this allowed me to explore the ways the Occident as coloniser created and represented the Orient and the Orientals, and on the other hand the manner in which the latter depicted their encounter with the Occident and the Occidentals, resulting in a representation of the Orient–Occident encounter from both sides of the relationship, bringing into the discussion characters and voices drawn from both the Oriental and the Occidental divides.

This discussion was animated by a wide array of discourses and narratives, and although the main focus of this book are the literary representations of the Maghrebi encounter with the Occident it also incorporates a good selection of primary sources including popular poetry, autobiography, political polemic, letters to the Occident (i.e., to Europeans) with recipients including politicians, authors, teachers or just friends and colonialist accounts of the conquest, amongst others.

Focusing in more depth on the early period (pre-1945) of the East–West encounter in the context of the Maghreb, has allowed me to explore a literary corpus often sidelined for its ideological content, and to rehabilitate it as an important part of Maghrebi literature. The few attempts at discussing these works, which took place after the publication of my first book, *Politics and Poetics in the Algerian Novel* (1999), have generally failed to engage with them in considerable breadth or depth. The novels in question are extremely rare and in some cases they have been printed in as few as 50 copies. Searching for them was close to a treasure hunt and bringing them into discussion with depth is my way to rehabilitate them and to share them with the academic community.

While for many decades this literature has been marginalised for political considerations due to the fact that its authors were in most cases the sons and daughters of the native aristocracy of Caïds and Aghas, who collaborated with colonial France to safeguard their interests, this sidelining resulted in the disregard of a wealth of discourse which reveals this early encounter like no other source.

Speaking of this first generation of French-educated native intellectuals Augustin Berque[13] criticised them for their 'unconscious mimicry' and their endeavour to look like Frenchmen through a total physical transformation which was preceded by an intellectual transformation. Their first stepping stone to the world of the Occident was of course the French school where they learnt to speak the French language as a vital tool which allowed them to read Occidental books and to travel through the world of European literature and culture. Having adopted this heritage as their own, they felt as though they belonged to the Occident while they also had their roots deeply anchored in the Orient among their own people, the Orientals. This position was problematised by the colonial factor and the dichotomy between the ideals of the French civilising mission and the lived reality in the colony, where the ravenousness of the European settlers intercepted all government projects for the bettering of the life of the colonised Orientals.

This condition was also exacerbated by the resentment of the majority of the natives who, after decades of armed resistance and rebellions, had to assent to their position of the defeated, and therefore ruthlessly exploited and dominated, Orientals whose living conditions had severely deteriorated as a result of land expropriation and the absence of social welfare. Then again, the vast majority of the authors from the pre-1945 period did not come from this social background. Their fathers were the allies of France who 'had a stake in the colonial system as native administrators and well-to-do landowners.'[14] Augustin Berque explains how such fathers worked towards the erasure of the colonial factor which resulted in a loss of memory of the French invasion among the first generation of native intellectuals.[15] Sending their children to French schools only deepened this amnesia and made the neophyte pupils think of themselves as sons and daughters of the Occident when the latter only treated them as its adoptive and not as its biological children. This condition of the adoptive children of the Occident created a mass of contradictions in the minds of this first generation of native intellectuals and authors who, while they knew they were the privileged minute minority of civilised Orientals, were keen to see their own people enter an evolutionary process to become civilised and cross the threshold into the world of the Occident. This dream was made hostage of their people's resistance to France's assimilationist project which targeted the total effacement of their cultural and religious identity, but most importantly the constant sabotage efforts of the European settlers who did not wish to see the natives other than a mass of illiterate people good for exploitation.

These two positions accentuated the feelings of loss experienced by the native intellectuals as they found themselves constantly straddling the worlds of the Orient and the Occident without successfully and permanently settling in either of the two. Their works therefore are a plea to the Occident to be more committed to its promise to civilise the native Orientals who, by their resistance to acculturation, became permanently tagged as uncivilisable.

Delving into this neglected literature in the way I did, is an attempt at filling a gap in the study of Maghrebi literature in general and Algerian literature in particular. Due to the political positions imposed by processes of decolonisation, critics worked tenaciously towards the effacement of the texts produced by the allies of the Occident, resulting thus in a severe amputation of the first part of the modern Maghrebi literature. Mainstream sources record 1950 as the date of birth of the Maghrebi novel while in reality this novel began at the turn of the twentieth century and having an array of artistically mature novels in the 1950s can only be the result of experimenting with the genre in the previous decades. As will be demonstrated throughout this book it is not possible to understand the encounter with the Occident from colonial to post-colonial times, evolving from a period of fascination (Occidentophilia) to a period of ambivalence, followed by total rejection of the Occident in the post-1945 period, without an in-depth study of the pre-1945 literature, a literature which documents how the encounter between the Orient and the Occident began in the Maghrebi context.

1

The Maghreb and the Occident: Towards the Construction of an Occidentalist Discourse

> *Et si parfois l'Occident triomphant chantait sa déperdition nietzschéenne, qu'en était-il de moi et de ma culture?*
>
> *[. . .] Aimer l'autre c'est parler le lieu perdu de la mémoire, et mon insurrection qui, dans un premier temps, n'était qu'une histoire imposée, se perpétue en ressemblance acceptée, parce que l'Occident est une partie de moi, que je ne peux nier que dans la mesure où je lutte contre tous les occidents et orients qui m'oppriment ou me désenchantent.*
>
> And if sometimes the triumphant Occident was singing its Nietzschean depredation, what would happen to me and my culture?
>
> To love the Other is to speak of the lost space of memory, and my insurrection which in an earlier time was nothing but a history imposed on me, now perpetuates itself in an acknowledged resemblance, for the Occident is part of me, a part that I can only deny insofar as I resist all the 'Occidents' and all the 'Orients' that oppress and disenchant me.
>
> Abdelkebir Khatibi[1]

Occidentalism *versus* Orientalism

Occidentalism is often defined as the counterpart of Orientalism. The word 'counterpart' signifies both the equivalent and the opposite, and in this case these two concepts are often presented as the two opposing poles of the gamut.

As a consequence, while 'Orient' is presented as the antonym of

'Occident', the lexical definition of 'Occidentalism' has been structured as the exact reverse of that of 'Orientalism' as follows: 'a quality, mannerism, or custom specific to or characteristic of the Occident', and 'scholarly knowledge of Occidental cultures, languages, and peoples.'[2] Although it is widely agreed that these functions are those pursued by Orientalism as an academic discipline, it is strictly not the case with Occidentalism which, it has to be emphasised, is not an academic discipline *per se* but merely a way or style of conceiving and representing the Occident, not in an academically scientific manner but mostly in a literary, artistic or polemical manner. This view is in fact highlighted by Said himself who asserts, 'to speak of scholarly specialization as a geographical "field" is, in the case of Orientalism, fairly revealing since no one is likely to imagine a field symmetrical to it called Occidentalism.'[3] Hassan Hanafi argues against Said's view above. He speaks of Occidentalism as a new science which he calls *ᶜilm al-istighrāb*, meaning Occidentology, and defines it as a counter-field of research, 'which can be developed in the Orient in order to study the West from a non-Western World point of view.'[4] He insists that Occidentalism is the opposite of Orientalism, or an Orientalism in reverse, and in a rather simplistic manner he imagines matters are being easily overturned. According to him:

> The object of study in Orientalism becomes the studying subject in Occidentalism, and the studying subject in Orientalism becomes the studying subject in Occidentalism. There is no eternal studying subject and no eternal object of study. It depends on the power relationship between peoples and cultures. Roles change throughout history . . . peoples and Islamic classical cultures were previously studying subjects and Europeans at the same time were objects of study. The role changed in modern times when Europeans became the studying subjects and the Muslim world became an object of study. The end of Orientalism and the beginning of Occidentalism means exchanging roles for a third time in the subject object relationship between the Self and the Other.[5]

What Hanafi seems to overlook is that what informs the process of representation in Orientalism is colonialism and domination, in other words 'power', and roles do not change as a result of some natural accident in which nations or peoples take turns in dominating each other. Furthermore, as will be explained later in this chapter, Arabs have not taken interest in studying people of the Occident in the same manner as the Occident studied those of the Orient, with the motive of better ruling over them, even at the time when the Arabo-Islamic Empire was at the peak of its glory.

Sadik Jalal Al-Azm casts doubt on the validity of Hanafi's project. He questions his call on the Arab intelligentsia to establish a science of *istighrāb* (Occidentology), for the purpose of systematically studying and scientifically understanding the West in the same way that the latter studied the Orient/Arabs in its science of *istishrāq* (Orientalism). Al-Azm begins his critique by doubting the term instigated by Hanafi: 'Unlike the term *istishrāq*, Hanafi's *istighrāb* is itself a strange and awkward word for naming a new scholarly discipline, considering its current usages, meanings, and connotations in Arabic, such as "to find strange, odd, queer, or far-fetched."'[6] From the onset, Al-Azm openly declares that he did not expect Hanafi's call to lead to any tangible results. He ascertains that it did not escape his attention that 'if this projected science of Occidentalism [Occidentology] is to amount to anything at all then it will have to seriously conform to international standards of scholarship, research, criticism, review, and argument that are in their turn almost wholly of Western origin and provenance.'[7] He enumerates the reasons for the failure of Hanafi's project beginning with the fact that it simply reaffirms and emulates Orientalism, and originates from feelings of acrimony for the ills done by the West to the East resulting in the undertaking of retaliation through 'Occidentology'. Furthermore, this project resuscitates the essentialism of Orientalism and 'gives up completely on the possibility of historically ever transcending this whole Orientalism/ Occidentalism problématique in the direction of a higher synthesis based on our common human concerns and shared scientific and scholarly interests (i.e., a scholarly horizon beyond both orientalism and Occidentalism)'.[8] Al-Azm concludes that Hanafi's Occidentology forms a classical instance of Orientalism in Reverse. In other words, it replicates Orientalism without transcending its pitfalls.

In his article 'Beyond Occidentalism: Towards Post-Imperial Geohistorical Categories',[9] Fernando Coronil refers to Said's 'Orientalists' as 'Occidentalists'. Coronil insists that this shift does not entail a reversal of focus from Orient to Occident, in other words from 'Other' to 'Self'. He explains that by directing our attention to the relational nature of representations of human collectivities, it brings to focus their genesis in asymmetrical relations of power, including the power to obscure their genesis in inequality, to undo their historical connections, and thus to present as the internal and separate attributes of bounded entities what are in fact historical outcomes of connected peoples. Coronil defines Occidentalism, not as the reverse of Orientalism but its condition of possibility, its dark side (as in a mirror). A simple reversal, he insists, would only be possible in the context of symmetrical relations between 'Self' and 'Other', which agrees with Said's view despite starting off by disagreeing with him. The end result of both arguments is that in the context of equal relations, difference would not be cast as Otherness. Therefore, to speak of Occidentalism as the exact reverse of Orientalism leads to the illusion that both Orient and Occident are equal which is not and has never been the case. The Orientalist *versus* Occidentalist condition is one of hegemony in which one was and still is the superior 'Self' and the second was and still remains the inferior 'Other'.

What Occidentalist representation attempts to do is to challenge Orientalism, especially its mode of representation in a 'counteracting', 'writing against' and 'writing back' manner, which as it were was the main surge behind the emergence of modern Maghrebi literature which saw the day under colonial France at the start of the twentieth century in the case of Algeria, the 1940s in the case of Tunisia and the 1950s in the case of Morocco.

It is important to emphasise that in the case of the Maghreb, unlike that of the Mashriq/ the Middle East, such literature was mainly written in the language of the coloniser which was mastered by native Maghrebi authors who were educated in colonial French schools and that the essence of this literature was to enter into a dialogue with the French coloniser in its own language, before it concerned itself with targeting Maghrebi readers who were practically non-existent, as the vast majority of the Maghrebi population during the colonial period was either totally illiterate or could only read Arabic.

This situation created a Francophone 'elite' from within the 'Other' who as a result of its education aspired to become part of the 'Self', but because of the colonial condition this elite was neither fully admitted to the ranks of the 'Self' nor did it accept its natural condition as the 'Other'. The affiliates of this particular elite can be positioned on the site of the border between Orient and Occident as they often rejected elements of their own culture which they saw as primitive though they could not radically extract themselves from it, while at the same time they opted for mimicking the Occident in looks and manners without being fully accepted into its ranks.

As such, the position of the colonised Francophone intellectuals is indeed very motivating. Instead of inhabiting a clearly defined marginal location they are positioned in a kind of liminal space which we may describe as a fluid location, for they became somehow 'dangerously' suspended between Orient and Occident, Other and Self without fully belonging to either of these categories. Ashcroft et al. call this space 'an in-between space in which cultural change may occur: the transcultural space in which strategies for personal or communal self-hood may be elaborated, a region in which there is a continual process of movement and interchange between different states.'[10] The colonised intellectuals resemble a pendulum that constantly sways left and right and never settles in either position. Their education instilled in their belief the fact that they belonged to the French civilisation, albeit through adoption rather than birth and that their loyalty and allegiance should perpetually be for their *mère-patrie* who bestowed on them the bounties of its civilisation. Yet, at the same time they could not totally detach themselves from their own people and cultural heritage. The ultimate outcome of this condition was the creation of cultural hybrids, who could not be accurately classified as either 'Oriental' or 'Occidental', 'Other' or 'Self', nor could they fully adhere to any of these possible categories. For Homi Bhabha[11] liminality and hybridity go hand in hand, making the eternal quest of the colonised intellectual towards striking a form of reconciliation between the two poles an impossible mission which thus results in their position as the diligent go-between; unable to satisfy either of the two poles. For their own people they were and continue to be the Occidentalised/Europeanised individuals who opted for the camp of the colonising Europeans and for the Europeans they remained the 'Other' no matter how deeply they assimilated European culture. Despite their keen endeavour to become and look European they were constantly thought of as the Other who was dissimilar and opposite to the Self. The ultimate reaction to this condition was to challenge colonialism and Orientalist Imperial discourse and their ways of Othering and representing the 'Other' as a homogenised collective often described in a stereotypical manner.

The resulting discourse took various forms including political polemics such as in the work of Ferhat Abbas, *Le Jeune Algérien* (The Young Algerian),[12] *J'accuse l'Europe* (I accuse Europe)[13] and *La Nuit coloniale* (The Colonial Night);[14] critical theory such as Albert Memmi's *Portrait du colonisé précédé du portrait du colonisateur* (The Colonizer and the Colonized),[15] Abdelkebir Khatibi's *La Mémoire tatouée* (The Tattooed Memory)[16] and *Amour bilingue* (Love in two Languages);[17] and Frantz Fanon's *Peau noire, masques blanc* (Black Skin, White Masks)[18] and *Les Damnés de la terre* (The Wretched of the Earth);[19] and works of fiction, which comprise the main bulk of the 'Occidentalist' discourse in terms of writing back to the Occident and literary representations of the Occident.

The consequence of challenging Orientalism, according to Coronil, is the disruption of Occidentalism as an ensemble of representational strategies and practices whose effect is to produce 'Selfhood' as well as 'Otherness'. He explains,

> ... by Occidentalism I refer to the complex ensemble of representational strategies engaged in the production of conceptions of the world that, separate its components into bounded units; 1) disaggregates their relational histories, 2) turns difference into hierarchy, 3) naturalises these representations; and, therefore, 4) intervenes, however unwittingly, in the reproduction of existing asymmetrical power relations.[20]

In lieu of disruption, challenging Orientalism is in fact the essence and the base-structure of Occidentalism which aims at all the functions listed by Coronil in the above citation. Let us take as an example Malek Alloula's book *The Oriental Harem*,[21] which examines a collection of phantasmagorical colonial/Orientalist photographs of native Maghrebi women. Alloula's book exposes the Orientalist mode of representation by publishing photographs produced by colonial photographers. By doing so, he does not change the generated situation of representation but merely exposes it and gives it wider circulation. This operation resulted in mixed reactions; while some criticised his method as doing further harm to the portrayed subject, others valued his work as a tool of challenging the Orientalist cannon through mere exposure. The resulting mixed feelings are in fact a reaction to the situation of 'Othering' from a prejudiced colonial lens, making the 'Self' rather uncomfortable at being exposed in such manner.

The Oriental Harem (1) disaggregates the relational histories of coloniser and colonised in order for its author to situate his book in its historical context. As to turning difference into hierarchy (2), Alloula's work highlights the difference between 'Self' and 'Other' in terms of hegemonic power relations. The subject of the photographs could not be reversed and interestingly enough the collection is made of photographs of 'Others' *only* and not of 'Self', or of the 'Self' together with its 'Other'. A clear delineation is evident in the colonial representations of the 'Other' as being separate from the 'Self'; this condition is a result of the intrinsic hegemony between colonisers and colonised and the resulting attitude of possessing and objectifying the colonised.

As to point (3) 'naturalizes these representations,'[22] the resulting critique of the book testifies to the opposite situation; that is the revoking of the exposed truth as a false representation. *The Oriental Harem* challenges the photographs as being true to life and exposes them as a result of the colonial euphoria and phantasm. Alloula explains that in their failure to find the constructed Orient and its imagined 'Others' in reality ('paradise found' which turns into 'paradise lost'), colonial photographers resorted to creating this illusory and sought-after situation of the Oriental harem in their studios. Such a reaction is a natural way to hide the deception felt at not finding the promised paradise where women roamed freely and at the disposal of the settlers of the new colony, who continued to deceive those in the metropolis that those lucky few who escaped industrial and suffocating Europe to the Orient/Maghreb were indeed enjoying its bounties. One photograph titled *Moorish Women of Algiers*, which represents two Oriental women sitting next to each other, was sent to acquaintances in the metropolis written on 'Anatoly's woman, R[. . .]'s woman'.[23] Alloula elucidates:

> Photography steps in to take the slack and reactivates the phantasm at its lowest level. The postcard does it one better; it becomes the poor man's phantasm: for a few pennies, display racks full of dreams. The postcard is everywhere, covering all the colonial space, immediately available to the tourist, the soldier, the colonist.[24]

The appropriation and exploitation of the colonial subjects, and in this case native Maghrebi women, made them thoroughly objectified and ruthlessly used in order to satisfy the colonialists' appetite for the exotic. In other words, they were inhumanely exposed to the Occident as proof of colonial supremacy and were displayed as human war booty. Marnia Lazreg problematises this condition in the following terms:

> Through Algerian women, French male writers [in this case male colonial photographers] could satisfy their own desires to penetrate Algerian men's intimate life by having their wives and daughters as spoils of conquest. At the same time, Algerian women gave men the opportunity to fantasize about the female sex in general. For, if one stripped the nineteenth- and twentieth-century discourse on Algerian women of its colonial trappings one would uncover French men's own prejudices against women in general. In addition, in Algerian women French authors found an inexhaustible subject to quench the public's thirst for what Fromentin called 'the bizarre'.[25]

And consequently, point (4) 'intervenes, however unwittingly, in the reproduction of existing asymmetrical power relations.'[26] Without the colonial condition of coloniser and colonised whereby power relations are asymmetrical, the whole Orientalist and the resulting Occidentalist concepts and discourse would not have existed. Power and conflict are at the base structure of these concepts and have always shaped their nature. What Alloula's work mainly revokes is the notion of the Orient and its women as the silent and passive 'Other' that lends itself to control and domination, and he adopts a retaliatory form of Occidentalist discourse. Alloula depicts the Occident through confronting it with its own portrayals of the Orient and bluntly states that his book is intended as a huge postcard returned to its sender to confront it with the truth about its unethical exposure of colonised women and its insatiable thirst for penetration. The book progresses from photographs of veiled women whose veils defeated the photographer's lens, to unveiled but dignified women in their interiors, which are here replicated in studios, to then end up with erotic images of semi-naked women. This progression reveals the desire for possession of these women as subjects and as war booty and at the same time the desire to penetrate the intimate life of the defeated Algerian men.

In a retaliatory effort, Alloula exposes these exotic postcards as the vulgar expression of colonial euphoria.[27] For him, it is sufficient to tell the world that the Occident had first fabricated its Orient and then went to find it in its new colonies. Unhappy with its discovery, and in order to surmount its crisis, the Occident stubbornly persisted in fabricating and propagating the same images of its own imagination albeit from the confines of fictitious photography studios.

The Crisis of Orientalism

In his seminal study 'Orientalism in Crisis', Anouar Abdel-Malek[28] argues that under colonial rule the Orient and its inhabitants almost automatically become an 'object' of study which was ' . . . stamped with otherness- – as all that is different whether it be 'subject' or 'object' but of a constitutive otherness, of an essentialist character . . . This 'object' of study will be as is customary, passive, non-participating, endowed with a 'historical' subjectivity, above all, non-active, non-autonomous, non-sovereign with regard to itself.'[29] Abdel Malek demonstrates that some Orientalist motivations were purely academic and could be ranked as positive, as highlighted by Youssef Asaad Dagher, who lists eight positive elements in the field of Arabic and Islamic studies as follows: the study of ancient civilisation, the collection of Arabic manuscripts in European libraries, the establishment of catalogues of manuscripts, the publication of numerous important works, the lesson of method thus given to Oriental scholars, the organisation of Orientalist congresses, the editing of studies, though frequently deficient and erroneous from a linguistic point of view, but precise in the method, and finally, that this movement contributed to arousing national consciousness in the different countries of the Orient and to activating the movement of scientific renaissance.[30] In the case of the Maghreb, Orientalist anthropology, archaeology and philology resulted in important scholarship which continues to be used as valuable references in the study of the region and its people.

In his article, 'Faut-it brûler l'Orientalisme?:on French Scholarship of North Africa', Abdelmajid Hannoum,[31] argues that French Orientalism, the bulk of knowledge that has been built in the context of colonisation, though it has changed through time, continues to operate today both in the discourse of the former colonised and that of the former coloniser. He contends that for the colonial machine, knowledge is not only a means of control and governance but it also contains categories by which imaginaries are shaped and colonial relations and attitudes perpetuated.[32] He explains that Orientalism condemned itself by becoming the tool of colonialism and demonstrates that in the Maghreb, French colonialism benefited from the expertise of the Orientalists to dominate and rule over the region. He highlights the important role played by De Sacy in the occupation of Algeria:

> It was he who was in charge of hiring interpreters, his own students, for the French army. He also determined the most important text for knowledge of North Africa, a book by Ibn Khaldūn, a universal history, whose section on the history of North Africa has become a central text for Orientalists. It was de Sacy's student, William de Slane, who translated it (De Slane, 1852–6). This text, with its colonial categories and objects, still conditions French writing on North Africa.[33]

Furthermore, Hannoum hypothesises that colonialism, as a political enterprise, was a major factor in consolidating the establishment of Orientalism. It is, without a doubt, colonialism that allowed the Orientalists 'to build whole Oriental libraries, by helping [them] to acquire, gather, and catalogue Oriental manuscripts, and to organize the study of the Orient in institutions founded and totally devoted to this purpose.'[34] In the same vein, Abdel Malek explains that this vision of academic Orientalism accomplished in the Universities and Scholarly societies, which he calls 'traditional' Orientalism, was not the dominant vision. He warns that despite all its good intentions it could not rid itself of some politico-philosophical concepts and methodological habits that often interfered with and compromised the results of their scientific findings. This leads to the second type of Orientalism which Abdel Malek qualifies as the Orientalism of the collaborators with colonial powers. He describes this group in the following terms:

> This latter group was formed by an amalgam of university dons, businessmen, military men, colonial officials, missionaries, publicists and adventurers, whose only objective was to gather intelligence information in the area to be occupied, to penetrate the consciousness of the people in order to better assure its enslavement to the European powers.[35]

In the case of the Maghreb, Abdel Malek comments on the work of the Arab Bureau mainly set up to control the lives of the natives. Based on

Jacques Berque's observations, he explains how these Bureaus were mainly installed by the colonial powers to supply them with intelligence:

> The optic of the Arab bureau, as Jacques Berque rightly observed, has led to the result that sustained, nourished at the same time and limited by action, the study of the North African societies has been oriented from the start.[36]

Abdel Malek explains that this phenomenon of generating knowledge about specific nations for the purpose of dominating them is built into the structure of the social sciences of the European countries in the period of imperialist penetration and implantation.

As to the view expressed in his title 'Orientalism in Crisis', Abdel Malek explains that this crisis occurs as a result of the rise of national liberation movements which brought the end of the age of colonial domination. Orientalist scholars faced a crisis because the territories they studied became liberated and were no longer controlled by their nations. This fact resulted in a change in the relationship between the researchers and their studied subject matter.

This view is also shared by Hannoum, who argues that because Orientalism made itself a tool of colonialism, both enterprises were linked together and shared the same fate. That is, the end of colonialism would automatically bring about the end of Orientalism. Although this may be correct to some extent, the mode of representation established by the colonisers towards the colonised continues to influence the ways the Orient and Occident view each other at the present. As ever, knowledge is not objective data about objects and subjects, but a form of social relations, a form of power by which and through which domination is assured and guaranteed. According to Michel Foucault,

> Knowledge linked to power, not only assumes the authority of 'the truth', but has the power to make itself true. All knowledge, once applied in the real world, has effects, and in that sense at least, 'becomes true'. Knowledge, once used to regulate the conduct of others, entails constraint, regulation and the disciplining of practice. Thus, there is no power relation without the correlative constitution of a field of knowledge, nor any knowledge that does not presuppose and constitute at the same time, power relations.[37]

Let us not ignore the fact that European Orientalism was generated in the colonial era, and in the light of Foucault's view we should ask the tantalising question of whether Arabs/Orientals cultivated a field of research that specialised in the study of other nations during the time of the expansion of the Islamic Empire.[38] Before doing so, we need to reiterate that the Occidentalist discourse, which makes the focus of this research is not the study of the people of the Occident and their manners or customs, as in the case of Western anthropology, but rather a matter of writing to (or back to) and about the Occident as a reaction and not as an enterprise initiated by the 'Orientals' to study the people of the Occident for any given purpose, hence the absence of Occidentalist scholarship on the one hand and its irrelevance on the other.

Furthermore, while Orientalism is a discipline which, according to Said, dates back to the seventeenth century with the appearance of Barthélemy d'Herbelot's *Bibliothèque orientale* (1697),[39] the Orient – and in this case we mean the Arab Muslim world – also engaged in the study of the conquered/Islamised nations including those from the Occident or again, in this context, the Christian world. Although the main aim of the Islamic expansions was to convert new nations into the new faith, and although in some cases this also meant a campaign of Arabisation as a means to enable the new Muslims to practise Islam and read the Qur'an without any language barriers, local cultures, while not totally erased, were largely Islamised. While practices which were deemed un-Islamic were banned, a process of fusion of cultures took place, especially in the case of the Maghreb where elements of the indigenous Amazigh culture continue to this very day to distinguish Maghrebi culture from that of the Middle East. Furthermore, the indigenous Maghrebi populations were not seen as colonised subjects but they in turn became members of the Muslim nation and partook in the Islamic expansionist project of taking Islam to new lands and people, as they did when Arab and Amazigh armies entered the Iberian Peninsula, subsequently known as Al-Andalus.

Although Arabs were criticised for their lack of interest in studying the arts, literature and historiography of the newly Islamised lands and peoples, this should in no way refute their influence on Arab thought. In his book *How Greek Science Passed to the Arabs* De Lacy argues that there is a lack of evidence of philosophical or theological speculation in Syria under the Umayyad dynasty and that such matters seem to have made very little appeal to Arab interest in that period.[40] This view is invalidated by Maghrebi scholar Ibn Khaldun (1332–1406) in his famous *The Muqaddimah* (An Introduction to History) which stands as the most important history of the pre-modern world; in it he laid the foundations for several fields of knowledge such as sociology, ethnography, economics and the philosophy of history. Written in 1377 as an introduction to *Kitāb al-ʿIbar* (Book of Advice), *The Muqaddimah* re-evaluates in an unparalleled manner every manifestation of highly developed civilisations and acknowledges that many civilisations preceded the Arab-Islamic civilisation and that many civilisations such as that of the Persians', the Copts', etc all joined up in its making. He asserts that the knowledge that has not reached us is larger than the knowledge that has, and contests the view which was popular during his time that nations of earlier times were believed to have been both physically and mentally better endowed for achieving a high and materially splendid civilisation than contemporary nations. In his opinion, it was merely the decay of political organisations and the power of government that gave his contemporaries the impression that the civilisation of their day was inferior to that of their predecessors. Ibn Khaldun believes there could be no essential difference between the faculties and achievements of former and contemporary generations, because political and cultural life was continuously evolving through never-ending cycles. He argues that human intellectual power is always constant and capable of producing the highest civilisation at any given time. He speaks of the sciences and civilisations of the Persians, the Chaldeans, the Syrians, the Babylonians, the Copts and the Greeks, yet remarks that the only sciences to have reached the Arabs are those of the Greeks thanks to the efforts of Caliph al-Maʾmūn who invested large resources to have them translated. On the other hand, he remarks with regret, that because of Caliph Umar Ibn al-Khattāb's hasty decision the books of the Persians and all the knowledge they contained were either burnt down or dumped in the river.[41] From *The Muqaddimah* it becomes evident that Ibn Khaldun's political theories have been influenced by Aristotle whose *Book of Politics* he cites several times.[42] He describes him as 'the greatest Greek scientist who enjoyed the greatest prestige and fame. He has been called "the first teacher". He became world-famous.'[43] Ibn Khaldun also speaks of Aristotle and his role in improving the methods of logic, and cites his work on logic as being called *al-Naṣṣ* (The Text); comprising eight books (volumes), which he describes one by one. Ibn Khaldun's knowledge of the cultures and civilisations of other nations is wide and diversified. What we find most interesting is his way of speaking of other nations and civilisations in a highly objective manner. In other words, there is no friend or foe in knowledge and his book displays no racial or religious bias. He speaks of Muslims, Christians and Jews as different people who belong to different faiths. He insists that these faiths did not stand as a stumbling block in the way of their interaction, and spoke of the Muslims as people who desired to learn the sciences of foreign nations. In doing so, they pressed them into the cast of their own views and surpassed the achievements of their authors in them.

This was happening during the golden ages of the Arab-Islamic civilisation when Arabs could, if they so wished, use other nations, whose lands they annexed to the Muslim Empire, as subject of study from a seat of power. Yet, it is difficult to find traces of this taking place in Islamic history. Ibn Khaldun and others before him speak of the harmony in which people of all faiths cohabited in Andalusia and the Maghreb and indeed, in the rest of the Muslim Empire.

While this is the case, the fear of Islam[44] and its expansion led the French to acquire knowledge of the enemy as early as the ninth and tenth centuries when Byzantine Greek texts on Islam were translated into Latin followed by the translation of the Qur'an in the twelfth century which was sponsored by Peter the Venerable (about 1092–1156), abbot of the Benedictine abbey of Cluny (1122–56). In his anti-Islamic polemic titled *Book against the Abominable Heresy or Sect of the Saracens*, Peter preached for the use of warfare against Islam. Such feelings culminated in the crusades in which the French knights constituted the largest group. Although Said claims that Barthélemy d'Herbelot's *Bibliothèque Orientale: ou Dictionnaire Universel* (1697) is the source wherein the Orient as a concept became formalised as it focused on the life of Prophet Mohammed and the history of the 'Saracens' as its main subject in a way which set up a new manner of viewing the Orient by Europeans for many centuries to come, I consider Peter's anti-Islamic polemic to be the first source which sets up the Orientalist mode. Like d'Herbelot, his illustrations of Prophet Mohammed as an impostor and founder of a heresy is undoubtedly the base for many prejudiced views about Prophet Mohammed which have been and continue to be produced even today in some extremist anti-Muslim media (note for instance the cartoons published in the Danish newspaper *Jyllands-Posten* on 30 September 2005).

Edward Said explains how, through the work of d'Herbelot, 'Europe discovered its capacities for encompassing and Orientalizing the Orient',[45] likewise Peter's work in the twelfth century clearly set up Christians and Muslims as enemies and preached for the use of warfare to rid the Christian world of Islam and the Muslim enemies. According to Irwin 'it was natural for Christian thinkers to interpret the unfamiliar and unexpected phenomenon of Islam in terms of what was familiar to them already. Therefore, they tended to present Islam to themselves not as a new religion, but rather as the variant of an old heresy.'[46] The image of Islam as a heretic religion is purely a reaction to it being a threat against Christianity as a result of its expansion into Christian lands, including Europe in the eighth century, and the incorporation of Sicily, as well as Spain and Portugal into the Islamic Empire as the province of Al-Andalus. The Arab and the Berber Muslims of the Maghreb who settled in Al-Andalus expanded north of the Pyrenees into the Frankish lands, defeated the Aquitanians at Bordeaux and went as far as Poitier where the Arab-Berber cavalry units were driven back repeatedly by an impenetrable Frankish resistance which eventually resulted in the defeat of the Muslims in the Battle of Tours-Poitiers on 25 October 732.[47] For many centuries later this victory was held as 'Christo auxiliante' and posed crescent and cross as enemies. In 1869, a time when France had occupied Algeria and was planning to expand into other Maghrebi territories, the Battle of Tours-Poitiers was described as 'a struggle between East and West, South and North, Asia and Europe, the Gospel and the Koran.'[48] This struggle has never ceased as hostile encounters between Muslims and Christians regularly occurred on the frontiers of Al-Andalus and the Francs, who, having already chased the Muslims from their kingdom, continued their attacks on them and chased them out of all Christian lands. Antoine Galland's translation of *The Thousand and One Nights* (1704–17) as a literary work, set the seal on the Orient in terms of representation; in addition to the attacks on Islam and its Prophet which were propagated through the work of Christian religious men,[49] *The Nights* added images of a totally imagined and distorted Orient as the place of sensuality, harems, eunuchs . . . which were extremely appealing to Western readers and contributed fundamentally to the establishing of

Orientalist art and literature. Such images were often misleading as their avatars often imagined an Orient which had no equivalent in reality; an Orient of extremes which is both violent and lascivious and essentially a place where the most bizarre things happen. Along with the above sources one has to take account of European travellers and soldiers, especially those in the Bonaparte Expedition in Egypt (1798–1801), and their accounts. Though often over exaggerated, and indeed outright fictitious, their reports served as trusted sources from which many laymen drew their fascination of and attraction to the Orient. In his book *Sexual Encounters in the Middle East*, Derek Hopwood explains how these sources were to feed the Western colonial imagination, and how the soldiers of the French conquest of the Maghreb built their imaginings on the basis of the reports composed by Bonaparte's soldiers in Egypt.[50] In addition to soldiers' reports and voyager's diaries, Napoleon's military expedition included a team of 167 scientists, mathematicians, naturalists, chemists and others whose work was published in the famous *Description de l'Égypte*.[51] It is believed that the work of this team generated a host of essentialist images, which were received as first-hand knowledge, and laid the foundations for a long tradition of Orientalism as a way of portraying and studying the 'Other' from a seat of power. The same enterprise of studying the locals as subjects of European anthropology took place as soon as the French occupation established itself in the Maghreb. This enterprise has, in effect, never ceased but continues to be perpetrated in post-colonial times. What *has* changed is the awareness brought about by the modern study of Orientalism as a discipline mostly in the aftermath of the publication of Said's *Orientalism*, but also, and this is important to highlight, through the emergence of anti-colonial and national liberation movements in Africa and Asia after the Second World War, and the victories achieved by these movements in the form of political independence. Abdel Malek argues that this new political condition is the main factor that plunged the Orientalist profession into a serious crisis, and that it became no longer natural that the Europeans rule the planet and enjoy direct control of Asia and Africa and their inhabitants.

Abdel Malek's critique was published in 1962, and was followed by Abdul Latif Tibawi's similar critique bearing the title 'English-Speaking Orientalists: a Critique of their Approach to Islam and Arab Nationalism' in

1964. Both studies have questioned European Orientalism well before Said's study *Orientalism* appeared in 1978.

Abdul Latif Tibawi, who was based at the University of London when he wrote his study, was rather disconcerted by the way Islamic topics and the 'Orient' in general, were taught at the School of Oriental and African Studies (University of London). He declared that he did not conceive his critique in any spirit of controversy and that it should not be taken as an apology for any creed, be it religious or national.[52] Tibawi's critique received a rather harsh evaluation by Irwin, who described it as 'a thesaurus of academic abuse' and lists all the 'abusive words' he used in his attack on the Orientalists and their works.[53] Irwin's defence of the Orientalists through vehement attacks on their enemies who all happen to be of Arab and Muslim descent, results in a host of direct assaults on individuals including Abdallah Laroui, Abdul Latif Tibawi and Anwar Abdel Malek, and a use of demeaning and aggressive discourse which does not benefit the tense relationship between Orient and Occident in any way. In this manner, Irwin positions himself as the faultless superior Self that does not accept criticism from its Other. As explained above, the discourse of Irwin's 'Enemies of the Orientalists' is a reaction to decades of stereotyping through a commissioned dominating discourse that accompanied colonial powers. It is the images of the Orient that made those of the Occident possible and at the same time as these reciprocal images of Orient and Occident proliferated, it became more and more obvious that the problems of the Orient and Occident are interconnected and rather common. Due to a lack of genuine efforts at rapprochement, essentialist images have been fashioned and often propagated. Such images of the 'Other/other' be they Oriental or Occidental, are never innocent nor are they free from hidden agendas that shape them and give them their final structure.

This situation ultimately results in each party handling the way they are portrayed with suspicion. This becomes even more so in academic fields such as anthropology. The way the studied subjects or communities (informants) in Western anthropology react to Western scholars, or even Arab anthropologists living in the West, who conduct research in the Middle East and the Maghreb, is a good example of this suspicion. I would like to refer to a study conducted by Lila Abu-Lughod in Upper Egypt. When she told her Egyptian host that the results of her field work in Egypt would be published in English, he told her 'it was a pity' as he wanted Egyptians rather than

Americans to know about its content. He then concluded 'Knowledge is power. The Americans and the British know everything. They want to know everything about people, about us. Then, if they come to a country, or come to rule it, they know what people need and they know how to rule.'[54] This reaction is not without foundation; its roots undoubtedly go back to Napoleon's invasion of Egypt and the crews of researchers who accompanied the armed forces. This same view is expressed by academics in their critique of Orientalism such as in Abdel Malek's study where he explains that the aim of European anthropology is to penetrate the consciousness of the people in order to better assure their enslavement to the European powers.[55] Abu-Lughod concludes, 'my Bedouin host had brought up an issue about the politics of scholarship that we as Western-oriented scholars have only recently begun to explore seriously.'[56] She elucidates that any discussion of anthropological theories about the Arab world must begin with this issue, meaning the politics of representation from a Saidian perspective. James Carrier confirms, 'while anthropologists conventionally see themselves as producing, and recently have debated their ability to produce, knowledge of societies and cultures outside the core of the West, Occidentalism is the silent partner of their work and debates.'[57] Carrier argues that Occident and Orient and the distinction between them are all shaped by political circumstance, which affects as well as explains the quality and terms of the encounter between Orient and Occident and makes their relationship so fluid.[58] He sets his book in motion with a short definition of Occidentalism as 'stylized images of the West' and concurs that Orientalism as defined by Said has become a generic term for a particular, suspect type of anthropological thought and that the criticism of anthropology as a discipline which concerns itself with the study of other nations draws on Said's *Orientalism*. This state of affairs puts modern anthropologists in a convoluted situation as the discipline has been so much tarnished by old style colonial modes of representation whereby alien/other societies were on the one hand seen as static and radically dissimilar from the complex and changing West, and on the other hand these studies were often informed by sets of preconceived ideas which have invariably influenced their enquiries resulting in a mode of essentializing other nations which Said criticises in the following terms, 'objects are what they are *because* they are what they are, for once, for all time, for ontological reasons that no empirical matter can either dislodge or alter.'[59] Being equipped with preconceived views of the 'Other' prior to the enquiry or encounter with this same 'Other' resulted in obstructing the vision and inquisitive mind of some colonial anthropologists, artists and authors. What intensified this situation is the colonial condition which made the 'Self' an eternal aggressor (even in post-colonial times) in the view of the 'Other/Oriental' who then handles the 'Self/Occidental' with eternal suspicion.

What I am trying to articulate at this point is that both parties have, as a consequence, developed and embedded a view of the other which cannot rid itself of essentialism. Both Orient and Occident essentialise each other and this condition can only be altered by changing the existing state of affairs of setting Orient and Occident apart, with a set of binaries attached to them which, despite the progression of these two poles from colonial to post-colonial conditions, locate these two worlds apart from each other.

Such binaries had indeed seen a temporal evolution of some kind prior to the 9/11 attacks but, in general, they have not lost the essence of setting one pole as the opposite of the other. In effect, the 9/11 attacks and subsequent terrorist events targeting the Occident have only intensified these binaries and deepened the gulf which separates Orient from Occident.

One very common example is that of the 'sexualised woman'; in Orientalist imagery the Oriental woman is portrayed as a veiled, passive and subservient victim, while in Occidentalist imagery the Western woman is often described as a devalued sex object, victim of sexual exploitation. In her article 'Orientalism, Occidentalism and the Control of Women'[60] Laura Nader denounces the political agenda, which lies behind such representations in both Orient and Occident. While the Muslim world uses the portrayals of Western women to contrast itself as one that values women and in which women are respected and therefore can be secure, Western societies highlight the victimisation and the passivity of Muslim women in contrast to independent and intellectually advanced Western women to both solidify and legitimise patriarchal gender relations in the West. In this, Nader insists, both societies are similar in the way they essentialise and simplify their depictions of 'Other/other' women as well as the way they maintain a patriarchal order in terms of gender relations.[61]

While I have so far argued that Occidentalism is produced by intellectuals from the countries of the 'Orient'/East mainly in a writing back fashion to the Occident, in their book, *Occidentalism: a Short History of Anti-Westernism*, Ian Buruma and Avishai Margalit, undertake another form of writing back process to the anti-Western Occidentalist discourse generated by the enemies of the West. Accordingly, they define Occidentalism as 'The dehumanizing picture of the West painted by its enemies,'[62] and insist that in this respect Occidentalism is worse than Orientalism:

> The view of the West in Occidentalism is like the worst aspects of its counterpart, Orientalism, which strips its human targets of their humanity. Some Orientalist prejudices made non-Western people seem less than fully adult human beings; they had the minds of children, and could thus be treated as lesser breeds.[63]

Buruma and Margalit argue that Occidentalism is at least as reductive; its chauvinism merely turns the Orientalist view upside down. Consequently, Occidentalism is a specific kind of discourse, which is often 'followed by violent actions,' stemming from the Arab and Muslim worlds. The sole purpose of this discourse is to denigrate, denounce and condemn the West in every imaginable means. They assert: 'to diminish an entire society or a civilisation to a mass of soulless, decadent, money-grubbing, rootless, faithless, unfeeling parasites is a form of intellectual destruction',[64] and affirm that pursuing Occidentalism as a nationalist and nativist resistance to the Occident only reproduces responses to forces of modernisation that have their roots in Western culture itself, among both utopian radicals and nationalist conservatives who see capitalism, liberalism and secularism as destructive forces. Buruma and Margalit's views are fairly unsophisticated and highly accusatory in the way they position the Orient and Occident as born enemies. They engage in a polemical mode of discourse which only sees one strand of Occidentalism and overlooks a long history of fascination with and mimesis of the Occident expressed both in literature and thought. To reduce Occidentalist literature to a meagre discourse of hatred which merely demonises the Occident and is often 'followed by violent action' is a grave oversight of the bulk of Occidentalist creativity. Their views are indeed easily rendered fallacious by the many diverse portrayals of the Occident by various Oriental writers who, while they may not escape generalisations and preconceived views of the Occident, hold divergent views which never failed to reflect on the contrasting facets of the Occident.

Buruma and Margalit's criticisms of and attacks on various anti-colonial intellectuals betray a Eurocentric stance and the whole book becomes rather speculative and loaded with words such as 'loathe', 'hate', 'violence', 'enemy'. Their attacks on named individuals are quite erratic such as in the following example where they deploy a fierce assault on the French humanist lawyer Jacques Vergès,

> A prominent supporter of Third World revolutionary causes, Arab terrorists, and other enemies of liberal democracy is the French lawyer Jacques Vergès. He has defended Algerian militants in court . . . Vergès might have personal motives for his hostility to the West. He was born in Réunion, an old French penal colony in the Indian Ocean, and his mother was Vietnamese, a circumstance that blocked his father's ambition to be a French diplomat. But the reason for bringing up this notorious but marginal figure is his eloquent argument against the banality of democracy. Vergès loathes 'cosmopolitanism'. He hates honour higher than morality and has a taste for violent Action.[65]

To categorise Occidentalism as the discourse of those who 'loathe' liberal democracy betrays Buruma and Margalit's lack of understanding of such a discourse on the one hand and their one-dimensional, and reactionary views on the other. The actions of humanists of the likes of Vergès, Fanon, De Beauvoir, Halimi[66] and many others, were in fact in the defence of liberal democracy and not the other way around. Vergès' defence of the victims of the French colonial machine and the revolutionary heroes of the Algerian War of Independence should in no way be classified as the defence of 'Arab terrorists'.[67] Such terminology feeds into the tendency to categorise all Arabs and Muslims as terrorist suspects, an image which intensified in the aftermath of the 9/11 terrorist attacks. Algerian nationalists and freedom fighters in the 1950s and 1960s were designated on the international level as Algerians and not as 'Arab terrorists'. Applying such terminology in retrospect is a way of falsifying history and labelling the legitimate cause of defending or liberating ones nation as an act of terrorism. Furthermore, accusing Vergès of having 'a taste for violent Action'[68] is contrary to the truth, as the people he defended were the *victims* of violent action in the form of colonial torture as a most inhumane type of violence directed at a person's dignity as well as their physical and mental integrity. Contrary to Buruma and Margalit's argument, Occidentalism as a discourse is not anti-Western in essence. It has to be made clear that exposing the Orientalist methodology and modes of representation, in no way aims to promote anti-Western feelings. Quite the contrary, the aim is to bring awareness to Western audiences that the created image of the Orient and the Orientals is not only erroneous but injurious. While such images are the product of the colonial machine, and were deployed to promote and at the same time reflect a colonial mindset, they have become both outmoded and irrelevant in the post-colonial era. However, what is exposed in the Occidentalist discourse is the durability and importance of such images, a fact that betrays the seemingly fixed mindset of the Occident vis-à-vis the Orient. Therefore, the main objective of such exposure is to change the ways the West views its 'Others' and vice versa. After all, most of the authors who produce the Occidentalist discourse are educated in the West, most of them continue to live in the West and have drawn their methods of evaluation and code of ethics of representation from Western understanding.

Telling the West about its failures and its inability to move beyond the colonial past in terms of essentialising its 'Others', and producing as well as propagating sets of misrepresentations about the East, as well as highlighting the contradictions inherent in its universal principles of human rights and democracy which exclude those from outside Europe, is almost a plea for bridge-building, cultural exchange and dialogue rather than the opposite. Furthermore, when attacking Occidentalism one should not mistake it for the fundamentalist discourse of Islamic terrorism, which Jean Baudrillard[69] calls 'Talibanish Occidentalism', as the main crux of the Occidentalist discourse I am pursuing in this study. While such extremist views do exist, it has to be highlighted that their authors do, in fact, produce radical attitudes against both the East/Orient and the West/Occident and should in no way be taken as a justification for labelling Occidentalism as solely the discourse of the hatred of the Occident.

Occidentalism as a Post-colonial Discourse

While the colonial period produced texts written in the colony and mostly in the language of the coloniser about the encounter with Western culture and civilisation, the post-colonial period offers the reader two categories of texts, the first of which comprises texts written in the Maghreb both in French and Arabic, whilst the second category consists of texts written in the Western Diaspora, mainly in French and English. It has to be noted that English has become in the last three decades very popular amongst the Maghrebi Diaspora in the United Kingdom, the United States and Canada, resulting in the Maghrebi Diasporic literature breaking its old European boundaries in terms of location and language.

The main questions which stem from the study of the post-colonial period would revolve around issues of Muslim identity and the element of diversity which should be borne in mind when looking at all Muslims as one uniform crowd. Aziz Al-Azmeh insists that 'Algerians in Aulney-sur-Bois, Kashmiris in Bradford, Kurds in Kreuzberg all live in similarly diverse conditions. Yet, we are repeatedly told, Muslims, Europeans or otherwise, are above all *Muslims* and that by this token alone they are distinctive and must be treated as such.'[70] Without doubt, Al-Azmeh's point is written against a tendency to group all Muslims under one umbrella regardless of their country of origin, colonial past and historical circumstances of migration. In the post-9/11-world the West engaged in a frenzy of forums and symposia around the issue of 'Islam in the West', mainly focusing on Islamophobia and Islamic terrorism, concepts which send us back to Orientalism and the colonial period when all Europe's 'Others' were viewed as 'the Orientals'.

Furthermore, while progressive forces from the Arab world are relentlessly battling against international Islam as a threat to national identity and individuality, the West, by classifying all Muslims in one category, whether consciously or otherwise, consolidates the existence of Islam as an identity and not simply as a faith which is practised in different ways from one country to another. The many literary works written by Maghrebi authors in the post-9/11 period focus on this element of diversity; instead of one Islam they speak of many Islam(s) and particularly of 'Maghrebi Islam'. The way Islam is performed as a faith is often nurtured by deeply cemented cultural elements which predate the advent of Islam in the region and fundamentally contribute to identity formations which go to distinguish one region from another. Targeting Islam in the diaspora space, such as the headscarf issue in France, bolsters the various Muslim communities in the diaspora into one community which then looks for stronger ties to form themselves as one resistance group against the imperialism and racism that situated such communities as one uniform group of Others.

According to Stuart Hall, Identity is not as transparent or unproblematic as we assume, and instead of thinking of it as an already accomplished fact, we should think of it as a production which is never complete but is in a continuous process of being fashioned within and not without representations.[71] How immigrant communities negotiate their identity is fundamentally shaped by a discourse that draws on the sacred to legitimise their authority. Mernissi explains that: 'Islam is a set of psychological devices about self-empowerment and making oneself at home everywhere around the globe'.[72] Muslim migrant communities often turn to Islam as an ideology and a psychological tool to empower them. This helps to explain the trend of reverting to Islam among many Muslim communities in Western countries. Moghissi argues that the shift of heightened Muslim identity does not represent increasing adherence to Islam as a religion, but to Islam as an ideology of resistance and the only force that, at present, seems to effectively challenge global power structures and domination systems.[73] Although Edward Said affirms that, unlike the United States, Europe has become more educated in matters of stereotyping the 'Other', describing migrant communities whose religion is Islam as 'Muslim communities in the West', demonstrates that not much has changed from the colonial period. In fact, the situation as we see it today is that the question of identity, which has been for the last two centuries the main dilemma of Europe's subjects, has now reached the centre itself, i.e., the Occident. Many studies have recently focused on the status of Europe in the post 9/11 attacks, and who gets to call themselves 'European'.

How have these events remodelled our understanding of Europe and the West? And how does Europe view itself in relation to the rest of the world, and more particularly the Maghreb? Many argue that while the French–Maghrebi situation was improving by the 1990s, it suffered a huge setback following 9/11 which was then further exacerbated by the November 2015 Paris attacks.

During the 1990s, particularly in major cosmopolitan cities such as London and Paris, the melding of cultures produced a society in which the creation of an 'Other', though not totally eliminated, was at least minimised.

Both active discrimination and the more passive or less perceptible stereotyping have dramatically increased in the years following 9/11, when discrimination has become religious-based as opposed to racial or ethnic-based as it was in the past. As a result, stereotyping can have a pernicious effect on individuals that is as disruptive to the formation of identity and a sense of belonging as direct discrimination can be, precisely because it is subtle and pervasive. Some questions to pose are: what do Europe's new and/or continuing internal divisions say about its own differentiated colonial histories? And, is it possible for Europe to conceive of itself as a 'post-colonial' space? How is Europe situated within current East–West and North–South cultural debates as shaped by 9/11 attacks and subsequent terrorist atrocities all the way through to the November 2015 attacks in Paris? And how do all these dilemmas shape the East–West relationship, becoming yet again 'the Muslim–Christian relations/encounters'?

What is Occidentalism?

To draw a final definition of Occidentalism, I would like to put forth a set of questions revolving around whether like in the case of Orientalism, as defined by Said, the texts produced by authors from the 'Orient' do belong to a collective formation which one may call 'Occidentalism', and whether there exists a synthesis between these texts and their authors and this complex collective formation to which they consciously or unconsciously contribute?.

In other words, do these authors consciously work towards the construction of a discourse and a way of thinking which one may call Occidentalist? A way of thinking that is charged with feelings of revulsion, anger and disgust in the same way as Orientalism is charged with feelings of domination and superiority towards an Orient which is depicted as barbaric, inferior and flaccid.

Is Occidentalism a rejection of, if not a rebellion against Orientalism? Have Occidentalist authors produced their texts as a counter-discourse against Orientalism? If so, are they motivated by a desire to change the negative and stereotypical images produced about them? Or to create an equally damaging set of mis/representations of the Occident that would dehumanise it, according to some, or unmask it for its inhumane deeds during and after colonisation whose legacy is seen as the main source of the ills of the present, according to some others?

And if so, what is the purpose of this endeavour? Is the Orient engaging in a war of words, which often justifies, either directly or indirectly, the many political wars which exist today between Orient and Occident?

On the other hand, isn't this intellectual dialogue between Orient and Occident an attempt at reconciliation and rapprochement? Isn't distortion in representation often a result of the lack of a genuine encounter?

The term 'Occidentalism' is often defined as an inversion of Orientalism which also entails an inversion of its function; while Orientalism is a mode of representation of the Orient in a stereotypical manner, Occidentalism is also defined as the stereotyped and often essentialised views on the Occident.

What is of major importance in this study is the evolution of the relationship between Orient and Occident, how it all began and how it developed. Is it really all about hatred and revulsion? If so, what are the reasons which resulted in such feelings and why is it that the Occident was and remains till this day a major attraction to people from the East/Orient? How could hatred and revulsion for the Occident make it at the same time a pole of attraction for people from the Orient both in colonial and post-colonial times? Could one speak of a love–hate relationship? Or, about a mission of revenge by the people of the Orient for the deeds of the Occident during the colonial period, and for the host of prejudices and misrepresentations it propagated about them?

El-Enany on the other hand insists, 'With few exceptions, Arab intellectuals, no matter in which period, have never demonized the European other or regarded him in sub-human terms'.[74] A view I would support but only to a certain extent because the Maghrebi encounter with the Occident differs in many aspects from the Middle Eastern encounter on which El-Enany focuses in his book *Arab Representations of the Occident: East–West Encounters in Arabic Fiction*. This is mainly due to the colonial past and the nature of the encounter with the Occident which has unsurprisingly shaped the quality of the resulting discourse. Consequently, reactions to the Occident from the Maghreb diverge from those from the Mashriq/Middle East, and cannot be classified into one and the same category.

Conclusion

While we may argue that Occidentalism is still an evolving concept being constantly nourished by the ongoing relationship between the Orient and the Occident, we should also bear in mind that there are many Occidentalisms. It is hoped that it is clearly evident from the above discussion that the word 'Occidentalism' seems very amorphous and resembles phantasmagoria. That is to say, if Orientalism has been the conception of the Orient by the Occident, Occidentalism is the conception of this latter by all the Orientals who include the people of the Middle East and the Maghreb . It is therefore, the multi-conceptions produced by multi-nations not only as a reaction against Orientalism, but also as the attitude of at least four continents out of six towards Western civilisation and Westernisation. From observing the diverse encounters with the Occident as reflected in Occidentalist discourse, we can identify three main and diverse forms of reactions which can be classified as follows:

(1) Love for the Occident: Occidentophilia
(2) Hatred of the Occident: Occidentophobia
(3) Ambivalence towards the Occident

The differing facets and meanings of Occidentalism in different theoretical perspectives should be interpreted as a sign that testifies to the power of the concept rather than its inadequacy.

2

From the Faraway Orient to the Reclaimed Occident: French Civilisation, Religious Conversion and Cultural Assimilation

> Let everyone, the soldier with his *sword*, the settler with his *plough*, the priest with his *prayer*, the native with his *submission*, form a group of forces and Algeria will then reach a splendid destiny which God has certainly prepared for it.
>
> Ministère de la guerre[1]

Introduction

To consolidate its rule in the newly conquered colonies in the Maghreb, France created a colonialist discourse championed by imperialist authors and Orientalists who worked tenaciously towards a discursive reversal of history while at the same time stripping its people from their own history. The starting point of this project was to remind those who might have forgotten, that before it became known as the Muslim's Occident, meaning the Arab Maghreb, the North of Africa was part of the Christian world which was invaded by the Arabs under the banner of the Islamic expansion, who then erased all Christian legacies from the region and Islamicised its people and their culture. Therefore, the mission of France was to redeem this stolen land and salvage its people from their status as the uncivilised and fanatical believers in a heretic religion, while at the same time transforming it from the Muslims' Occident into the Occident's Orient.

This mission was sustained by many French authors whose thirst for all things Oriental was so ravenous to the point of making a location South of Europe which is only sixty nautical miles away from its shores, become yet another Orient. According to Marnia Lazreg 'The French fascination with the "Orient", spurred by Napoleon during his foray into Egypt in 1797, could not be satisfied',[2] mainly because it was short-lived and as such remains a curtailed dream in French imagination. However, while they found the task of identifying with the North African location as a new Orient unproblematic, they failed to make the local people part of this location which they persistently claimed as a land returned to the bosom of the Roman Empire on some occasions, and the Christian Creed on others. They have therefore, portrayed the North African natives as undeserving of such an idyllic location which they neglected and failed to elevate to the level of civilised countries mainly because they were lazy and unintelligent. Over and over again, these Orientals whom they often called the 'Arabs' are lumped together as one uniform group of uncivilised and indolent people whose country was in a dire need of a civilising power to rescue it from total decadence. This aspect of being 'uncivilised' and keeping the Orient in a primitive and decadent state, gave the colonial armies the authority and legitimacy to forcibly occupy the Orient in order to salvage it from becoming totally ruined, and save its primitive people from their own destructive barbarity by bestowing on them the benefits of civilisation. In other words the mission to civilise overlapped with, and justified, the mission to colonise.

Joseph Fourier articulates this point in the same way in his discussion of the Napoleonic expedition to Egypt, which he depicts in the following terms:

> This country [Egypt], which has transmitted its knowledge to so many nations, is today plunged into barbarism ... Napoleon wanted to offer a useful European example to the Orient, and finally also to make the inhabitants' lives more pleasant, as well as to procure for them the advantages of a perfected civilisation.[3]

Orientalising the Maghreb

The meaning of the word 'Maghreb' in Arabic is 'Occident' or the place where the sun sets, in other words the West. This appellation highlights the geographical setting of this region in comparison to the Arab Mashriq/East which gave it this name. However, to call a region that knows itself as being the Maghreb/Maghrib an 'Orient' meaning Sharq/Mashriq, is far from being an appropriate label, especially because this region is situated south of France and not in its East. What makes this situation even more ironical is how France was content to call the Maghreb its Orient when it did not designate the Maghrebi people as *Orientaux*/Orientals, but as *les arabes*/the Arabs. This therefore betrays the fact that France Orientalised the Maghreb as a geographical site that is not inhabited by Orientals but by Arabs.

The French Orientalisation of the Maghreb preceded the occupation of Algeria in 1830 by many decades. Being part of the Ottoman Empire France situated the regency of Algiers with its tales of piracy and captivity to which a host of legendary stories of treasures, riches, odalisques and sensuality were attached, as part of the tropes of the Orient. Chronicles of the early days of the conquest are laden with accounts of treasure-hunting in the Casbah of Algiers and the capture of women as Oriental odalisques.[4] By the end of the nineteenth and early twentieth century an important volume of literature was written by French authors to rationalise France's conquest of the Maghrebi/North African Orient, which they sometimes called 'Africa', and other times 'the Orient'.

J.-R. Henry explains the position of the French towards this new Orient which they found more accessible to their Orientalist imaginary than they did Egypt under Napoleon Bonaparte. Considering the geographical locations of these two regions which make Egypt more to the East of France than the Maghreb, one finds this view rather unsettling. Henry describes this state of affairs in the following terms:

> *Bien plus que l'Égypte de Bonaparte, l'Algérie, puis le désert et l'Afrique du Nord dans son ensemble ont été l'espace de référence privilégié où se sont déployés et mis en forme nos fantasmes Orientaux . . . Au feu du rapport à cet Orient concret, et a ses hommes, nous avons testé, et parfois forgé nos mythes: progrès, libéralisme, égalité, laïcité . . . ; nous nous sommes révélés en usant de l'Orient nord-africain comme d'un miroir.*[5]

> Much more than Bonaparte's Egypt, Algeria, the Sahara desert, and North Africa as a whole have become the privileged space of reference where our Orientalist phantasms have unfolded and taken shape . . . in the heat of our relationship with this *real Orient* and its people we have experimented and sometimes forged our myths of scientific progress, liberalism, equality,

secularism . . . ; we revealed ourselves by using the North African Orient as a mirror.

A Journey to the Orient: The Literary Orient of the Occidental Authors

Guy de Maupassant (1850–93) opens his novel *Au Soleil* (1884), with a description of the monotonous European life he escaped and his new attraction to the African Orient. He speaks of an intense desire and a deep nostalgia for the 'mysterious', yet 'enthralling' desert:

> *On rêve toujours d'un pays préféré . . . Moi, je me sentais attiré vers l'Afrique par un impérieux besoin, par la nostalgie du désert ignoré, comme par le pressentiment d'une passion qui va naitre.*[6]

> One always dreams of a favourite location . . . For me, I felt attracted to Africa by an exultant need, by the longing to the mysterious desert, as if by a sensation for a new passion.

Maupassant left Paris on 6 July 1881 and meticulously recorded his Oriental journey to Algeria as a new horizon but also as a lieu of escape. He not only describes his own impressions but also records the different views of the various Frenchmen (sailors, engineers, doctors and laymen) who were heading in the same direction. Although their views greatly diverged from his own, they all seem to share the same aim of finding what should work best to manage Algeria as a new French overseas department, which they saw as a land of opportunities for spiritual and material enrichment. However, beyond any economic or political considerations, what attracted Maupassant to Algeria was a journey for self-fulfilment through a personal pursuit of the unknown. On approaching Algiers from the Mediterranean Sea at dawn, he expressed his elation at what he saw:

> *Quel réveil! Une longue côte, et là-bas, en face, une tache blanche qui grandit- Alger ! [. . .] Féerie inespérée et qui ravie l'esprit ! [. . .] qu'elle est jolie, la ville de neige sous l'éblouissante lumière.*[7]

> What an awakening! Such a long coast, and over there a white stain that evolves-Algiers! [. . .] what an unexpected enchantment that delights the soul! [. . .] What a beauty, a snow white city under the enchanting light.

Using a host of Orientalist motifs, Pierre Raynal (1920–2008) describes the same city as being both attractive and repulsive at the same time. While he found the climate 'excellent' and the land 'admirable', he declared that nothing could equal 'the bizarre ugliness of Algiers', and 'nothing could equal its magnificence either'.

On the women of Algiers Raynal writes in a disappointed tone that they 'seem to have fled Africa (another name given to Algeria)', reflecting the Orientalists' expectation to find women roaming everywhere and at hand in the Orient.

Another Orientalist favourite motif is the Turkish baths, of which Raynal says, 'the baths here are part of a woman's life and the most jealous of husbands, in this country of Othellos, cannot prevent his wife from going there'.[8] As to Oriental music, which he calls 'Moorish music' he describes it as simply barbaric.[9]

The view of some French authors from the metropolis about the French civilising mission diverged greatly from that of the European authors who settled in Algeria. In his novel *Les Misérables* (1862) Victor Hugo (1802–85) contests this tendency to colonise in order to civilise. He speaks of Algeria as a country conquered with more barbarity than civilisation,[10] and demonstrates that one cannot civilise and colonise all at the same time, especially when colonisation is associated with extreme military violence. As to Guy de Maupassant, he criticises the tendency of the French conquerors to impose their way of life, their values, culture, architecture and manners on a country and a people for whom they are totally alien. He cites Napoléon III whose wise words he finds pertinent:

'Ce qu'il faut à l'Algérie, ce ne sont pas des conquérants, mais des initiateurs'. Or, nous sommes restés des conquérants brutaux, maladroits, infatués de nos idées toutes faites.[11]

'What Algeria needs, is not conquerors but motivators'. Nonetheless, we remained brutal conquerors, clumsy, and infatuated with our own ready-made ideas.

Maupassant criticises the French view of civilisation and argues that French projects in Algeria should harmonise with the indigenous style of architecture imposed by the climate and local culture. Instead, the settlers brought with them their own culture and architecture and imposed them onto an environment where they did not fit, and in an architectural setting where they did not match anything. He opines that by doing so, the settlers were doing violence to the native people as well as to their environment. Not to mention the shock that such projects brought to the locals and the difficulty they encountered with accepting them as part of their surroundings. In other words instead of adapting to their new North African environment the settlers Europeanised it and transformed it into an extension as well as a regeneration of the places they had come from, destroying therefore the sought after Orient the authors used to escape to and turning it into another piece of the Occident. For French litterateurs and artists, Algeria was viewed in exotic terms and mostly as a lieu of refuge and escape from a monotonous and complicated industrialised Europe, and for this they opposed the Europeanisation of their much sought after Orient as a source of inspiration for their works and an idyllic refuge from industrialised Europe.

From the Exotic Orient to the Latin Reconquista: Reclaiming Roman and Christian Legacy in France's New Orient

Louis Bertrand (1866–1941) brought an end to the literature of exoticism produced by the avatars of the Orientalist canon in the Maghreb. His position was not that of a traveller discovering bizarre locations and enchanting sites, but that of a crusader recovering a land stolen from the Latin world. In his book, *Le Sang des races* (1899),[12] he explains how his journey to the Maghreb was actually a journey to rediscover his Latin ancestors and reconquer their land. He declares that French intervention in Africa was motivated by the recovery of a province which had been lost to the Latin world: 'French Africa today is the Africa of the Romans, an Africa which is still alive and has never lost its vitality, even during the most troublesome, barbarous times.'[13] This Latin theme was used by Louis Bertrand not only to rationalise the French conquest but more importantly to create a common identity which would bring together the European settlers who came from different parts of southern Europe to settle back into the land of their Roman ancestors and forge a new race capable of restoring its past glories which were effaced by the ruin brought about by the Arab Muslim conquerors.

Such views were in circulation well before the French conquest of 1830. In a book published in 1785 titled, *Voyage dans les états barbaresques de Maroc, Alger, Tunis et Tripoli*, the anonymous author expresses similar views to Bertrand's, which may in effect have influenced the latter's opinion. He writes,

> *Les monuments augustes, quoique ruinés par les temps et les Barbares, nous font assez voir quelles étaient autrefois en ce pays la gloire et la puissance des Romains, ces hommes extraordinaires qui avaient l'art de donner une empreinte d'immortalité a tout ce qu'ils touchaient, la vue seule des décombres de la superbe Carthage, mérite bien notre attention, elle nous fait éprouver un sentiment douloureux.*[14]

These majestic monuments, though ruined by time and the Barbarians, are there to show us the grandeur and influence enjoyed by the Romans in this country. They were extraordinary people who had the power to bestow immortality on everything they touched. The sight of the remnants of the superb Carthage merits our attention, though it gives us painful feelings.

Louis Bertrand, however, insists that in addition to the recovery of the Latin heritage the French paid a high price for Algeria:

> *Les Français ont acheté l'Algérie avec le sang de leurs soldats, avec la mort empoisonnée des défricheurs, avec l'intelligence, l'énergie et l'argent dépensé sans compter . . .*[15]

The French bought Algeria with the blood of their soldiers, with the poisoned deaths of the first settlers, with their intelligence, energy and the inestimable funds spent on it . . .

More determined than ever, he adds in a reassuring tone while speaking on behalf of the new settlers:

> *Nous, Français, sommes chez nous en Algérie. Nous nous sommes rendus maître du pays par la force, car une conquête ne peut se réaliser que par la force, et implique nécessairement le fait qu'il y a eu des vainqueurs et des vaincus. Lorsque ceux-ci ont été matés, nous avons pu organiser le pays et cette organisation affirme encore l'idée de supériorité du vainqueur sur le vaincu, du civilisé sur l'homme inférieur.*[16]

We, the French, are at home in Algeria. We made ourselves the masters of the land by force, because a conquest can only be achieved by the use of force and that necessarily implies that there are conquerors and conquered. When the latter were subdued, we managed to build and organise the country and this organisation confirms once more the superiority of the conquerors over the conquered and of the civilised people over the inferior [uncivilised] people.

In an article he published four years later (1926) in the newspaper *Le Figaro* Bertrand expounds on how to dominate and rule among the uncivilised:

Pour réussir auprès de ceux-ci, il faut leur en imposer. Présentons-nous à eux comme les successeurs de l'Empire romain et comme une nation forte; C'est la seule politique africaine raisonnable.[17]

To succeed amongst them [the North Africans], we have to impose ourselves on them. We have to present ourselves as the successors of the Roman Empire and as a powerful nation. This is the only reasonable African strategy.

In 1865, *Le Tell*, a settler's journal, published a statement explaining the manner in which the new Algeria should be shaped:

Let everyone, the soldier with his *sword*, the settler with his *plough*, the priest with his *prayer*, the native with his *submission*, form a group of forces and Algeria will then reach a splendid destiny which God has certainly prepared for it.[18]

This colonial and racial ideology is summed up in Marshal Bugeaud's famous slogan '*Ense et Arato*: By the Sword and the Plough'. While the above statement delineates that no progress could be made without the total submission of the natives, in other words their 'effacement' and becoming a soulless malleable group of people primed to be used by the three main actors in the colonialist project; the settler, the soldier and the priest, who emerged as the main forces capable of changing the destiny of Algeria, Bugeaud's slogan testifies to the colonial method of conquest and land appropriation.

Aldrich explains how 'Algeria provided refuge to a heterogeneous population held together by the desire to make a new life in better conditions, feelings of superiority to native Algerians and links with France, mother country for some and protector of all Europeans in the colony'.[19] This demonstrates that while the new colony may have been considered a recovered Latin province by some, it was also 'vaunted as a new America, a haven for the poverty-stricken masses'[20] by many others, which explains the extreme use of force by the French conquerors who adopted a policy of ethnic cleansing and genocide especially in the early years of the conquest. In his book *Le Jeune Algérien* (1931), Ferhat Abbas (1899–1985) quotes some excerpts from the Letters of Maréchal de Saint-Arnaud as war reports. He writes,

> *Le pays des Béni-Menasser est superbe et l'un des plus riches que j'ai vus en Afrique. Les villages et les habitations sont très rapprochés. Nous avons tout détruit. Oh! La guerre! La guerre! Que de femmes et d'enfants, refugiés dans les neiges de l'Atlas, y sont morts de froid et de misère!*[21]

> The Béni-Menasser region is superb. It is one of the wealthiest that I have seen in Africa. The villages and their inhabitants are close to each other. We destroyed everything ... so many women and children took refuge in the snowy Atlas Mountains to end up perishing from the cold and misery.

In the same vein, Benjamin Stora lists some of the atrocities of the conquest in the following passage:

> In 1842, Saint-Arnaud destroyed part of Blida; Cavaignac inaugurated 'smoke-outs', asphyxiating rebels in caves on the west bank of the Chéliff; Canrobert razed a village in the Aurès to 'terrorize the tribes'; Pélissier, colonel of Bugeaud's column, smoked out a thousand men[22] from the Ouled Riah tribe who had sought refuge in the caves.[23]

Marie-Cecile Thoral describes the smoke-out and the reaction of French public opinion in the Metropole in the following terms:

> Some 800 members of that tribe had retreated before the advance of the French army and the razzias committed on neighbouring tribes and had sought shelter in a complex of caves or caverns in the nearby Dahra Mountains. The French pursued them and, after unsuccessfully ordering them to surrender and get out of those caves, piled wood at the entrances of the caves and set it ablaze, asphyxiating the Algerians who were trapped inside. This was the deadliest and most widely publicised case of *enfumade*

[smoke-out] but it was not the only one and there were a few other cases in subsequent years. This atrocity committed by the French army against rebellious tribes could not be kept secret or censored, despite the efforts of the War Minister Marshal Soult to cover it up, and, when leaked to the press, was strongly condemned by the French public.[24]

Despite Bugeaud's and many other army officers' justifications of the use of extreme violence against the native populations, these brutalities were widely criticised in metropolitan France by liberal journalists, some members of parliament and the general public who saw these massacres as immoral, barbaric and negating the moral justification of France's civilising mission.

As early as 1843, a member of the investigating commission formed by the kingdom of France following the smoke-out of the Ouled Riah tribe declared: 'We have surpassed in barbarism the barbarians we came to civilise'.[25] Such views, however, did not perturb the European settlers whose numbers increased dramatically over the years following the conquest but especially after Paris had extended citizenship to all Algerian-born Europeans in 1889.

The European population in Algeria soared from 37,000 in 1841 to 279.700 only 30 years later,[26] and with it grew the size of expropriated land. By the end of the 1860s, one third of the Algerian land had been confiscated and redistributed to the settlers, and by the time of the centenary of French occupation (1930) the settlers owned 40 per cent of the Algerian agricultural estate leaving only land of inferior quality to the natives[27] . . . The settlers, also known as the *colons* and the *pied noir*, came from various European countries including Spain, Italy, Sicily, Malta, Poland and France to settle in France's new colonies where they sought social and economic opportunities they did not have in Europe. French social reformers saw the colonies as an opportunity to provide homes and land to destitute Europeans whose social status could only be improved by seeking opportunities in the newly conquered colonies. According to Aldrich the colonies supplied land

> [. . .] for landless peasants, the urban unemployed and even orphans. Those convicted of criminal offences or political crimes could be transported to the colonies to rid France of dangerous elements in the body politic, supply the empire with settlers and rehabilitate wrongdoers.[28]

Watson explains how coming from such dubious social backgrounds contributed to the fact that the *colons* were a group of unscrupulous exploiters of the natives, and an unruly group of people who challenged the authority of various French governor generals appointed from the metropolis.[29] Their major aim was as ever to appropriate the land, exploit it and ruthlessly take advantage of the local people without abiding by any rules or caring about France's *Mission Civilisatrice*. In order to preserve the cheap unskilled labour force supplied by the natives, they fiercely opposed any reform programmes which would benefit them. The ultimate result was the creation of an indigent native population deprived of all citizenship rights, and a group of newly rich *colons* who employed them as daily labourers on what used to be their own land. At the turn of the twentieth century, this heterogeneous population positioned itself as the new Algerian race, while the locals became 'the Arabs' irrespective of whether they were actually Arabs or Berbers. Through a set of extreme binaries Louis Bertrand glorified this new race for its hard working qualities, strength and adroitness and criticised 'the Arabs' for being lazy, feeble and maladroit making them not worthy of their own land, which visibly justified its appropriation. Edward Said explains this point in the following excerpt:

> A civilised man, it was believed, could cultivate the land because it meant something to him; on it accordingly he bred useful arts and crafts, he created, he accomplished, he built. For an uncivilised people land was either farmed badly or it was left to rot. From this string of ideas, by which whole native societies who live on American, African, and Asian territories for centuries were suddenly denied their right to live on that land, came the great dispossessing movements of modern European colonialism, and with them all the schemes for redeeming the land, resettling the natives, civilising them, taming their savage customs, turning them into useful beings under European rule.[30]

Convinced that the Algerian land would be better looked after by the European settlers, Louis Bertrand boasts of the latter's arduous work and of their ability to transform the landscape into a vibrant scene after they laboured the land with modern machinery and tended the vineyards which became the bastion of the country's export economy. The settlers are the ones who built modern cities in the Maghreb, laid the rail lines, and opened modern schools and hospitals. Unlike the indolent Orientals the settlers are an active race capable of surmounting the difficulties of their new environment.

Nevertheless, Aldrich insists, no matter how firmly established the *colons* felt in the Maghreb, they lived among millions of native Maghrebis whom they often saw as ever threatening famished faces, from whom only the colonial power of France guaranteed their security and position.[31] One way to overcome this threat and fear in literary texts, and often in reality, was by pretending the natives did not exist, which explains their overall absence from French colonial literature. Commenting on Bertrand's literary works Patricia Lorcin posits,

> His African novels, which created his literary reputation, had no place for either Arab or Berber, being primarily concerned with the 'new Latin race'. The only interest the indigenous population held for him was as a 'walk-on in beautiful surroundings'. With the Latins of Africa, on the other hand, he had a 'multitude of affinities' and was drawn to them as much by nature as by literary predilection. His novels were a celebration of the virility and vitality of the settlers. In contrast he saw the indigenous population as a negation of these attributes.[32]

Bertrand's work is loaded with overt hatred of the natives and their religion which only brought decrepitude and ruin to what used to be a civilised land.

Comparing the discourse of the French authors from the metropolis to that of the European settlers in the colonies shows the huge disparity that exists between them, resulting therefore in two types of Europe, one that clung to France's republican values and somehow believed in France's mission to 'civilise the uncivilised', and another whose aims were purely colonial, almost campaigning for the total extermination of the native populations after stripping them of their best land and most importantly of their 'Algerianity' which they appropriated to become a term used to designate the new settlers while the original Algerians were all lumped together as 'les arabes/ the Arabs'.

France and its Mission of Assimilation and Civilisation

France's first assimilationist project goes back to the seventeenth century. The royal edicts of 1635 and 1642 state that the natives were to be considered citizens and Frenchmen *only* once they had converted to Catholicism.[33] No sooner did France pacify its Maghrebi colonies in the nineteenth century, and achieve its mission of the abolition of the enslavement of Christians, the destruction of piracy, and the end of humiliating tributes that European states have had to pay to the Ottoman Regency, it had to find a new motive for maintaining itself in its new colonies. The humanitarian mission to civilise the 'barbarians' soon became the fundamental drive for establishing itself in the Maghreb. Although the means to carry out this mission may have varied from one Maghrebi country to another, France's principal objective was occupation and domination but not civilisation. In the case of Algeria, Napoleon III wrote to Governor-general Pélissier[34] about his idea of 'the Arab Kingdom', where Arabs and Berbers would be associated with the European settlers under the aegis of France's civilising mission. The letter, which resembles Napoleon Bonaparte's letter to the Egyptians,[35] states that 'we have not come to Algeria to oppress and exploit them [the native Algerians], but to bring them the benefits of civilisation.'[36] In February 1863 Napoleon III instigated the creation of the Arab kingdom chiefly as a means to alter the image of France as a callous aggressor and to protect the native population against the systematic dismantling of its socio-cultural and economic fabric, which was fiercely inflicted by the conquering armies, and increasingly carried out by the European settlers in the decades following the occupation. In a study on population size in African countries[37] Mohammed Mazouz demonstrates that a population of 3 million Algerians in 1830 was reduced to 2.3 million in 1856. He explains that this regression is most likely due to the excess mortality caused by the unusually violent intrusion of the French colonial conquest, which weakened Algerian social development by destroying its socio-economic structure.[38] Charles Robert Ageron states that the country was devastated through the arbitrary policy adopted by the French occupants to impoverish the native populations. As a result of regular, improvised, and unremitting attacks on their sources of livelihood (pillaging of grain silos; stealing of herds; felling of trees), their economic situation became critical.

Following this the undernourished population was hit by epidemics.[39] In contrast, Droz and Lever testify that Napoleon III, 'tried with an admirable sense of commitment to heal the terrible sufferings of the previous decade, to improve the living standards of the natives and to set up a legal system respectful of Muslim customs'.[40] However, following France's defeat at the hands of Prussia in 1870 on the one hand, and due to the settlers' harsh opposition to this project which they saw as an obstacle to their expansionist aspirations on the other hand, Napoleon's venture of an Arab kingdom never took off the ground. In the centennial history of French Algeria produced by Augustin Bernard in 1930, the attitude of French administrators vis-à-vis France's colonies in the Muslim world is presented in the following terms:

> Now we did not go to Algeria merely to bring order into the native administration or to equip the country and then see it break away, retaining perhaps some gratitude towards us. No, our ultimate aim was always, as it still is, to *found an overseas France* where our *language* and our *civilisation* would live again through ever-closer cooperation of the natives with France – in other words, by *their being made Frenchmen*.(My emphasis.) [41]

The above citation refutes Napoleon's statement, and demonstrates that in accordance with its new republican principles of Liberty, Equality and Fraternity, and its mission to bestow civilisation on uncivilised nations, France's policies in its overseas territories evolved in order to bring together all its subjects under one roof and unify them through French language and culture. In other words, turn them into Frenchmen.

This remodelling of the Other to the image of the Self implies that the Other is imperfect *de facto*, and is therefore compelled to evolve to facilitate its becoming a facsimile of the Self so as to enter the realm of 'civilised' people, in other words to become French. To achieve this goal France deployed two principal institutions, namely the Catholic Church and colonial French schools.

While conversion to Catholicism was a condition for naturalisation, French education was tailored as a corrective tool to adjust environmental differences, seen as deficiencies, between the Self and its Other,[42] though it has to be underlined that this project could not be extended to the whole population but merely to an insignificant minority who were the children of France's allies. This elite were referred to as the '*Évolués*' who were the 'Frenchified' chosen few who graduated from French schools and adopted French looks and lifestyles. Although the term '*Évolués*' was proudly adopted as an epithet that gave a distinguished status to its bearers, it is nevertheless loaded with racist and denigrating meanings which stipulate that the members of this elite have undergone a process of evolution from their primitive state, while their parents and the majority of their people remained primitive. This state of affairs created division among the natives into various categories comprising those who chose to become allies of the French and those who were determined to resist acculturation and naturalisation and remain loyal to their people and their faith. On the other hand, it is worth stating that France's assimilation project was more of a metropolitan ideal than a concrete programme on the ground, mainly because the European settlers never believed in assimilation nor did they want to elevate the natives to the status of civilised people. They consistently opposed all assimilationist measures and undermined Metropolitan attempts at introducing any reforms to improve the conditions of the natives, whom they dubbed as '*incivilisable*' *de facto*. In Jules Ferry's words,

> It is difficult to make the European settler understand that there exist rights other than his in an Arab country . . . Rare are those *colons* who believe in the '*mission éducatrice et civilisatrice*' of the superior race; more rare still are those who believe in the possible improvement of the conquered race.[43]

Between the idealism and the policies of the French rulers in the metropolis and the influence and rapaciousness of the European settlers on the ground, native Maghrebis were often exposed to contradicting facets of France. Beyond the extreme violence of the conquest, especially so in the case of Algeria, Maghrebis were caught between a discourse which promised civilisation and education and a lived reality which was that of impoverishing the natives by expropriating their sources of livelihood and turning them into daily labourers in the farms of the *colons* which used to be their own.

The Catholic Mission and Assimilation through Religious Conversion

Just like Louis Bertrand believed the occupation of North Africa was an act of reclaiming a land stolen from the Romans, 'French Africa today is the Africa of the Romans, an Africa which is still alive and has never lost its vitality, even during the most troublesome, barbarous times',[44] the Catholic Church considered the occupation of the Maghreb a Christian victory over Islam, and an act of justice against the barbarians who for many centuries have not only captured and enslaved Christians through the work of the Barbary corsairs, but obstinately worked for the erasure of the Christian Creed from Africa. It was the Muslim conquest of the Maghreb that eradicated Christianity from it and erased its legacy to the ground. Motivated to restore Christianity in Africa as a whole and in the Maghreb in particular to what it was before the advent of Islam, Catholic and Protestant missionaries worked in earnest to convert Maghrebi Muslims and Jews into Christianity. In this, conversion was often mixed up with civilisation. To civilise also meant to convert in the same way as to become French also meant to become Christian. In the early years of the French occupation the church and the school worked hand in hand to convert, assimilate and civilise.

According to Raymond Betts, France's idea of assimilation is not a French invention but an idea which goes back to the Roman Empire. He claims:

> ... Roman expansion led to Latinisation of barbarian[45] regions, as was particularly evident in Caesar's times ... long before the French embodied assimilation in colonial theory, its practice had been apparent in diverse forms.[46]

He explains how, with the decline of the Roman Empire and the advent of Christianity, conversion into the new faith became a new form of assimilation resulting in the conversion of much of the Western world into Christianity. This spirit never ceased; 'To encourage the propagation of the faith, Spanish, Portuguese, and French missionaries, among others, carried the Christian message to the lands newly submitted to the control of their respective countries.'[47] Likewise, Walter Rodney considers Christian missionaries 'as much part of the colonizing forces as were the explorers, traders and soldiers ... missionaries were agents of colonialism in the practical sense, whether or not they saw themselves in that light.'[48] In the same vein, Daughton argues that the French civilising mission was an alibi to justify France's colonial project in the same way as the Christian missionaries had nothing to do with civilisation. He exposes the latter's true aspirations by saying:

The term 'civilisation' was of secondary importance to the Catholic missionary movement from its regeneration in the 1820s until at least the mid-1880s. For decades civilisation was little more than a positive by-product of the religious, spiritual, and moral awakening that missionaries brought to neophyte communities. Overwhelmingly, missionaries were committed to one goal: winning souls. Conversion was an essential precondition of (and, frankly, more important than) spreading civilisation.[49]

For the missionaries, the chief objective was the establishment of a Christian kingdom on earth and for this purpose they made conversion to Christianity a pre-requisite for becoming a candidate for French citizenship. They believed that teaching Christian life to the Maghrebi natives would automatically engender in them civilisation and grant them entry into the Christian kingdom.

This vision of civilisation, explains Daughton, 'made room for the missionary agenda of old: conversion and the acquisition of a "Christian" mode of behaviour were necessary preconditions of civilisation'.[50] Consequently, resisting conversion from the part of the natives equally meant resisting civilisation which in turn resulted in the label 'uncivilisable', as a condition of one who would not give up their own obscurantist faith exemplified in Islam, to enter the realm of civilisation through becoming Christian. This same token was made a pre-requisite for French naturalisation and citizenship. To become a French citizen also signified renouncing one's personal status, and interestingly enough preserving one's faith during the colonial epoch became symbolic of preserving one's own identity. In the absence of a political nation state, religion became the stronghold which kept the colonised together as one force of resistance against the invaders. On the popular level, the French occupation of Algeria was mostly understood as the prolongation of the crusades and an aggression of the *Kuffār* (infidels) against the Muslims, making it therefore a main duty to defend and preserve one's faith and remain Muslim in order to resist the invasion at least on the religious and cultural levels.

This popular view was heightened by the colonists' attacks on local religious institutions and the systematic closures of the *Zawāyā*[51] as religious centres which, in addition to teaching people the Qur'an and Arabic language they also taught them to actively fight against French occupation as a religious duty (*jihad*). This view is consolidated by the very fact that all popular uprisings have the *Zāwiya* as a starting and unifying base. The first Algerian popular armed resistance which lasted from 1832 to 1847 was led by the Emir Abdel Kader (1808–83)[52] who from the *Zāwiya al-qādiriya* to which he belonged, rallied all the local *Zawāyā* under the call for *jihad*. In the face of all forms of oppressive measures exercised by colonial France against the *Zawāyā*, these latter institutions played a fundamental role in preserving Arab and Islamic heritage as well as holding together the social fabric of the colonised society. Well aware of this vital role played by the *Zawāyā* the colonisers deployed all means to forcibly close them and brand them as centres of fanaticism and backwardness. Instead, they presented the Catholic priests and missionaries along with the French teachers as agents of civilisation and enlightenment, whom the majority of native Maghrebis feared and mistrusted because they considered their endeavours a direct assault and an alluring weapon against their faith and identity as Muslims. They therefore rejected 'this civilisation' not only because it came in the wake of a violent conquest, but also because it targeted their national/religious identity. According to Daughton, who unmasks the true aspirations of the Christian missionaries, the natives' views were not unfounded. This interpretation is shared by Walter Rodney in his book *How Europe Underdeveloped Africa*, where he argues that Europe failed to bring civilisation to Africans and contends instead that the Christian missionaries were mere agents of imperialism:

> The Christian missionaries were as much part of the colonizing forces as were the explorers, traders and soldiers ... missionaries were agents of colonialism in the practical sense, whether or not they saw themselves in that light.[53]

Cardinal Lavigerie and the Work of the White Fathers

Cardinal Charles Martial Allemand Lavigerie (1885–92)[54] is often remembered in the Maghreb for rescuing sick orphans during a famine, only to then convert them to Catholicism refusing to return them to their relatives when they recovered from illness, lest they would leave their new faith and fall back to their barbarity.

Genuinely believing in the conversion of North Africa to Christianity,

Lavigerie was alarmed by the absence of all Christian thought in France's early administration of Algeria. He declared that he was unable to understand France's 'blindness and impotence' for leaving the native Algerians for more than thirty years of French presence to their '*barbarity and their Koran*, instead of leading them to civilisation and the true faith.'[55] (My emphasis.)

For Lavigerie, Algeria was not a land of Muslims but a land of Islamised Christians. He believed that beneath the veneer of the Muslim faith lay the Christian conviction which pre-existed the advent of Islam. He worked tenaciously to revive the era of a Christian Africa which, for him, continued to be alive under the sediments of a recent Islamisation process. Lavigerie and his followers believed that these populations were forcibly converted to Islam and were therefore eager to be rescued and return to the faith of their glorious Berber ancestors who not only were Christian but played leading roles in the propagation of the faith as did Saint Augustine of Hippo (354–430 CE).[56] As soon as he was appointed to the position of Archbishop of Algiers on 27 March 1867, Lavigerie reversed the French policy of neutrality towards the Muslims and initiated a strong movement of assimilation and conversion. For this purpose he founded the White Fathers in 1868 and the White Sisters in 1869. He then deployed them to run and maintain the orphan asylums, the schools, hospitals, and agricultural settlements, which he established at great cost in order to bring the natives under the influence of the Gospel. This mission was expanded to Tunisia as soon as it became a French protectorate.

In 1881 Lavigerie won the title of Cardinal and became the first primate of the newly restored See of Carthage in 1884, retaining meanwhile the See of Algiers. In these two countries his legacy stands to this day in the form of the Basilicas of Notre-Dame d'Afrique in Algiers, of St Louis in Carthage, and the Cathedral of St Vincent de Paul in Tunis as testimonies of his re-Christianisation project.

In her book *Chrétiens de Kabylie, 1873–1954: une action missionnaire dans l'Algérie coloniale*, Karima Dirèche-Slimani[57] explains how following the 1857, 1864, 1867 and the 1871 popular uprisings against French occupation the Kabylie region became extremely impoverished, with its best lands being seized, its notables being killed or exiled, and its sources of livelihood annihilated by the French military. This was followed by a series of famines, of which the most notorious was the 1867–8 famine[58] which claimed a huge number of lives, and the outbreak of epidemics of cholera, tuberculosis and smallpox resulting in high rates of infant mortality and loss of life in general. These dire conditions made the Kabyle people a vulnerable target for Lavigerie's mission. Capitalising on the age-old Kabyle myth which distinguished between Algerian Arabs and the Kabyles on the basis that the latter might be of Indo-European rather than of Semitic origins,[59] his reconversion/re-Christianisation project targeted five tribes in the heart of the Djurdjura Mountains.[60] These are the Ath Smaïl, Ath Menguellet, Ath Yenni, Beni Douala and the Ouadhia. By distributing food to the famished population, by taking in orphans, and curing the sick, the missionaries soon became indispensable. Old people, orphans and widows who were unable to provide for their children were among the first to be converted to Christianity. In some cases destitute parents who were unable to feed their children would entrust them to the orphanages where they would be cured and fed and eventually converted to Christianity. Dirèche-Slimani calls this conversion process 'conversions de la misère', and a rare occurrence in the whole Maghreb.

It is in these circumstances that the White Sisters came to play a vital role in helping the poor, tending the sick and spreading the Christian faith.[61] In no time at all they became part of the social fabric, infiltrating deep into the Kabyle society to the point of being called the *Roumi's Marabout*, meaning the religious sisters of the French. They were highly regarded by the Kabyles who found in them a helping hand to tend the sick and to give advice on various issues relating to the health of the community. As nurses in the mission's hospitals the White Sisters helped the locals trust modern medicine and discard the customary local cures which proved less efficient. These conversions, however, constituted a bone of contention for both the missionaries and the Muslim population. While the first group sought to start its mission of converting the whole country by converting the Kabyles, who were known for their relaxed approach to religion in general, the Muslim Algerians were utterly alarmed by this move as a way to divide the nation.

Those who opted to convert to Christianity were castigated for their disaffiliation from their own people. Although under colonial conditions the converts were not subjected to capital punishment for deserting their religion, as would be the case under normal circumstances, they were nevertheless ostracised by the majority of their fellow natives who afflicted them with all kinds of stigmatising names such as *M'tourni* (turncoats), *Kuffār* (renegades), and *Murtad* (apostate) etc . . . when at the same time the French never saw their transformation as genuine or their shift to Christian ways as masterly or successful, but viewed them as pretentious imitators. In addition to this, their conversion did not lead to their naturalisation to become French citizens but they were instead classified by the colonial administration as non-citizens. As such, they were stripped from their status as Muslim Algerians and became Christians but not French citizens, making them losers on all fronts. Dirèche-Slimani explains:

> *La conversion confondue avec la naturalisation accentuera l'ambigüité de leur identité. Chrétiens sans être français, indigènes sans être musulmans, leur position bascule d'un sens à un autre, d'une définition à une autre sans jamais être vraiment satisfaisante.*[62]

> Conversion confused with naturalisation only accentuated the ambiguity of their identity. Christian without being French, native Algerian but no longer Muslims, their position swayed from one pole to another, from one characterisation to another without ever being truly adequate.

Over and above, this condition resulted in a deep and painful identity crisis for converts who, in effect, became a category of people rejected by all. A good example of this dilemma is the case of the Amrouche family of authors who turned their sentiments of alienation into the central theme of their literary oeuvre . . .

In her autobiography, *My Life Story* (1968), Fadhma Amrouche (1882–1967) explains how she was vilified by her in-laws as the renegade who had stolen their favourite son. She describes herself as the Christian among the Muslims, and the Kabyle among the Arabs. She says, 'I remain for ever the eternal exile, the woman who has never felt at home anywhere.'[63] This view is shared by her son Jean Amrouche (1906–62) who on 18 August 1959 wrote in his diary:

> *J'avais onze ans. Petit Kabyle Chrétien, j'étais roulé entre les puissantes masses que constituaient mes condisciples: renégat pour les musulmans, carne venduta (puttain, litt.viande vendue) pour les italiens, bicôt au regard des français . . .*[64]

I was an eleven-year-old young Kabyle Christian boy. For this I was lashed by my classmates: renegade for the Muslims, *carne venduta* (whore, lit. sold flesh) for the Italians and *bicôt* (kid) for the French.

In his novel *Les Chemins qui montent* (1955),[65] which is the only literary text which discusses the subject of the Kabyle converts, Mouloud Feraoun (1913–62) portrays them in ironic terms. He claims that they would worship at both the church and the mosque as they would celebrate both the Muslim and the Christian festivals:

Ils jurent par les saints du pays, pratiquent la circoncision comme les bons musulmans et célèbrent les Aids aussi bien que la Noël.[66]

They swear by the local saints, they circumcise their children as would do the Muslims, and they celebrate the Eids as well as Christmas.

Feraoun also speaks about the insincere conversion which many of them had undergone in order to improve their social status and how, when they failed to gain acceptance by the French regardless of their new faith, they then turned on Jesus and the priests. Indeed, many of them confused conversion with naturalisation.

This way of ostracising the converts remained unchanged for the length of the colonial period. After independence Maghrebi Christians became even more alienated and for fear of reprisals from their Muslim compatriots they had to flee their native villages, cities or even in some cases, their countries.

On the ground, however, while the number of converts was minimal, amounting to a few thousand persons out of a population of 300,000 Kabyles in 1870,[67] most of them were not profoundly persuaded and many ended up reverting to Islam. Those who remained Christian were strongly attached to their Kabyle culture which they practised along with their Muslim compatriots, especially in terms of male circumcision, endogamous marriages and other matrimonial practices. In some cases, it is reported that the converts would celebrate both the Muslim and the Christian feasts, visit the local saints and even attend the mosque on Fridays and the church on Sundays.[68] Although the families of the converts were closely supervised as well as coached by the missionaries, it became obvious that Kabyle customs were stronger than the new faith, a fact that had to be accepted by the church in the end. Following the death of Cardinal Lavigerie in 1892, the White Fathers admitted to the failure of their re-conversion project and had totally given up on this idea by the 1930s.

Assimilation through French Education

Because the Catholic missionaries used the school as another route towards conversion to Christianity and Christian ways, missionary schools were not popular among the natives. In fact they often operated as orphanages that recruited orphans and as French schools to which the children of France's allies were enrolled in the hope of securing high profile positions in the French administration. As to ordinary natives, they boycotted these schools to preserve their children from conversion and the loss of their cultural identity.[69]

While the position of the Maghrebis vis-à-vis the missionaries' schools remained reasonably unchanged all the way to the turn of the twentieth century, their attitude towards secular French education evolved from a total rejection in the nineteenth century to a gradual acceptance in the early years of the twentieth century.

Although it was generally perceived that this change of position had been influenced by the natives' declining economic conditions and the impossibility to gain access to decent jobs to which the sole key was French education, one should not overlook the efforts made by the first educated native elites, the *Évolués*, to build bridges and close the gap which separated the Orient from the Occident. Through their writings, political activities, and social networks they deployed all the means they possessed to reassure the former that the latter had indeed brought the key to salvation through modern education.

French Schools as Workshops for Assimilation and Acculturation

Secular French education became free and compulsory for native Algerians in the 1880s. Believing in the school as a vehicle which would carry over the natives from their own decadent culture to the realm of French civilisation, Jules Ferry set up the *Certificat d'études indigènes* which was modelled on the metropolitan prototype but destined for indigenous populations.

In Algeria, the number of such schools grew from 23 in 1882 with 3,200 pupils, to 124 schools and 12,300 pupils ten years later, to reach 228 schools and 25,300 pupils in 1901.[70] While educating Maghrebi elites was intended to eventually fill the lower ranks of the colonial civil service, it was officially declared that, 'education for the natives . . . will effectively bridge the gap and, by helping them to live with the same concepts, will teach them to see themselves and act as members of the same human family, of the same nation'.[71] Although the prime objective of French education was assimilation through the teaching of French language and culture, it was received by the Maghrebis as a key to the realm of European civilisation; 'C'est par l'éducation que nous arriverons à la civilisation'.[72] However, it remains to say that up until the independence of the whole of the Maghreb, French education remained the privilege of a very small minority and this was not solely owing to resistance from the part of the natives but was mainly attributable to the European settlers' interference with the project of educating native Maghrebis.

After destroying the local public educational networks in Algeria, which though mostly traditional generated high rates of literacy, French rule laid the foundations of a colonial education destined for a very select elite. Mahfoud Bennoune provides some statistics which affirm that by 1944 only 8 per cent of school-age children were attending school. In other words, out of the eight million Algerians in the 1940s, seven million were illiterate.[73] On the eve of the Algerian War of Independence in 1954, as many as 85 per cent of the total Algerian population were illiterate, with women's illiteracy rate being at 98 per cent.[74] Lazreg gives the following figures: the number of Algerian boys attending schools by 1954 had reached 225,289 while that of girls was only 81,448.[75] Not only did the settlers fear that the schools would nurture educated nationalist elites who would then be pitted against the brutal exploitation of their people, but most importantly they wanted to keep the natives as an uneducated working class which constituted a cheap labour force. This dichotomy between the views of the French in the Metropole and those of the settlers in the colony shaped colonial rule and decision making throughout the colonial period, with the first believing in the French Civilising Mission and the latter rejecting the unrealistic ideals of the Metropole.

Based on their colonialist ideology, the settlers claimed that they knew the natives very well through direct contact on the ground, and therefore they were better positioned to establish that they were not worthy of civilisation.

On this account Jules Ferry, a fervent colonialist who believed that it was the right and the duty of superior races to bring civilisation to inferior races, wrote in a tone of regret:

> *Bien rares sont les colons pénétrés de la mission éducatrice et civilisatrice . . . ils ne comprennent guère vis-à-vis de ces trois millions d'hommes que la compression.*[76]
>
> Very rare are the settlers who have embraced the mission to educate and civilise the natives. They only envisage containment with regard to these three million natives.

Ferry was convinced that the attitudes of the settlers in relation to the natives would result in the demise of the colonial endeavour, and that education was the most efficient tool to disseminate civilisation, and in consequence to fully integrate the native population into the French nation. The French textbooks studied in the new primary schools were replete with images of a bountiful France unreservedly extending its generosity to all its citizens including the uncivilised people of the colonies.

In Morocco, Resident-General Louis-Hubert Lyautey, known as the architect of the French domestication of Morocco, aspired to realise the Arab dream which Napoleon III had failed to achieve in Algeria through his Arab Kingdom project. Lyautey proclaimed,

> What I dream of, what many of you dream of along with me, is that among all these disorders that are shaking the world to the point that one asks when and how it will ever regain its equilibrium, in Morocco a solid edifice will be built, orderly and harmonious; that it will offer the sight of a group of humanity where men of such diverse origins, habits, professions and races, pursue, without abdicating any of their individual conceptions, a search for a common ideal and a common rationale of life. Yes, I have dreamed that Morocco would appear one of the most solid bastions of order against the sea of anarchy.[77]

A devoted advocate of the civilising virtues of colonialism, which were fiercely opposed by the Algerian settlers through the uncivilised and ruthless manner they treated the natives, and their constant opposition to any French reforms which would improve the Algerian natives' social and economic status, Lyautey believed that colonialism could lead to progress if its mission was not interrupted. In Morocco he called for the collaboration of the indigenous elites to help establish a civilizing protectorate.[78] Lyautey's project greatly benefited from the mistakes committed in Algeria and in consequence he did not press for the assimilationist attitudes which aimed at suppressing the diversity and difference between the coloniser and the colonised, but respected and accepted the fact that Moroccans were dissimilar to the French, which in his view was key to forging a more magnanimous relationship between France and its subjects.

Having said this, Lyautey's mission was not opposed to a colonialist agenda which aimed to rule and dominate the conquered population, albeit in a more restrained manner, which was in his view a more efficient means to achieve his colonial ambitions. Although he held opposing views to those of the Algerian settlers and their callous approach when dealing with the natives, he did not differ from them in his loathing of the culture and politics of the Metropole as too idealistic and not fit to be applied in the colonies. According to Spencer Segalla,

> After many years of military service in the colonies, Lyautey had developed disdain for republican France, which he found alien [and] decadent ... For Lyautey, the remedy to Parisian decadence could only come from the periphery, from the aristocratic traditions of provincial France and from the colonies, where the rigors and privations of life would purge the French character of weakness.[79]

In this, Lyautey's views largely concurred with those of the Algerian settlers, and like them he also believed that the colony was the birthplace of a 'New' France. Herein, his 'muscular philosophy' did not differ from that of Louis Bertrand, who sung the glories of the new French Algerians (the *colons/* settlers) whose hard work and virility forged the new Algerian nation, that of the new French–Algerian race.

Lyautey alleged that in order to build the new Morocco, he did not need the assistance of any 'Molière-type doctors in pointed caps speaking Latin, but sturdy practitioners who roll up their sleeves and get down to work',[80] which falls in harmony with Marshal Bugeaud's famous slogan 'Ense *et Arato*: By the Sword and the Plough'. Much like the settlers in Algeria, he did not believe in assimilation or conversion of the natives into the French ways and Christian religion. Based on his conviction as to the values of conservatism, Lyautey built his colonial views on 'respect' of the natives' particularities in terms of religion and culture and therefore did not favour educational institutions which would bring the Moroccans into direct contact with the French, as a means of promoting the separation of cultures and social classes. This stark segregation of the races was, for Lyautey, key to preserving European dominance, and this was reflected in every aspect of colonial Morocco including urban planning. His major endeavour was to oppose and prevent any occurrence of miscegenation between the native Moroccans and the French occupants at all levels, be they social, racial/biological or cultural.

Furthermore, while colonial schools were generally viewed as sites of close interaction between colonised and coloniser/Orient and Occident, and a favourable loci of cultural contact and exchange, in the case of Morocco they were mainly seen as cites for creating new collaborators who would serve the coloniser and help maintain the colonial order. Segalla confirms this view: 'Colonial schools aimed to produce willing collaborators among the colonised',[81] and although French-run schools in Morocco were supposed to reinforce French hegemony by convincing the locals that it was in their best interest to comply with the French colonial agenda, they, just like in the neighbouring Algeria and Tunisia, 'became focal points of contestation'.[82]

The Évolués as Bridge-builders between Orient and Occident

Commonly known as the *Évolués* (in Algeria they were known as Les Jeunes Algériens (the Young Algerians), and in Tunisia as Les Jeunes Tunisiens(the Young Tunisians)),[83] the first Maghrebi French-educated elite worked tenaciously to help find ways to bridge the gap that separated their people from the Occident. The first step towards this was to help them view French schools not simply as workshops for converting their children from their religious and cultural identity, but also as a means to gain a modern education and therefore secure a better future. Believing in the sincerity of the French civilising mission, the work of the *Évolués* was that of the mediators between their own people and their civilisers. They mobilised their compatriots on the ground while they communicated with the French through their letters and published papers.

In a letter addressed to the members of the French senate in charge of debating necessary reforms in Algeria, Louis Khodja tried to correct the image held by the French of Islam as a fanatical religion and of Muslims as harbouring hatred against Christians. He insisted that the Qur'an, which was consistently blamed for the fanaticism of the Muslims, does not contain any hatred against non-Muslims and in no way forbids the assimilation of the Arabs (meaning Algerians) to French ways:

> ... *le Coran ne s'opposait pas à l'assimilation de l'Arabe. Tout d'abord, je ne vois, dans ce livre sacré des musulmans, aucun texte qui lui défend de s'instruire, et partant, de se ranger à la civilisation européenne, ou qui lui commande, comme on se plait à le lui attribuer, la haine du 'Roumi' (du français).*[84]

> The Qur'an is not against the assimilation of the Arabs. I see in this sacred book no text forbidding the education of the Muslims, and from here nothing that would prevent them from embracing European civilisation nor, as many tend to believe, to harbour hatred against the 'Roumis' (the French).

To assimilate the Arabs to French ways, Khodja advises the French to change their political attitude which stipulates religious conversion as a pre-requisite for French citizenship. Although he himself converted to Christianity he knew well that not many natives would choose the same path as his parents did. He, therefore, was negotiating an important political reform through arguing for the acceptance of the status of the Français Musulman, meaning to be French while remaining a Muslim. This would imply that France as a nation would have to accept the inclusion of a new religion under its banner. In other words, since Algeria was politically annexed to France, then it would become a reality that not all French people living in Algeria were Christian. As a result, Islam ought to be recognised as the second religion of the French nation.

While it would appear that Khodja was simply pleading for the right of his own people to accede to French citizenship without having to give up their personal status, he was in real fact asking for a fundamental political and cultural change in what it means 'to be French': an issue which continues to be debated to this very day by Muslim communities living in France as they negotiate their identity as French Muslims. Keen to be heard and understood, Khodja skilfully drew a plan which he put forth to the French authorities. He advised them as follows:

Pour assimiler l'Arabe, il faut, 1– L'instruire, l'attirer dans vos écoles, 2– Il faut lui apprendre à distinguer entre le nom Français qui est celui d'un peuple, et le nom de Catholique, qui est le nom d'une religion; il faut lui montrer que l'on peut être bon Français en même temps que fervent Musulman. (My emphasis.)[85]

In order to assimilate the Arabs, one must, 1– educate them, attract them to your schools, 2– one must make them distinguish between the name French which is that of a people, and the name Catholic, which is that of a religion; *one must demonstrate to them that it is perfectly possible to be a good French person and at the same time a fervent Muslim.*

In the same vein, Mejdoub ben Khalfat, one of the first trained native Algerian school teachers wrote an article explaining to the French authorities his strategy to attract Muslim children to French schools. In his attempt to understand the reasons which held back the natives from educating their children in French schools, he maintained that there was much resentment between them and the 'new rulers of the country'. Such defiance, which was according to the French view mainly intensified by the natives' religious fanaticism, would persist for as long as they remained illiterate and ignorant. To break this cycle of mistrust and prejudice Ben Khalfat advised the French authorities that:

. . . il faut amener l'enfant arabe à l'école; il faut l'arracher des parents ignorants et fanatiques, incapables de comprendre les bienfaits de l'instruction et de la civilisation française.[86]

One must bring Arab children to [French] schools; one must remove them away from their ignorant and fanatic parents, who are incapable of appreciating the benefits of French education and civilisation.

In his effort to understand the reasons for this fanaticism, which in real terms is the native's cultural resistance to acculturation, Ben Khalfat concluded that the memory of the crusades, as a religious war against Islam and Muslims, was still alive in the natives' minds and as a consequence they continued to believe that the primary aim of the French teachers was to convert their children to Christianity.

Furthermore, one should not neglect to mention the extreme violence of the French invasion and the horrors inflicted by the French armies on the native populations in the not-too-distant past. However, what anchored this sentiment of mistrust in the minds of the natives is the work of the missionaries who forcibly converted orphans and destitute people, especially in the course of famines. This was seen by the natives as a direct attack on Islam and their cultural identity as Muslims before all else.

In order to change this situation and win the trust of the native parents, Ben Khalfat suggests that native teachers should be trained and then employed to teach native children. In this way their Muslim parents would not fear conversion to Christianity, meanwhile conversion into French ways and culture was not seen as an irresolvable problem; native children were brought back to their parents' way of life as soon as they stepped out of the school's vicinity.

Strongly believing that French education was the only route to civilisation, the first generation of native Maghrebi intellectuals saw French schools as a locus for producing bridge-builders between the Orient and the Occident. After all, it was not in the highly segregated colonial public space, but in the vicinity of the school that Maghrebi children came into direct contact with the Occident as the benefactor who came to civilise the people in their colonies – albeit after decades of bloody resistance.

If the main aim of French education was to turn the natives into Frenchmen, and since what seemed to be of prime importance for the native population was to preserve their religion and religious identity, then it did not matter so much to become a Frenchman as long as one remained a Muslim. This is manifest in the opinion of many Maghrebi intellectuals including Ferhat Abbas who, in 1931, was happy to count Algerians as Frenchmen with Muslim personal identities.

In 1936 Abbas went so far as to identify with France and openly proclaim 'La France, c'est moi', in an article he published in *L'Entente franco-musulmane*, a cultural and political journal he himself established and edited, and whose title indicates his full dedication to France's assimilationist project.

Not only did Abbas express his personal fusion with the Occident by declaring that he was France and France was him, but he was happy and proud to consider Algeria a fundamental part of France; an idealised France of which he read in his books and whom he loved through his love for its authors, intellectuals and the universal principles of *Liberté, Egalité, Fraternité*.

Fully immersed in the ideals of his adoptive nation, Abbas went as far as marrying a French woman, which was very uncommon at that time, and was happy to think of himself as fully French and declare that 'the Algerian nation' was a myth and that it had never existed as a nation state:

L'Algérie en tant que patrie est un mythe. Je ne l'ai pas découverte. J'ai interrogé l'histoire; j'ai interrogé les morts et les vivants; j'ai visité les cimetières: personne ne m'en a parlé.[87]

The Algerian nation is a myth. I have not encountered it. I have questioned history; I have questioned the quick and the dead; I have visited cemeteries. No one has spoken to me of such a thing.

For Abbas, total self-denial and becoming part of the glorious France while remaining Muslim was the ultimate opportunity for his fellow Algerians to join the ranks of civilised people and redeem themselves from their own barbarity.

However, the reality on the ground was different. His deep reflection on the relationship between France as the Occident and Algeria as the Orient, made him identify two possible political options; the first is the emancipation of the natives through French education under the rule of a French civil administration which would grant full citizenship rights to all native Algerians, while the second is a traditional colonialist regime which exploits the natives and suppresses their rights of citizenship.

Abbas describes the first option as an ideal possibility where a genuine marriage between the Occident and the Orient would occur and be made possible through France's reconciliation with Islam thereby generating an *Oriental France* with a *Franco-Muslim culture*, which would therefore create the most beautiful miracle of the modern times; the fusion of two civilisations, that of the Occident with that of the Orient.

As for the second option, this is when the colonialists opt for appropriating the colony and its native inhabitants and claiming them as their own and at their service. In the case of Algeria, Abbas refers to Louis Bertrand's project of claiming the land of his Latin ancestors in Africa. With deep regret Abbas remarks that the second option was the most prevalent one resulting thus in a colonialist regime which instead of genuinely bridging the gap between the two peoples and their two cultures they put their emphasis on the differences between them.

This gap became even wider following the 8 May 1945 massacres which resulted in the killing of 45,000 Algerians.[88] On the day the armistice was signed Muslim Algerians paraded in major cities with banners bearing the slogan 'Down with colonialism', and 'Long Live Algeria, Free and Independent'. The colonial police was alarmed to see for the first time in the history of modern Algeria the demonstrators waving the Algerian flag, which they tried to confiscate. Being met with strong resistance the police shot the demonstrators resulting in the angry reaction of the crowds and the fury of the settlers who intervened with firearms. According to Stora 'Shooting and summary executions among the civilian population continued for several days ... Villages were bombed by the air force, and the navy fired on the coast'.[89] The result was a tragedy which unified all native Algerians, regardless of their political orientation, against colonialism. For them these bloody events destroyed any confidence they might have had in France and the date of 8 May 1945 came to be known in the annals of modern Algerian history as the point of no return which ultimately led to the Algerian War of Independence (1954–62). This political divorce created long debates among Algerian intellectuals and French liberals. For the assimilated Algerians it signalled the deepening of their identity crisis because the fortress they used to believe in had started to disintegrate and to show the ugly face of the colonial Occident. For the French liberals this episode also resulted in a deep anxiety and the fear of an uncertain future. Although intellectuals like Camus, Amrouche and Abbas continued to debate what they called 'the Algerian Problem', they did not disagree that May 1945 was a violent tremor that shook fundamental beliefs to the core.

Conclusion

While the political, economic and administrative institutions in the colony were easily assimilated to those of the metropolis, cultural assimilation of

Maghrebi people proved to be more difficult. This is so, especially because assimilation and/or naturalisation implied renouncing one's statutory rights, '*statut personnel*' under Islamic law, which was deemed an act of apostasy, and although the native educated elite tried very hard to explain the Occident to the Orient and the Orient to the Occident, the latter's intentions about civilising the former were not always forthright.

It has become clear from this discussion that the Algerian 'Oriental' encountered so many different 'Occidentals' that are so dissimilar to the point of creating confusion about how to draw a definitive portrait of the Occident. Four distinctive types from the Occidental became very prominent during the colonial period as follows:

(1) The French authors and intellectuals who propagated humanitarian and republican values for which they were deeply admired by the Orientals.
(2) The Christian missionaries: their prime aim was the re-Christianisation of Africa through the 're-conversion' of the natives to Christianity, with the assumption that they were eagerly waiting to be saved from their barbarity through conversion.
(3) Metropolitan politicians: whose republican ideals and projects for the colony were often sabotaged by the European settlers on the ground. While they are often portrayed by both the European settlers and the native Algerians as being very far from the lived reality in the colony, the natives saw them as less harmful and more genuine in their claims to bring civilisation to them but were constantly being hindered by the European settlers.
(4) The European Settlers: they came to the colony for material gain and did not believe in the French's civilising mission. For them the only thing that mattered was land appropriation with its native inhabitants merely viewed as a subhuman class good for exploitation.

This categorisation indicates that the natives did not lump all Europeans together as ruthless colonisers, as they were themselves lumped together as uncivilised Orientals in need of saving by the Occident from their own barbarity, and therefore at this stage the Orientals did not Occidentalise the Occident in the same way as the Occident Orientalised the Maghreb.

Although native intellectuals have not spared any effort to bring Orient and Occident closer to each other, Abbas and his fellow native intellectuals were convinced that France did not do enough for this ideal to become a reality, and therefore that it should not persist in blaming the native population for being eternally uncivilisable. He says:

La vérité, cependant est simple à concevoir. Dominée par le problème du peuplement européen et par les intérêts particuliers, la colonisation a très peu fait pour la société musulmane et pour l'entente et la réconciliation des races.[90]

The truth, however, is simple to comprehend. Preoccupied by the problem of European settlement and the specific needs of the settlers, colonisation has done very little for the Muslim community and for promoting mutual understanding and reconciliation between the two races.

Seeing that the European settlers had positioned themselves as a stumbling block in the natives' way to progress and civilisation, and that they did everything in their might to keep the two communities both separated and unequal, Abbas presents a powerful depiction of this condition in the following excerpt:

Nous la voyons se dresser contre nous, cette société dont le meilleur élément a été chassé de l'Europe par la misère.

La France a conçu l'instruction des indigènes, réalisé en 1890 par le regretté Jeanmaire: la Colonie a été hostile à cet enseignement . . . La France a ouvert son pays à l'ouvrier algérien: la Colonie a été hostile à l'exode de cet ouvrier en France . . .[91]

It is obvious to us that the settlers are against us; they are a group of colonists the best of whom had left Europe by dint of their poverty.

France has put in place a programme for the instruction of the natives, engineered in 1890 by the late Jeanmaire: the settlers were hostile to this programme . . . France opened its country for the Algerian workers: the settlers were hostile to the exodus of these workers to France.

3

The Occident and the Barbary Corsairs: Pre-colonial Maghrebi Encounters with the Occident

The Arabs and the West: it is a long complicated story, and like a good complicated story it has plenty of conflict in it, and plenty of love and hate. The relationship is as old as Islam: attraction and repulsion between them have co-existed to an exhilarating degree, sometimes to a tragic degree.

Jabra Ibrahim Jabra[1]

Introduction: Pre-colonial Encounters

According to Albion Small, 'Conditions are what they are, events occur as they do, because, a long chain of antecedent conditions and occurrences has set the stage and furnished the motives'.[2] Without deconstructing the links which make this long chain of antecedent conditions and occurrences, it would be challenging to gain a fuller understanding of the encounter between the Maghreb and Europe. Situating the Maghreb region in the historical context which preceded the French occupation of Algeria in 1830 and its presence in the region all the way to 1962 will help us gain a better understanding of many aspects of this encounter and a deeper appreciation of the literature which represents it.

Prior to becoming known as the 'Maghreb' under the Umayyad's reign, North Africa encountered many occupants and was given many different names. From the Phoenician era (333–149 BCE), to the Hellenistic period and the arrival of the Vandals in the fifth century, the last European occupants of the North African region were the Romans, who preceded the advent of Islam and the creation of the Maghreb as part of the Islamic Empire in the seventh century. Therefore the image of the Romans, locally referred to as '*Roumis*', is the most anchored in popular memory and is vastly recorded in vernacular poetry. Up to the present day, white people from Europe are referred to as *Roumis* in colloquial North African languages. Not only this, but to this day the visibility of Roman relics especially in Algeria and Tunisia testifies to the great material influence the Romans had on this region. H. V. Canter testifies that, 'There is no other part of the world that Rome governed, not even southern France, where her genius is to this day more clearly to be recognised or where imposing material remains, mosaics and inscriptions, are more abundant.'[3] The reverse encounter between the Muslim Maghreb and Europe occurred in the first half of the eighth century. And just like all that is left in the Maghreb from the Roman Empire is its material relics, all that remains of the Islamic Empire in the Iberian Peninsula are its architectural vestiges.

Under the banner of the Islamic expansion Tariq ibn Ziyād led Arab and Amazigh (Berber) armies from the Maghreb to conquer the Visigothic Kingdom of Spain in 711, which was from then on named the province of Al-Andalus. From there Muslim armies expanded northwards into Aquitaine and the Rhône valley in the Frankish lands where they were met with a strong resistance by an impenetrable Frankish infantry which, on 25 October 732 dealt them a serious defeat at the Battle of Tours-Poitiers.[4] For many centuries to come this battle was hailed as the decisive moment when the Cross defeated the Crescent with the help of Christ, *Christo auxiliante*, and made the Frankish Kingdom the triumphant country who had, unlike its neighbours, not only resisted Muslim expansion but chased the Muslims from all the lands they occupied in their Kingdom. The Frankish policy of resistance to the Muslims was soon turned by Charlemagne (r. 768–814) into military campaigns against all Muslims in all Christian lands including the Iberian Peninsula. The religious aspect of this encounter motivated the many conquests led by the Frankish warriors and later by the French armies against Muslim territories in the southern Mediterranean region and the Levant including the crusades (1095–1300), the Napoleonic conquest of Egypt (1798–1801) and the occupation of the Maghreb which began with the takeover of Algiers in 1830, as part of France's empire-building project in Muslim lands. For many decades and for many generations this conquest was held as a victorious act to rid the Mediterranean sea of the evil work of the Barbary corsairs.

Prior to the 1830 invasion, the French military were active in the Maghreb as early as the period of the crusades. In 1270 the crusaders led by Louis IX, took Carthage in Tunisia and hoped to convert its Hafsid ruler Abu ᶜAbd Allah Muhammad al-Muntaṣir to Catholicism. Struck by an epidemic of dysentery which killed vast numbers of crusaders including Louis IX on 25 August 1270, the French had to leave Carthage and retreat to France.[5] Likewise, the Spanish Reconquista (1492) in which the French participated, originally started as a war of conquest to regain Christian territories from the Muslim occupants and soon became a religiously justified war whose main aim was the re-Christianisation of the Iberian Peninsula. The vanquished Muslim and Jewish inhabitants of Al-Andalus were obligated to convert to Christianity if they were to remain in the Kingdom. By 1610, however, all Muslims and Jews were either expelled from Spain or killed.

The Spanish war against the Moors did not stop at this level but turned into attacks on the Maghrebi coastal cities of Morocco and Algeria which hosted the Muslim and Jewish communities who escaped from Spain. While Algeria called upon the help of the brothers ᶜArrouj and Khair Eddine Barbarossa to ward off the Spanish attacks to become later on part of the Ottoman Empire, Morocco decided to keep its sovereignty under the Wattāssid sultans. In consequence, with the exception of Morocco, the Ottomans established themselves on the coast of the Maghreb, beginning with Algeria – which formally became an Ottoman province in 1512, followed by Libya in 1551 and Tunisia in 1574. This ultimately deepened Europe's fear of Muslims, making the Ottoman incursion into what used to be Christian lands a fundamental reason for the European–Ottoman rivalry which was enhanced by the establishment of centres of piracy along the Maghrebi coast.

The Barbary corsairs, as they were called, controlled the Mediterranean waters and became notorious for piracy and hostage taking, which became the main reason for the Christian–Muslim conflict in the region. Clissold explains:

> North Africa had four main 'Barbary pirate' states – the sultanate of Morocco, and the three Ottoman regencies (Maghrebi proxies of the

Turks) in the *pashalik* of Algiers, the Husaynid *beylik* in Tunis, and the Qaramanlid *beylik* in Tripoli. During the heyday of the Barbary pirates in the sixteenth and seventeenth centuries, Morocco typically held 10,000 European slaves; Algiers, 25,000; Tunis, 7,000; and Tripoli, 1,500.[6]

To suppress the piracy against Christian Ships and free Christian slaves, as well as ending the practice of enslaving Europeans, gave justification to many military aggressions against the coastal cities of the Maghreb. In July 1775 Spain made a thwarted attempt to invade Algiers resulting in severe losses to their artillery and armies. The same city was bombarded in 1815 by a US naval squadron led by Captain Stephen Decatur who forced the governor of Algiers to sign a treaty banning piracy against their ships. One year later in 1816 an AngloDutch fleet under the command of Admiral Lord Exmouth[7] also bombarded Algiers resulting in the Dey freeing some 3,000 slaves and signing a treaty to end the practice of piracy and enslavement of Europeans.[8] This same cause was stated as one of the main reasons for the French occupation of Algeria in 1830, although many other economic reasons lay behind the occupation as Watson clarifies:

> While the slave trade provided the context for French hostility toward the Maghreb, nationalism and other economic issues lay behind the decision to commit French forces to the conquest of Algeria. France had purchased grain from the Dey of Algiers in the Republican and Napoleonic imperial periods. A complicated financial dispute emerged between the French government, the Dey, and Algerian Jewish merchant families who had negotiated a grain deal in 1805 with Napoleon.[9]

Furthermore, European powers engaged in political negotiations to share between themselves the Arab provinces under the weakening Ottoman Empire. In 1881 Tunisia became a French protectorate and was followed by Morocco in 1912. In the same year Libya was occupied by Italy, following a secret agreement with France, while Britain made a pact with the latter to secure its acceptance of British occupation of Egypt in return for allowing France freedom of action in Morocco.[10] As a result, Morocco became a colony divided between France and Spain, the latter of whom took the northern tenth of the country including its historic enclaves of Ceuta and Melilla which it has occupied since 1497 and 1580 respectively, while France occupied the rest of the country following the treaty of Fez, by which time the powerless Alawite Sultan Abdel Hafiz accepted the French protectorate, though he still reigned as sultan over his entire country except for the parts occupied by Spain.[11] This demonstrates that from the time of the Roman Empire and the time of the Islamic expansion into the Maghreb and Al-Andalus, to the crusades and the period under the Ottoman regency which ended with the epoch of European colonialism, the encounter between the Maghreb and the Occident was primarily an encounter of war and military battles which after the advent of Islam essentially became fuelled by religious sentiments. Cross and Crescent often faced each other in battlefields and this resulted in endless feuds in which the Occident justified its actions by claiming back what the Orient had taken from it by force under the banner of Islam.

Such military encounters, however, did not prevent profound cultural encounters and exchanges from taking place between the Maghreb and the Occident. Ira M. Lapidus explains,

> From Spain, Islamic scientific and philosophical thought was transmitted to Europe . . . Hispano-Islamic culture had a strong and immediate influence upon Christian style. Nobles and churchmen built their houses in the Moorish manner and borrowed Hispanic-Islamic motifs for their heraldry. They dressed in Arab fabrics, and had Jewish and Muslim literatures translated into Castilian and Latin. Alfonso X arranged for the translation of the Bible, the Talmud, and the Quran into Castilian . . . the works of Ptolemy were translated. The Muslim philosophers, al-Kindi, al-Farabi, and Avicenna were also translated into Latin, making the thought of Aristotle available to Europeans . . . between 1220 and 1250 Averroes's commentaries on Aristotle and the works of Maimonides were rendered into Latin, and were quoted by St Thomas Aquinas. Thus, Greek philosophic thought came through the Arab world to Europe.[12]

From Empire to Colony: Representations of the Fall of Algiers

The fall of Algiers in 1830 passes largely unnoticed by Arab intellectuals in their accounts of their journeys to the Occident in the nineteenth century; one such example is the well-known Rifāʿa al-Ṭahṭāwī who was still in Paris at the time of the invasion.¹³ His book *Takhlīṣ al-ibrīz fī talkhīṣ bārīz*,¹⁴ which he published in 1834, does not mention France's colonial endeavours nor its occupation of neighbouring Muslim lands. His account is one of fascination and admiration for French civilisation and culture regardless of its colonial project. Likewise, Al-Shidyāq's Book *Al-Sāq ᶜala al-sāq fī mā huwa al-fariyāq*,¹⁵ published in 1855, ignores the image of France as a colonial aggressor and solely sings the praises of Paris, his deep fascination with its beauty and his enthralment with its culture, civilisation and intellectual progress. El-Enany explains that the same reaction is true about the Napoleonic invasion of Egypt (1798–1801). He says:

> ᶜAbd al-Rahman al-Jabartī gave us a record in his annals of the first brief but violent encounter between the West and the Arab East, a record that conveyed both the horror and the fascination, with the latter arguably being the dominant sentiment. By the time Rifāᶜa al-Ṭahṭāwī came to publish his *Takhlīṣ al-Ibrīz* in 1834 based on his study years in Paris, the horror had gone leaving no trace, and only fascination speaks out of his book, a sentiment still shared by al-Shidyāq in his *al-Sāq ᶜala al-Sāq* of 1855, where the fascination continues, tempered only by occasional light-hearted social satire of the Europeans.¹⁶

Julia Clancy-Smith, on the other hand,¹⁷ explains that the fall of Algiers was a rude shock not only to the capital's inhabitants but also to most people in the regency, the Maghreb and the wider Muslim world. Most Algerians, both ordinary and elite, looked in vain to the Ottoman sultan in Istanbul for deliverance and could not comprehend the disappearance of the Dey of Algiers without putting up a resistance to the occupants or calling for *jihad* to oust the invaders. On the local scale, however, literary accounts in the vernacular which portray the French invasion speak of a ruthless aggressor who brought death and misery to Muslims. Yet, feelings of stupefaction, fear and at the same time fascination about France's modern weaponry were manifest in most texts. The French armies were therefore described as being superior and invincible, as in the following extract:

> *On dit que les Français sont puissants;*
> *Qu'en guerre leurs soldats sont courageux;*

Qu'au moment du combat leurs rangs frémissent;
Qu'au bout de leurs fusils, ils portent des lances.[18]

They say the French are powerful;
In battle their soldiers are brave;
In combat their ranks are pulsating
At the tip of their riffles they carry lances.

On the popular level, the French conquest was seen as an attack by 'infidels' against the Maghrebi Muslims, while at the same time it brought to mind the various invasions incurred by the Greeks and the Romans on the coasts of North Africa prior to the advent of Islam. The French were therefore, generally called '*Roumis*', referring to the Roman conquerors, and also called *Kuffār* (infidels), referring here to the crusaders and believing that the French armies of occupation were a prolongation of the crusades. As such, popular resistance was fuelled by religious sentiments, making it therefore a main duty of all Muslims to defend the land of Islam and preserve their faith in order to resist the invasion at least on the cultural level. This idea is clearly voiced in a vernacular poem recited at the time of the conquest:

Le sabre nous sépare du chrétien
C'est l'ennemi de notre foi;
Mais ceux qui croient et se soumettent
Auront certes le paradis pour séjour

Les infidèles se sont emparés d'Alger,
Les terres, ils les ont dispersés;
Puis ils se sont rués sur nos campagnes
Sauterelles venues en leur temps.[19]

The sword separates us from the Christians
They are the enemies of our faith;
Though those who believe and submit to the will of God
For sure, will attain the havens for abode

The infidels have captured Algiers,
Between them they shared the lands;

To the countryside they then headed
Such as a plague of locusts arriving in their term.

Organised popular resistance in Algeria and Morocco rallied masses of volunteers who responded to their religious leaders' calls for *jihad*. Such resistance groups inflicted serious defeats on the conquerors resulting in the signing of several treaties and in the loss of armies from both sides. Popular armed resistance and rebellions in Algeria began with the resistance of the Emir Abdel-Kader lasting from 1832 to 1847,[20] and ended with the defeat of the Bouamama uprising in 1884,[21] leaving Algerians seriously impoverished with their best lands having been expropriated for the benefit of European settlers/*colons*. The native chroniclers of these rebellions were mostly poets who composed both in classical Arabic and in the vernacular, and whose poetry was recited to incite people to join the rebellion against the occupants as well as a means to preserve the memory of the conquest. To defeat the Algerian resistance and ensuing popular uprisings, French armies terrorised and starved the population into submission, and although the French Prime Minister Polignac wrote on 12 March 1839 that France's objective in the occupation of Algeria was: '[. . .] humanitarian. We are seeking, in addition to satisfaction for our grievances,[22] the abolition of the enslavement of Christians, the destruction of piracy, and the end of humiliating tributes that the European states are having [sic] to pay to the Regency',[23] it has become evident that the primary objective was to turn Algeria into a colony of settlement.

Although in Tunisia and Morocco, which were both protectorates, the French imperial hand was much lighter, this did not prevent the upsurge of popular uprisings which strongly opposed the occupation. In Morocco Abdel Karim al-Khattabi resisted the occupants and defeated a Spanish army of 20,000 soldiers at Anoual in 1921. This victory consolidated his control over the Rif Mountains until his final defeat in 1926 at the hands of a joint French and Spanish force, numbering some 250,000 men. [24]

After defeating all forms of resistance and popular uprisings, what ensued across the Maghreb was a long colonial night which ended in Morocco and Tunisia in 1956 but lasted in Algeria until 1962, thereby singling it out as the centrepiece of the French Empire and the colony of settlement it was never willing to relinquish.

Early Literary Encounters between the Maghreb and the Occident: From Barbarity to Civilisation

The first Maghrebi encounters with the Occident documented in works of literature took place in the colony rather than in Europe, and were recounted by the first French-educated elite in the Maghreb. In this they differ greatly from the early Middle Eastern literary encounters with the Occident, which were in the majority accounts of Arab intellectuals on their journey to seek knowledge in Europe and were written in Arabic. The different nature of these encounters resulted in divergent accounts, and while in the case of the Middle East/Mashriq they mainly documented their authors' fascination with the Occident in terms of its culture and civilisation and discussed the East's spirituality versus the Occident's materialism, the early Maghrebi accounts are rather convoluted, having at their core the colonial encounter which brought the two sides (Maghreb/Orient and Occident) together and thereafter informed and shaped this encounter in all its aspects.

Furthermore, while Berber, vernacular Arabic, and classical Arabic poetry are replete with images of the *Roumis*/the French invaders, merely as the brutal aggressors who conquered the land of Islam and spread terror and destruction amongst the Muslims but seldom as civilisers, images of the French in the early Francophone novels differ greatly in that they present the reader with a plethora of European people who mainly include the soldier, the teacher, the priest and the settler as agents of civilisation. Such texts do not refrain from boasting about the work of the French civilisers to the extent of making the reader doubt their authenticity, as they appear distant from the lived reality of the locals. See for example these excerpts taken from Mohammed Ould Cheikh's first novel *Myriem dans les Palmes*:[25] '*La France est bienfaisante et juste* (France is charitable and just)';[26] '*la France . . . leur envoya des éducateurs et leurs offrit sa protection* (France sent them teachers and bestowed on them its protection)';[27] '*La France est une nation protectrice des musulmans* (France is a nation who protects the Muslim peoples)';[28] '*C'est une nation noble et généreuse* (It is a noble and generous nation)'.[29] Furthermore, '*Les Arabes ont gagné beaucoup au contact des Français* (The Arabs gained a great deal from their contact with the French)' amongst other examples.[30] These works failed to document the trauma experienced by a people who was exposed to extreme forms of violence, which in some cases amounted to genocide. Moreover, they seldom mention the systematic land appropriation to which people were subjected, ending up totally dispossessed of their sources of livelihood having had their land forcibly taken away from them. In this way the images they produced fluctuate significantly from those found in the Berber and Arabic vernacular and classical poetry of the same period, which has as its main focus the colonial assault on the land of Islam and meticulously records the suffering and feelings of loss experienced by the masses, though in almost every poem the final lines resonate with hope and a belief that just like the Romans before them the new invaders would sooner or later be vanquished. One poem even speaks of exacting revenge on the French not only by evicting them from the Maghreb but also by conquering Paris, from which the Muslims would then seize the rest of the French territories:

> *Nous prendrons Paris, nous y réunirons;*
> *Puis nous nous emparerons des autres États;*
> *Et nous leurs apprendrons l'unité du vrai Dieu*
> *N'allez pas dire, 'cela n'est pas possible';*
> *Rien ne prévaut contre la volonté de Dieu!*
>
> ...
>
> *O mon Dieu, la chose est dans ta main:*
> *Ordonne que les Musulmans triomphent,*
> *Et que les Français leur soient soumis.*[31]
>
> We will capture Paris, and there we will congregate;
> We will then conquer the other states;
> And we will teach them the unity behind the one true God
> Do not say, 'This is impossible';
> Nothing prevails against the will of God!
>
> ...
>
> O my God, this matter is in your hands:
> Make it that the Muslims triumph,
> And that the French would submit to them

Prayers and deep faith in the triumph of Islam over the conquerors was the stronghold that kept the nation alive in the hearts and minds of the defeated Maghrebi people from the date of the invasion of their homeland all the way through to its liberation, one century and thirty two years later in the case of Algeria.[32] It has to be born in mind, nevertheless, that such images were the product of ordinary people as they came into contact with the French armies of occupation, while the images in the first Francophone texts were the product of the educated Maghrebi elites whose encounter with the Occident was first of all through their education in French schools and subsequently in the workplace and in society in general. These authors were a direct product of colonial education and in most cases their novels reflect the assimilationist ideology to which they had been subjected. This first generation of novelists was in Bourdieu's words caught *'entre le doute sur soi et la complaisance orgueilleuse en soi-même, entre l'adhésion à autrui et la défense farouche du quand à soi*:[33] between self-doubt and a conceited complaisance with one's Self, between devotion to the Other and a fierce safeguarding of the Self'. Such an ambivalent position between Self and Other and not fully knowing where to belong is a direct result of an educational system whose primary objective was to assimilate and 'civilise' a 'savage' people and turn them into 'Frenchmen'. The first starting point was to make them believe that they were 'barbarians' whom the civilisers transformed into French-educated individuals, and then subsequently elevated to the realm of civilised people. In fact, in the Maghrebi context this represents the starting point in the coloniser/Occident–colonised/Orient encounter. From here the relationship becomes informed by this very reality which condemns the Orientals to be eternally indebted to the Occident for saving them from the dark alleys of ignorance and fanaticism.

In *The Wretched of the Earth*, Fanon explains how the principal objective of colonialism, be it in Africa or in the Arab world was 'to plant deep in the minds of the native population the idea that before the advent of colonialism their history was one which was dominated by barbarism',[34] and this very fact not only justifies the Occident's 'charitable' act of saving the Barbarians from their barbarity but most importantly that the colonisers should stay there forever lest the colonised would fall back into their primitive state and waist their civilisers' colossal efforts invested in this endeavour. Fanon argues that 'the effect sought by colonialism was to drive into the natives' heads the idea that if the settlers were to leave, they would at once fall back into barbarism, degradation and bestiality'.³⁵ In their venture to become civilised French citizens, the native intellectuals started to evaluate matters from a French lens to the point of seeing their own people as inferior folks and ignorant barbarians, and therefore rejected their own cultural heritage as shameful and barbaric.

Jean Amrouche, the son of converted parents whose education was entirely in French, speaks of his experience as a pupil in a colonial French school where he was taught shameful truths about his barbarian ancestors, as in the following passage:

> *Le premier fait historique nous touchant, nous l'avons reçu à la figure sous les regards ironiques des écoliers européens, comme une justification anticipée de nos abaissements passés, présents et à venir. Nos ancêtres ne sont entrés dans l'histoire que pour s'offrir à la massue de Charles Martel . . . Ils reparaîtront pour opposer une absurde résistance aux croisés bardés d'armures et de nobles idéaux, et prouver leur méchanceté en capturant le bon Saint-Louis. Les siècles perdent à nouveau la trace de notre existence. Alors le méchant Dey Hussein frappe un Consul de France de son éventail. Pour venger l'affront et purger la Méditerranée des pirates barbaresques, la France arrive dans ce pays misérable . . . Ou Arabes et Kabyles se dévoraient périodiquement . . . Nous éprouvions un mélange de honte et d'irritation, de désarroi et de colère . . .*³⁶

The first historical facts directly concerning us [native children] were flung at us under the mocking looks of the European pupils as an anticipated justification for our past, present and future abasements. Our ancestors only entered the pages of history to take the staggering blow of Charles Martel . . . they would reappear but only to stage an absurd resistance to the crusaders who were well equipped with armouries and noble ideals, but regardless, my ancestors would prove their evilness once more by capturing the kind Saint-Louis. Centuries would lose our trail but then the evil Dey Hussein would strike a French ambassador with his fly whisk. To exact revenge on him and to save the Mediterranean Sea from the Barbaresque pirates, France arrived in this wretched country where Arabs and Berbers were constantly fighting each other . . . We felt a mixture of shame and irritation, of disarray and anger.

Great emphasis was put in French schools on the image of France as intervening in the Maghreb as a saviour and liberator of the Maghrebis from the rule of the tyrannical Ottomans and not as a conqueror. Its mission was to rescue Maghrebi people from centuries of obscurantism, fanaticism and terror experienced at the hands of the cruel Ottoman rulers, while in fact, the terror in question was more felt by the Europeans north of the Mediterranean Sea and not by the people of the Maghreb. For the Algerians, Tunisians and Libyans the Ottomans came to guard their major cities from European attacks.

After the Reconquista, Spain occupied the following Moroccan cities: Ceuta in 1415, Tangier in 1471, and Melilla in 1497. In Algeria, it seized Mers El-Kébir in 1505, and in 1508 it occupied Oran in the west. Expanding further eastwards, Spain captured Béjaïa and the Pennon of Algiers in 1512. Consequently, the Ottoman intervention in Algeria represents a genuine Muslim Reconquista which gave the Ottomans legitimacy to free the occupied Algerian cities as the guardians of the lands of the Muslim people. Meanwhile in Morocco, which was not part of the Ottoman Empire, the cities of Ceuta and Melilla remain to this day under Spanish occupation.

In his book *Les Corsaires barbaresques: la fin d'une épopée, 1800–1820* Daniel Panzac explains that while the Barbary corsairs posed a serious threat to the European and American ships that crossed the Mediterranean Sea, for the inhabitants of the Maghreb they represented 'les fers de lance de l'Islam et l'orgueil des musulmans',[37] in other words, the defenders of Islam and the Muslims' source of pride. This image is totally reversed in France's colonialist discourse, which emphasised *ad infinitum* that it held a Universalist mission. It entered the Maghreb not only to end the rule of the Barbaresque corsairs who unjustly captured and enslaved Europeans but also to put an end to the tribal wars which were tearing apart the Maghreb, as was the case with the Tafilalet[38] tribes in Morocco where, according to colonial accounts, France pacified the warring tribes and established security and peace after years of instability, while in reality this meant putting an end to popular resistance to French occupation. This went very far towards justifying the French mission to civilise the uncivilised as much as it justified its use of force to bring peace and harmony to the warring tribes. Once the region was pacified and the native populations freed from the grips of the tyrannical Ottoman corsairs the French began their mission to bring peace and civilisation to the whole Mediterranean region. Jules Ferry states,

Can you deny, can anyone deny that there is more justice, more material and moral order, more equity, more social virtue in North Africa since France carried out its conquest? When *we went to Algiers to destroy piracy* and assure freedom of commerce in the Mediterranean, were we doing the work of corsairs, of conquistadors, of destroyers? . . . is it possible to deny that it is the good fortune of the miserable population of Africa to come under the protection of the French nation . . . ? (My emphasis.)[39]

Ferry's statement became a colonial truth adopted and propagated by the authors of the early decades of the twentieth century. In *Myriem dans les Palmes*, Ould Cheikh opens his novel with a statement which endorses this state of affairs. He presents it as a hymn to the glorious deeds of France who freed his people from the persecution of the Barbaresque tyrants; '*C'est l'histoire d'un peuple longtemps persécuté par des tyrans barbaresques*: It is the story of a people who for a long time were persecuted by the Barbary Corsairs.'[40] Although such statements are recurrent in the writings of the Francophone authors of this period, the only work which is fully dedicated to this subject is Chukri Khodja's novel *El-Euldj: Captif des Barbaresques*.[41]

Chukri Khodja (1891–1967): *El-Euldj: Captif des Barbaresques*

Through the reproduction of French colonial clichés, *El-Euldj: Captif des Barbaresques* casts a harsh criticism on the work of the Barbary corsairs as if it were written by a French author. The novel highlights the pain inflicted by the corsairs upon their Christian captives and the inhumane way they handled them in captivity. It takes pains to describe the loving families they left behind and the good life they used to have in contrast to the degrading conditions they were forced to endure in captivity.

Seeing through French eyes, Chukri Khodja [42] adopts a discursive reversal of history. From the onset the novel portrays Algiers, a city known as 'Europe's breadbasket' which used to supply France with grain, as traversing a period of famine.[43] Such famines could only be circumvented by the capture of a French fleet traversing the Mediterranean Sea by a notorious Ottoman corsair nicknamed Catchadiablo – a title which designates his evil character. The author insists that famines were very frequent in the regency[44] which, in lieu of remaining the centre of commerce it had been known as during the Ottoman era, is now described as existing in tumultuous times not only because of the scarcity of livelihoods and the recurrent famines but also because of the spread of fear among the locals and lack of security. The ruler of the regency is described as a ruthless, blood-thirsty despot who terrorises everyone including his own men.[45] At the port of Algiers the captured French sailors were ordered to unload the ship of its contents of coffee, rice, wheat, and other items, as they were scorned by the Janissaries who were watching over them and hurling insults at them '*kelb, melᶜoun . . . yahoudi, kafer.* Dog, damned, Jew, reprobate . . .'[46] Khodja further laments the fate of the European captives through a dialogue between two Turkish notables, who agree that the cruelty experienced by the captives at the hands of their captors was barely humane:

J'ai vu des chrétiens capturés descendre de plusieurs galiotes; ces chrétiens avaient été arrachés a leurs affections et a leurs familles, simplement pour démontrer notre force . . . croyez-vous qu'il n'est pas déshonorant d'entretenir ainsi des troupeaux humains, de charger les prisonniers de chaines et de fer, de les laisser couverts de haillons, déguenillés, et, ce qui plus est, de les priver de nourriture?[47]

I saw Christian captives alighting several ships; these Christians have been torn away from their loved ones and their families for the simple reason for us to exhibit our supremacy . . . Do you think it is not shameful to detain in this way human herds, to burden them with iron chains and leave them in rags and on top of all this, deprive them of food?

The novel sheds light on the cruelty of the Muslims towards the Christians and the feelings of revulsion and hatred expressed by both parties against the other. High tension reigns in the novel and outbursts of violence are likely to occur at any time. The author clearly shows that the unfair treatment of the Christians was unjustified and hard to endure by the captives who look at their assailants with anger and disdain. To intensify the captives' feelings of undeserved suffering the author speaks repeatedly of their qualities, knowledge and intelligence, which the corsairs could have benefited from, by integrating them rather than using them for forced manual labour, 'Ces médecins, ces savants qui moisissent dans les sous-sols humides ne pourraient-ils pas nous être utiles?: These doctors, these educated men who rot in humid dungeons, should they not have been made more useful for us?'[48] To further dramatise this condition, Chukri's novel has a French captive as the central character after whom the story is narrated. He is called Bernard Ledieux (a connotation of Bernard the God) and is one of the members of the captured French flotilla who, after a period of forced labour, was lucky to end up a slave in the house of Ismail Hadji, one of the city's notables, who was kind to him. To escape his condition of a captive slave Ledieux converts to Islam and marries the daughter of his master. His new status leads him to a new occupation as guardian of the captives which, though it gave him importance and earned him respect among the Muslims, quickly brings on him the scorn and rage of his fellow captives, but especially that of his close friend Cuisinier. This latter describes Ledieux's conversion as a monstrosity, a betrayal and a great injustice not only against his initial faith but also against his family and himself.[49] Cuisinier explains to him the consequences of his action,

> *Après une transformation pareille, c'est la méfiance entre nous. C'est la conséquence logique de ton transfuge. D'ailleurs les Turcs ne t'épargneront pas, de temps a autre, leurs sarcasmes. On t'appellera 'Euldj' pour marquer ton origine, pour la stigmatiser même. Nous autres, captives, nous te désignerons sous le nom de renégat.*[50]

> After this conversion of yours, there will be mistrust between us. It is the logical result of your treason. The Turks will not spare you their sarcasms from time to time. They will call you 'Euldj/renegade' to evoke your origin, and even to disgrace you. As for us the captives, we will call you an apostate.

From Cuisinier's reaction it becomes even more obvious that in his view Christians and Muslims are born enemies who can neither cohabitate wth nor accept one another. Despite being close friends with Ledieux, mistrust replaces their initial friendship which he decides to end as he bids him farewell.

While Ledieux is happy to become part of the Muslim community through conversion and alliance, for Cuisinier the Muslims are an inferior race against whom he holds so many grudges and an enormous set of preconceived ideas some of which he read in *The Arabian Nights*.[51] He is convinced that the Muslims are nothing but barbarians whose customs are revolting and whose cruelty against Christians is unsurpassed to the point of making the novel an outcry for ending such injustice. In other words, it justifies the French occupation of Algeria not only as an act of vengeance but also as an act of justice to bring an end to the rule of the barbarian corsairs. In one such instance Cuisinier tells Ledieux about his irritation and horror at the treatment of European captives:

> *Quelles mœurs, mon ami, quelle mentalité! Ne crois-tu pas qu'un jour viendra où cette façon de se jouer de l'Europe et de faire le jeu de massacre avec des existences humaines prendra fin?*[52]

> What customs my friend and what a mentality! Don't you think there will come a day when this facetious way of treating Europe and flippantly massacring human existence will come to an end?

In another instance a priest held in captivity along with Cuisinier reassures him by telling him:

> *Mais ne supposez pas, mon bon et fidèle Cuisinier, que notre malheur actuel soit sans fin, d'autres souffriront après nous longtemps encore, c'est possible; mais le jour ou le Seigneur délivrera l'humanité de la flibusterie africaine est déjà fixé par lui. Nos neveux, nos petits-neveux ou nos arrière-petits-neveux, ceux de dix générations après nous, peut-être, connaitront, je n'en doute pas, ce moment béni et l'humanité verra alors poindre l'aube de la vraie civilisation.*[53]

> But you should not think my kind and loyal Cuisinier, that our actual adversity is interminable, others will suffer after us for even longer, this is possible. But, the day when the Lord will deliver humanity from African pirates is already known to Him. Our nephews, our grandnephews or even our great-nephews, ten generations latter may be, will witness, and I have no doubt about this, the blessed moment when humankind will see the breaking dawn of true civilisation.

The above quotations attempt to justify the French occupation of the Maghreb as an act of universal and divine justice to free European captives, bringing an end to piracy in the Mediterranean Sea and liberating the native people from the tyranny of the Ottoman rulers.

Such concepts are among the 'inverted truths' that were propagated by colonial ideology and were taught to native pupils in French schools. To prove that they had well assimilated their education, the French-educated elite internalised and propagated these learned truths as if to reassure their 'civilisers' that their undertaking has been well received. In the course of building the image of France as the benefactor who landed in the Maghreb to liberate the native people from the tyrannical Ottomans, French colonial ideology erects an image of the natives as uncivilised barbarians who were trapped under the rule of the Ottoman despots and were therefore in need of a saviour. Fanon explains this phenomenon of devaluing pre-colonial history in the following terms:

> . . . colonialism is not simply content to impose its rule upon the present and the future of a dominated country. Colonialism is not satisfied merely with holding a people in its grip and emptying the native's brain of all form and content. By a kind of perverted logic, it turns to the past of the oppressed people, and distorts, disfigures and destroys it.[54]

This act results in feelings of embarrassment about one's past and ancestors as expressed by Jean Amrouche. Such feelings have often led many Maghrebi intellectuals to a total rejection and denial of their own cultural heritage, to the level of speaking from the standpoint of the French – as is the case with Chukri Khodja, the author of *El-Euldj*. This novel not only accentuates the suffering of the Christians at the hands of the Muslims and justifies the French occupation as an act of justice and legitimate defence, but also engages in explaining the cruelty of the Muslims vis-à-vis those who convert to Christianity while in the opposite case the Christians restrain themselves to praying for the converts to find reason and return to their initial faith.[55] Witnessing such cruelty makes Ledieux, whose son Youssef becomes a Muslim theologian, renounce his new faith and return to Christianity. Portrayed as a victim of history Ledieux ends up demented and dies of remorse for betraying his initial faith. While *El-Euldj* discusses pre-colonial concerns to somehow justify the act of colonising Algeria, it also stages French and European Christian characters as they encounter Maghrebi Muslims through their experience of captivity. The portrayal of these characters follows a binary line which displays wicked people as opposed to good people, cruelty as opposed to kindness, and barbarity as opposed to civilisation. The reader of this text is at a loss with regard to the identity of its author and his intentions in writing such a novel. This situation resulted in some critics having to resort to evaluating Chukri's work as an attempt to demonstrate to the French as well as to his own people that the assimilationist project of the former was bound to fail just as Ledieux's attempt to become a Muslim has failed in the novel. It was evaluated as an indirect response to the work of the Christian missionaries and their relentless campaigns to convert Muslims into Christianity.

In his article, 'Un Romancier de l'identité perturbée et de l'assimilation impossible: Chukri Khoja',[56] Abdelkader Djeghloul builds a thesis which argues that the novel is a kind of reverse criticism of the colonialists' assimilationist project and that it interrogates the implicit meanings and the many things it could not say 'le non-dit' rather than the things it could say. Djeghloul consolidates this view through the insinuations the novelist puts forth demonstrating that if the powerful Ottoman rule in Algeria came to an end at the hands of the French occupiers, these latter would without any doubt meet the same fate. The novel also insinuates that there is no barbarity that surpasses the barbarity of compelling a weak people to convert to the religion and the culture of the dominant people. Djeghloul insists that the aim of the novel *El-Euldj* is 'to demonstrate that ultimate assimilation is an impossible mission whether in the sixteenth or the twentieth century, whether for a Christian individual or for an Algerian Muslim intellectual'.[57] *. . . de démontrer l'impossibilité de l'assimilation définitive au 16e siècle comme au 20e siècle, pour un Chrétien comme pour un intellectuel algérien*'.[58] By opting to reverse the roles and the truths in the novel, the novelist makes the protagonist Ledieux, a French convert, go through the painful transition from his religion to that of the dominant Ottomans and demonstrates that deep inside any human being genuine conversion or assimilation does not occur effectively. Such a concept remains an artificial apparatus that an individual might adopt for political motives or out of personal apprehensions. Ledieux's renouncing of his new faith was not for any reason but to get rid of this new being 'Omar Lediouse'[59] with whom he could no longer identify himself. Chukri demonstrates that in this implicit way no matter how much 'the Self' would try to become 'the Other', this effort would not reach the core of 'the Self' but will only give it a resemblance of 'the Other'. While this interpretation of the novel *El-Euldj* is perfectly possible, it also proposes a new model of assimilation which was adopted by the first generation of Maghrebi intellectuals at the turn of the twentieth century. This 'new model' is explicitly demonstrated through the character of Youssef, the son of Ledieux. In other words 'le fils Musulman d'un Français', who carries in himself Arab pride fused with the knightly spirit of the French.[60] Youssef teaches Islamic divinity in the mosques of Algiers and at the same time speaks the French language fluently. Of this language he says that he could not resist '*à la curiosité de gouter les fruits du jardin de la rhétorique française* (the curiosity to taste the fruit from the garden of French rhetoric)',[61] as if entering the Garden of Eden and not being able to resist the forbidden fruit. This point is very revealing seeing that the French language as a vehicle for French culture and civilisation did seduce Maghrebi intellectuals who engaged, and indulged, unreservedly in learning it and speaking it – often times with the fluency of native speakers. Likewise, Youssef declares that he did not feel ashamed of speaking the French language of his father (symbolising the fatherland) and equally he was not embarrassed to be a Muslim like his mother (symbolising the motherland). Perhaps the author is alluding to the marriage of the two nations coming together as one inseparable entity as experienced by Youssef, whose statement also sums up the new identity sought after by Maghrebi intellectuals during the first three decades of the twentieth century, that of the 'Français Musulmans', the French Muslims, who may have accepted French language and culture, but strongly resisted conversion into Christianity, and at the same time defended Islam as a religion which accepts and has the ability to adapt to modernity and not as an obscurantist, fatalist and fanatic religion as it was often described by the French colonialists.

This very point is consolidated in the novel *El-Euldj* through Youssef, who preaches a modernist Islam to his students in the mosques of Algiers. A discussion between the Imam and his students reveals the major issues of Islam and modernity as experienced by Maghrebi intellectuals in the early years of the twentieth century. At one stage the issue of Europeanisation is brought to the fore. One student proclaims that there would come a time when Muslim countries would fervently follow an evolutionist movement which would lead them to Europeanisation: 'les pays musulmans se jetteront, avec une frénésie diabolique, dans un mouvement évolutionniste qui les emportera dans le courant impétueux de ce que nous appelons l'européanisation.'[62] At another instance it was professed that faith would become a matter concerning the individual and it would not be necessary to display signs of one's religion through religious attire. At this point the inhabitants of the globe would adopt one similar fashion of clothing which is the European style of dress suggesting that it would be perfectly possible for Muslims to dress in European attire without having to renounce their faith, and insisting that the supposed 'perfect Muslim gear' is proscribed nowhere in the Qur'an; '*il est évident que la religion musulmane n'impose aux croyants aucune coiffure déterminée, ni aucun habit special*: It is obvious that Islam does not impose any specific head gear or any special form of dress to its followers.'[63]

Conclusion

It has become evident from the above discussion that religion is central to the pre-colonial and early Maghrebi encounter with the Occident. What we have seen is that the threat posed by the Islamic expansion into Europe and the massive waves of conversion that ensued resulted in an obvious overhaul of Christianity's ability to stand in the face of this major threat.

The Spanish Reconquista and the ousting of the Muslims and Jews from Al-Andalus was a Christian victory over the expansion of Islam, which empowered Spain not only to oust the Moors from its territories but to conquer Muslim lands south of the Mediterranean Sea.

The rule of the Ottomans in Algeria, Tunisia and Libya not only liberated the cities occupied by Spain but posed a new threat to North Europe exacerbated by the piracy activity exercised by the Barbary corsairs, not only in the territories that came under the Ottoman Empire, but also in Morocco which similarly participated in piracy activity.

While it is common knowledge that the French occupation of Algeria, followed by Tunisia and Morocco respectively, was outwardly motivated by economic concerns, at the core of the matter religion seemed to also play a pivotal role as demonstrated in the discussion above.

Although *El-Euldj* is a historical novel set in the sixteenth century which mainly addresses the theme of the Barbary corsairs, their control of the Mediterranean Sea and their tyranny against Christian captives, as if written from the perspective of a European author, its last part clearly concerns itself with the twentieth century's issues as experienced by Maghrebi intellectuals in general and particularly by the Jeunes Algériens, the group of 'Young Algerians' during the 1930s.

The main concerns discussed by Youssef with his students in the last part of the novel *El-Euldj*, examine the complexity as well as the impossibility of religious conversion on the one hand and the intricacies of adopting French civilisation and culture on the other. These two facts constitute the main themes addressed by the Francophone Maghrebi novels of the first half of the twentieth century, which mainly focused on the early encounters with the Occident within the Maghreb itself.

The novel *El-Euldj* is almost a plea to the Occident, here the French occupants, to give up on its policy of making conversion to Catholicism a condition for naturalisation, and at the same time demonstrating in an ardent manner that it is perfectly possible to become French and remain Muslim, building thus upon the thesis of the 'Français Musulman', which will in the twentieth century become the status of naturalised Algerians.

As such, through his novel, Chukri Khodja presents an ambivalent position vis-à-vis the Occident which diverges greatly from the position expressed in the vernacular and classical Arabic poetry which is unreservedly 'Occidentophobic', constantly swearing revenge for France's horrific deeds to the point of aspiring to not only oust the colonists from the land of Islam but furthermore to conquer France, arriving all the way at the heart of Paris:

> We will capture Paris, and there we will congregate;
> We will then conquer the other states;
> And we will teach them the unity behind the one true God
> Do not say, 'This is impossible';
> Nothing prevails against the will of God!

4

'La France, c'est moi':[1]
Love and Infatuation with the Occident

Comme je connais les savants français, leurs travaux, leurs découvertes, comme je connais les Voltaire, les Boileau, les Pascal, les Musset et autres, je ne saurais faire autrement que de les aimer d'un amour profond. Et les aimer n'est-ce pas aimer leur Patrie ?

J'aime la France d'un amour profond. Je l'aime d'autant mieux que je l'ai visitée. Je connais son beau paysage, ses habitants séduisants, ses belles choses.

Because I know the French scientists, their achievements, their discoveries, because I know the likes of Voltaire, of Boileau, of Pascal, of Musset and many others, I cannot but love them all intensely. And by loving them, does that not also mean loving their nation?

I love France profoundly. I love it even more since I visited it. I discovered its beautiful scenery, its seductive inhabitants and all its fine-looking things.

Chukri Khodja[2]

Introduction: For the Love of the *Mère-patrie*

The infatuation of the first generation of educated Maghrebis with the Occident became the central theme of various texts including poems and novels written in French not only as an expression of the authors' loyalty to their *mère-patrie*, but most importantly as a means to express their deep assimilation of the language of their civilisers, and their ability to express themselves with no linguistic barriers. Writing in the language of their colonisers/ civilisers signals that they have fully assimilated themselves to the realm of the Occident. According to Ashcroft et al., 'The producers [of such works] signify by the very fact of writing in the language of the dominant culture that they have temporarily or permanently entered a specific and privileged class endowed with the language, education, and leisure necessary to produce such works.'[3] The early Francophone novels, which mainly addressed the French reader, were produced as channels of communication with the Occident and as a tool for establishing a platform where the newly affiliated subjects could enter into a dialogue with their civilisers, a dialogue often epitomised either by a French teacher, or sometimes a Catholic priest, who is portrayed as a generous source of knowledge, tirelessly providing advice and guidance to his neophyte but knowledge-thirsty native disciple.

Departing from the putative notion that the Orientals were generally uncivilised and often uncivilisable, the *Évolués* committed themselves to a process of demonstrating that they had indeed evolved from their primitive state to that of the civilised people. To make this message more perceptible they, through literary discourse, put into action characters who not only represented them and their often painful evolutionary process, but also voiced their sentiments and views about their encounter with the Occident through their benevolent civilisers.

At this stage the image of the Occident was very much idealised and principally based on the portrait the very Occident drew about itself, and which it conveyed to its pupils in the French schools, as the first site of the encounter with the Occident as a benefactor.

This acceptance into the realm of the Occident, in other words into the world of the civilised, puts the 'learner' in the position of becoming embarrassed by his own uncivilised people, their heritage and customs, which he was made to see through French eyes and therefore appeared to him as strange, ugly and barbaric. Ultimately, he resorted to denying his inner self and rejecting his own people as the 'Other' and eagerly yearned to cross over to the rank of the civilised 'Self'. In order to do so, he engaged in a process of blind mimicry by adopting the appearance, the manners as well as the language of the awe-inspiring Occidental.

Bhabha defines colonial mimicry as 'the desire for a reformed, recognizable

Other, as *a subject of a difference that is almost the same, but not quite*.[4] Not quite, because despite adopting an appearance which is that of civilised people in terms of dress and learned manners there will always be a deeper side in the native's ego which civilisation can never reach. For this reason, he became suspended between Self and Other both in the literal/physical sense and symbolically. On the literal/physical front the native intellectual became a go-between agent whose role was to convince his own people that not only did he choose the right path but that they too should join him and follow his example in order for them to become civilised and redeem themselves from their barbarity. His European appearance and acquisition of the French language allowed him to enter both locations with relative ease; that of the Self (because he adopted their looks and spoke their language), and that of the Other (because he still belonged to his people). This go-between condition is in fact a third location wherein elements of the Self and the Other exist in a constant process of cultural miscegenation albeit through perpetual conflict. Symbolically, this conflict inhabited not only his location but also his inner self which persistently swayed like a pendulum between Self and Other, Occident and Orient, without managing to permanently settle in either of the two locations.

The expected role of the native intellectual of this period was to interiorise, reproduce and propagate Occidental values. For him, the Occident was the epitome of civilisation, and its main mission was to save the colonised from the ills of their savagery and primitive life. In return, the 'lucky few' native beneficiaries were duty-bound to sing the praises of their civilisers, to diligently show their loyalty, and as a sign of gratitude they were eager to demonstrate to their own people and to the whole world how what used to be barbaric locations before the coming of the French, were transformed, as if with a magic wand, into buoyant hubs of progress and development. In a preface to Mohammed El Aziz Kessous's book, *La vérité sur le malaise algérien* Dr Bendjelloul writes with a tone of amazement:

> *Nous voyons bien . . . que l'Algérie a pris un essor prodigieux depuis le jour où les trois couleurs ont flotté sur la blanche Alger.*[5]

> It is evident that Algeria has taken an extraordinary leap since the day the French tricolour was raised over Algiers.

Such views were typical of the Maghrebi *Évolués* at the eve of the centenary of the French presence in Algeria (1930). Not only amongst the French-educated intellectuals, which can be seen as expected and understandable, but also among those who studied in Islamic universities, which is rather surprising. Sheikh Abdul Hamid Ibn Badis, the leader of the Algerian Muslim ᶜUlama declared,

> *Le peuple algérien est un peuple faible et insuffisamment évolué. Il éprouve la nécessité vitale d'être sous l'aile protectrice d'une nation forte, juste et civilisée qui lui permette de progresser dans la voie de la civilisation et du développement. De telles qualités, il les trouve en la France, à laquelle il se sent attaché par les liens d'intérêt et d'amitié.*[6]

The Algerian people are weak and have not sufficiently evolved. They are aware of the vital necessity to be under the protective wing of a strong, just and civilised nation that will allow them to progress on the path to civilisation and development. Such qualities are to be found in France to which they feel attached both for their interests and friendship ties.

Totally infatuated by the Occident's progress and development, the native intellectual saw in it the embodiment of perfection. He would rather put the blame on himself and his own people for being 'uncivilised' and for their feelings of alienation and any kind of misfortune they may have experienced, rather than hold their civilisers accountable. Following rigid sets of binary oppositions, all the wrongs were placed within the world of the ignorant, naive, fanatical and uncivilised 'Oriental', whom the knowledgeable, sophisticated, rational and civilised, Occidental was eagerly trying to save from his own dangerous and harmful destructive powers fuelled by his own witlessness.

This chapter will discuss three novels which are rarely deconstructed with any degree of depth as part of Maghrebi literature. Written early in the twentieth century by French-educated intellectuals whose parents were often the privileged 'Friends of France', these works were seen as tokens of gratitude expressed by their authors for all the efforts deployed by the Occident to civilise them, but also as gestures of appreciation and signs of loyalty to their civilisers. As such it would be unimaginable to expect these texts to be critical of the Occident in any direct manner. On the contrary, they are, in most cases, demonstrations of their authors' infatuation with the Occident, falling therefore into the Occidentophilia category of Occidentalist discourse outlined above.

Abdelkader Hadj Hamou, *Zohra la femme du mineur* or *Méliani the Husband of Zohra*

In *Zohra la femme du mineur* (1925),[7] Abdelkader Hadj Hamou (1891–1953)[8] portrays Miliana, a town in North West Algeria, as being totally transformed from an unknown ragged place before French occupation, into a modern municipality which then boasted European schools, train stations, factories, modern farms and many vital amenities. It is inhabited by people from all over the Mediterranean Sea and despite their different religions (Muslims, Jews and Christians) and diverse origins (Italians, Spaniards, Maltese and French along with Arabs, Kabyles and Mozabites) they all live side by side in peace and harmony.

It all appears as if a genuine fusion of Mediterranean races and religions is taking place in this mining town, thus confirming that France's policy of assimilation and its republican principles of *Liberté, Egalité* and *Fraternité* are actually working. Méliani's close friend, the Italian Grimecci, repeats *ad infinitum* that Jews, Arabs, Italians and French, are all alike and equal: 'Juifs, Arabes, Italiens, Français, tout les hommes se ressemblent, sont égaux.'[9] This statement is, nevertheless continuously being controverted in the novel which demonstrates time and again that only those Europeans who are of French origin are portrayed as being genuinely good people, and every time a European person acts inappropriately their non-French Origins are quickly underlined. For example, the French headteacher of the city's school is designated as 'Le bon directeur'.[10] Likewise, the manager of the mine is described thus:

> *Un Français d'origine; ce qui d'ailleurs retenait encore dans ces immenses mines les centaines d'ouvriers musulmans c'était justement la bonté et l'impartialité du directeur.*[11]

He is of French origins; unsurprisingly, what kept the hundreds of Muslim workers in these immense mines, is the kindness and fairness of the director.

In contrast the non-French Europeans, of whom the Spaniards make the largest majority, are portrayed as the source of all the tribulations brought upon the society.

Méliani, the novel's main protagonist, is the archetype of the *Évolués* group of the early 1920s who ultimately became the typical central characters of the early Francophone novels in the Maghreb. He is an individual of noble descent, son of a Caïd, and grandson of an Agha,[12] yet life seems to have taken a different turn for him to descend from the local aristocracy and become a member of the working class. He left his original tribe and his 'primitive' way of life to settle in a modern city, not as a student or as an intellectual, as is generally the case in the rest of the novels of this period, but as a miner. He is first portrayed as a devout Muslim man who performed his five daily prayers regularly and never swayed from the right path, yet in the long run he was contaminated by European civilisation and its perils:

> *Méliani eut beau résister par la suite aux tentations de boire, haïr les ivrognes, . . . détester les Musulmans dépravés qui croyaient être dans la bonne voie, en prenant pour la civilisation française l'alcoolisme et la prostitution, . . . il arriva un jour où malgré lui, pour la première fois de sa vie, il approcha de ses lèvres le verre.*[13]

> Méliani tried very hard to resist the temptation of drinking alcohol; he hated drunkards and detested depraved Muslims who mistakenly associated civilisation with drinking and visiting the prostitutes . . . Nonetheless the day came when, against himself, he took the glass to his mouth for the first time ever.

Although alcohol is always disapproved of as one of the ills brought by the Europeans, the novelist insists that the Occident should not be blamed for this, and casts full liability on those who were not able to guard themselves against alcoholism: '*Quand on a des yeux et de l'intelligence, on doit se méfier soi-même . . . des jolies bouteilles qui renferment le poison*: When one has eyes and intelligence, one must guard oneself against the pretty bottles which contained poison.'[14] Accordingly, it is urban life and bad company that affected Méliani negatively and made him neglect his faith. He who refrained from casting a simple gaze at other women, and religiously observed his prayers, not only became an alcoholic but also an adulterer,

Celui-ci ne faisait plus les cinq prières quotidiennes . . . Autrefois, il s'interdisait de regarder le visage d'une femme même européenne, il devint moins sévère pour lui-même.[15]

This latter stopped performing his five daily prayers ... In the past he would not even allow himself to glance at a woman's face, not even that of a European woman, he clearly became less strict with himself.

Furthermore, due to his naivety Méliani fell for the games of Thérèse, Grimecci's wife, who drew him into an adulterous relationship in order to fire up her husband's jealousy and detract him from his mistress Rosette, a young Jewish seductress.

Along with this transformation at the level of the individual is the general view held about the Occident and the success of France's assimilationist policy. The deeper we delve into the storyline of this novel the more we see the Occident developing into both a symbol of debauchery and a cause of alienation for the protagonist, whose trajectory as a character yearning for European civilisation transforms him from being a positive character widely respected in his entourage for his noble lineage, personal qualities and values, into becoming the example of total degradation who is in consequence is rejected by his own people for deserting his religion, neglecting his family and becoming an alcoholic.

Nevertheless, the blame is never cast on the infallible France nor its civilisation but on the fallen individual and the non-French Europeans whose doubtful past made them negative characters devoid of noble values. In this instance the Italian Grimecci is portrayed as the epitome of the dubious settler who spread vice and led Méliani to his downfall through peer pressure. The novel plainly establishes that while Islam is generally presented as *fanatique* (fanatical), the same label is given to those who performed their prayers and refrained from drinking alcohol. In contrast, the epithet *civilisé* (civilised) is given to those who befriended Europeans, drank alcohol and became relaxed about their religious and cultural values.[16] In other words, they blindly imitated the Europeans in order to resemble them but in this instance the imitation was only superficial and negative. Frantz Fanon argues that 'A national culture under colonial domination is a contested culture whose destruction is sought in systematic fashion. It very quickly becomes a culture condemned to secrecy'.[17] In other words, a culture that is performed and preserved in the home and whose custodians are women who, through their roles as guardians of national culture, not only assure the continuance of this culture but also create in their homes a safe and uncontaminated haven where the men, and the children who go to work and French schools, find a location where they can be true to themselves and perform their inner identity and culture in a relaxed and natural way. In *Zohra la femme du mineur*, although Zohra is given second position as the wife of the miner, she is also portrayed as actively playing the important role of the one who resists Occidental influence, while at the same time she is represented as the passive victim of the very culture she was trying to preserve from European contamination. This becomes particularly obvious when the demise of Méliani is contrasted with the suffering of Zohra as she helplessly watches his downfall without being able to save him. However, this does not make her the passive victim of her own culture as seen and portrayed by the Europeans, but rather, the victim of 'European civilisation' which infected her husband for whom she left her tribe and her loved ones to live with in the city where she became secluded, totally alienated and very unhappy.

However, Zohra remained firm in her rejection of any form of interaction with the Europeans and did not allow Western influence to penetrate into her home. When Grimecci came to see Méliani, for example, he was never invited in but had to wait for him at the entrance. She therefore remained 'pure' and kept herself and her home 'uncontaminated' by European civilisation and influence, which she rejected and resisted albeit in a passive manner, and thus symbolically became the guardian of her native culture and identity, while Méliani, who thought himself to have become an integrated *civilisé* transformed into the archetype of the anti-hero whose trajectory goes to prove the misleading side of European culture and civilisation, is here portrayed as nothing but a chimera which deviates the infatuated neophyte Muslim Algerians from their faith and culture and leads them to their demise.

This role of the guardian of native culture was seen as a barrier to European influence and penetration. In *Les Compagnons du jardin* a book in a form of a dialogue between Robert Randau and Abdelkader Fikri (the pseudonym of Abdelkader Hadj Hamou) about the East–West encounter, Randau openly declares that without integrating native women into the workings of the French civilising mission the latter would not be successful,

> *Notre action civilisatrice ne s'appliquera pas seulement aux hommes, mais, pour être efficace, atteindra les femmes, qui croupissent dans la plus épaisse ignorance au fond du gourbi. Car ce sont elles qui, plus que les hommes, forment, égarées par l'esprit de superstition, bloc contre l'Europe.*[18]

> Our civilising mission does not just apply to men. For it to be efficient it should also be extended to native women who hide behind the densest ignorance in the depths of their huts. It is them, more than the men, who due to their superstitions constitute a solid obstacle in the way of Europe.

Well aware of the value of integrating women into the workings of the civilising mission to the Europeans, Hadj Hamou's portrayal of the demise of Méliani in *Zohra la femme du mineur* is, in a way, a well elaborated response to his colleague Randau showing him how the male character who opted wholeheartedly for European civilisation almost walked blindfolded towards the abyss, losing out on all fronts.

At the end of his trajectory Méliani is only awakened from his delusion to face the nightmarish reality of Zohra's silent death, which came as the culmination of her suffering mostly caused by his neglect, and the shame he brought to her by his imprisonment – albeit for a crime he did not commit. Albert Memmi explains that the colonised is always guilty in the eyes of colonial justice 'being suspect by definition, why should he not be guilty?'[19] Seen as a criminal and a traitor, Méliani was totally rejected by both his own people and the unforgiving Europeans for killing his friend Grimecci, which was seen as a sign of ingratitude. To escape his solitude and the stigma of his dubious trajectory, he decides to leave his city and take refuge in Morocco as a self-imposed exile where he became known under the emblematic appellation of *El-menssi*, meaning the forgetful one for forgetting his wife Zohra while he was indulging in his sins, but also signifying the fact that in his quest to resemble the Europeans, he had forgotten his own cultural values which Zohra was desperately trying to safeguard in the safety of her home.

Zohra la femme du mineur is a thought-provoking novel which, while it tries to demonstrate that the French project of assimilation and civilisation was perfectly working thanks to the generosity and understanding of the Occident, contains in its pages a significant number of contradictions. For example, when Zohra blames the Europeans for her husband's downfall, the narrator intervenes to make it unequivocal that 'La douce France'[20] did not just bring alcohol; it also brought peace and justice, it opened modern schools, paved the roads and lined the railways, and most importantly, it respected the culture and religion of the Muslim Algerians. Similarly, when Méliani portrays his city as a cosmopolitan heaven and affirms that the people in his entourage live in harmony despite their different religions and origins, as demonstrated above, he then questions the use of racist nicknames used by each racial group to label the other:

> *Pourquoi ces mots 'bicôt'[21] pour les arabes et 'youpin'[22] pour les juifs? Et pourquoi les arabes entre eux appellent les Européens 'gaouris'?[23] C'est idiot! C'est enfantin tout cela! Pourtant nous nous ressemblons tous!*[24]

> Why do we use such words as 'bicôt' [wog] for the Arabs and 'youpin' [kike] for the Jews? And why do the Arabs call Europeans 'gaouris'? This is all silly and very childish! Surely, we do resemble each other!

Furthermore, to defend French civilisation and culture for all their negative aspects, the author would either blame the falling native individuals for being negligent, or the European settlers of the likes of the Italian Grimecci who, in any case, were not *Français de souche* (not of pure French lineage), not only so but they often have a dubious past. Grimecci escaped Italy after he murdered his brother's assassin, and fearing for his own life he fled to Algeria where he met his adulterous wife Thérèse whose father is also not of French ancestry but of Spanish origins.

Another contradiction contained in the novel is when Méliani, along with Thérèse, are accused of killing Grimecci who was shot by his own wife with Méliani's rifle. French justice is hailed for prosecuting not just Méliani, the Arab, but also Thérèse the European. This is quickly contradicted when the reader learns that Méliani is sentenced to five years in jail while Thérèse, the actual murderer, is only jailed for one year. This demonstrates, though in the subtext rather than directly, that this idealised 'modern/European' environment is highly racist and contains multiple layers of discrimination based on class and origins. While superficially the society is divided into two main categories, namely Europeans and Arabs, each of these categories is also subdivided into further groupings.

In *Zohra la femme du mineur*, unlike the colonisers/Europeans who see all the natives as being alike, 'they are all the same',[25] the natives did not see all Europeans as being the same. They distinguish between the French from France, who occupy the upper positions in society and are generally seen as noble and imbued with republican values, and the *other* Europeans who are seen as opportunists and whose past is generally suspicious. Unlike the civilised French they are portrayed as greedy and rough in their attitude with the native populations, and perfidious in the way they conduct their business. According to Memmi, even though the French colonists were not all the same, and that some may have held republican values and have been devoid of racist colonial ideology before coming to the colony, these values quickly evaporated upon their arrival in the colony as they entered into the settler/colonist category. Memmi adds that it did not take long for the European newcomers to the colony to put aside their values and become part and parcel of the established settlers; 'Let us suppose that there is a naïve person who lands just by chance, as though he were going to Toulouse or Colmar. Would it take him long to discover the advantages of his new situation?'[26] When drawing his portrait of the European coloniser, Memmi explains that what brings a European settler to the colony is not a mission to civilise the uncivilised but mere profitable economic gain,

> You go to the colony because jobs are guaranteed, wages high, careers more rapid and business more profitable. The young graduate is offered a position, the public servant a higher rank, the businessman substantially lower taxes, the industrialist raw materials and labor at attractive prices.[27]

Memmi challenges the stereotypical image of the coloniser as a 'tall man, bronzed by the sun, wearing Wellington boots, proudly leaning on a shovel as he rivets his gaze far away on the horizon of his land',[28] as unsustainable and owhere to be found in the colonies. This negative opinion about the non-French Europeans also reflects the general discontent among the natives with seeing their country become a colony of settlement opened up for Europeans from all walks of life to settle in Algeria and appropriate the land of the natives, and because most of them came from dubious backgrounds they spread vice and degrading values.²⁹ However, the infatuation of Abdelkader Hadj Hamou with the Occident and its civilising mission somehow blinded him from seeing this reality. Instead he saw his own people 'the Orientals', as refusing to be saved from their status as uncivilised people. They were at fault for not wanting to benefit from the opportunities brought to them by the Occident. From reading *Zohra la femme du mineur*, one feels the constant presence of a secondary but watchful narrative voice in the text which emerges at every turn to come to the defence of the good and magnanimous France and its civilising mission, despite the sad tone and the tragic aspect of the novel which clearly shows that the natives were not thriving under the auspices of the French civilising mission. The reader is left wondering whether this lack of condemnation was out of a fear of censorship and persecution or whether the author was so deeply infatuated with the Occident to the point of seeing it as it wanted to be seen, in other words as the flawless benefactor. Either way, through the pages of this novel, the author infallibly confirmed his 'unqualified assimilation'³⁰ of European culture and civilisation and deep infatuation with the occident.

Chukri Khodja, *Mamoun: L'Ébauche d'un idéal* or The Disrupted Dream of Emancipation?

An analogous trajectory to that of Méliani is to be found in Chukri Khodja's first novel *Mamoun: L'Ébauche d'un idéal* (1928).³¹ Like Méliani in *Zohra la femme du mineur,* Mamoun, the novel's protagonist, is also a son of a Caïd but unlike him he did not move to the city for work but to study in a French high school. Motivated by the dream that his son Mamoun would become a doctor or a lawyer in the future, his affluent father, Caïd Bouderbala, enrolled him in the French Lycée of Algiers despite his mother's opposition to the idea, for fear that her son would be lost to French ways.

Just like Zohra, Mamoun's mother Haddehoum is presented as the guardian of the native culture against the acculturation project brought by the Occident. However, despite her opposition to her husband's plans for their son, she clearly had no say in the matter. The author portrays her as unsophisticated and superstitious '*comme toutes les femmes arabes du bled*³² (just like all Arab women in the country)', presenting thus a negative image of native women but also homogenising them in an Orientalist manner. It is clear that the novel does not empathise with Haddehoum nor condemn the violent and demeaning way she was dealt with by her husband in order to silence her. Nevertheless, ignorant as she might have been, she guessed right and her fears for Mamoun proved to be real. After a few years in Algiers, Mamoun became the perfect example of the French-educated and totally assimilated individual who threw himself unreservedly into Occidental culture while he rejected his tribe and its primitive culture; he is the embodiment of the Maghrebi intellectual of the 1920s–1930s, making this novel the first in a long line of Maghrebi novels on the encounter with the Occident through colonial education, often epitomised by the character of the French teacher.

From the first pages of *Mamoun: L'Ébauche d'un idéal* the reader is exposed to a set of rigid binary oppositions between the 'Self' and its 'Other', 'coloniser' and 'colonised', 'civiliser' and 'uncivilised', 'light' and 'darkness', 'modern' and 'archaic', etc . . . These are followed by '*rejet de soi* (self-rejection)' *versus* '*adhésion à l'autre* (adhesion to the other)', a severe criticism of Qur'anic schools as centres of ignorance and fanaticism,[33] and a total fascination with French schools as centres of enlightenment. These binaries emphasise the view that the Self is the exact opposite of its Other, which brings to mind Lord Cromer's statement about the Egyptians, who he described as the precise opposite of the Europeans. He declared: 'I content myself with noting the fact that somehow or other the Oriental generally acts, speaks, and thinks in a manner exactly opposite to the European.'[34] Edward Said elaborates on this by explaining how Orientals are seen as almost nearly the same almost everywhere in the world and how the Occident sees them as a phenomenon possessing regular characteristics: 'On the one hand there are Westerners, and on the other there are Arab-Orientals; the former are rational, peaceful, liberal, logical, capable of holding real values, without natural suspicion; the latter are none of these things.'[35] It is now an established fact that such precepts are the views held by the Occident about the Orient, yet making the assimilated Oriental not only become the mouthpiece of the Occident who brought him civilisation, but also deeply believe in these ideas and make them his own, creates an extra layer of Othering as the assimilated/educated Oriental aspires to become part of the Self and actively participates in the Othering process of his own people who are yet to reap the fruit of the

French civilising mission. Consequently, Chukri Khodja's novel presents us with the Other of the Other as opposed to the Self, and the Other aspiring to-become-another or at least part of the Self.

Furthermore, through the pages of this novel Khodja makes every effort to demonstrate that Algeria was blessed with a civilising mission which transformed every aspect of life in it. It is thanks to the hard work of the colonists that the city of Algiers went through a miraculous transformation to become a splendid place which he describes in the following terms,

> *Les allées symétriques, les plates-bandes clairsemées de dessins fleuris et les sveltes silhouettes féminines qui se profilaient devant lui. Et cette vision pleine de charme et d'enchantement l'amenait à raisonner en soi sur les beautés du siècle, sur les splendeurs de la vie civilisée, sur le mérite de la France qui, en moins d'un siècle, a fait de l'Algérie un véritable Eden.*[36]

Symmetrical alleys, flat sections of land garnished with flowery patterns, and graceful feminine silhouettes that roamed in front of his sight. This charming and enchanting view made him ponder on the beauties of the century, the splendours of civilised life and the merit of France who in less than a century transformed Algeria into a genuine Garden of Eden.

These splendours are juxtaposed with the ugliness of the natives' primitive Bedouin dwellings in the desert where Mamoun comes from. These are no longer described as the enthralling exotic locations portrayed in the works of Orientalist artists and voyagers but as the most repugnant habitat,

> *Les gourbis, en cette région mi- primitive, se ressemblent tous; les même objets, les mêmes décors naïfs, les mêmes ustensiles se trouvent éparpilles çà et là, sans ordre, sans méthode et sans harmonie. C'est dans ce mélange de pourriture, dans cette ambiance morbide, que grouillent des êtres rustres et malpropres et pleins de vermine.*[37]

The huts, in this semi-primitive region are all alike; the same objects, the same ingenuous decor, and the same utensils are to be found scattered here and there with no order, no method or harmony. In this mix of dirt and gloomy atmosphere swarm some loutish and dirty beings covered with vermin.

From these contrasting images and the way the author describes them, it becomes evident that he became estranged from these locations to the point of casting an outsider's view on his own native people both as a way to rationalise his own repugnance at such uncivilised beings and to vindicate his decisive choice to move over to the camp of the civilised. Fanon skilfully describes this condition in *The Wretched of the Earth* where he explains how 'The intellectual throws himself in frenzied fashion into the frantic acquisition of the culture of the occupying power and takes every opportunity of unfavourably criticising his own culture.'[38] Nonetheless, this is not a new feature brought by European colonialism. Many centuries before Fanon, Ibn Khaldun (1332–1406) wrote extensively on the age-old phenomenon of the imitation of the victor by the vanquished people. According to him,

> The vanquished always seek to imitate their victors in their dress, insignia, belief, and other customs and usages. This is because men are always inclined to attribute perfection to those who have defeated and subjugated them. Men do this either because the reverence they feel for their conqueror makes them see perfection in them or because they refuse to admit that their defeat could have been brought about by ordinary causes, and hence they suppose that it is due to the perfection of the conquerors. Should this belief persist long, it will change into a profound conviction and will lead to the adoption of all the tenets of the victors and the imitation of all their characteristics.[39]

Ibn Khaldun explains that the imitation of the victor/coloniser by the vanquished/colonised may be an unconscious phenomenon, or else consciously due to a mistaken belief that the victory of the victor/coloniser was attributed not to their superiority and power, but to the inherent inferiority of the customs and beliefs of the vanquished/colonised. He argues that the purpose of the imitation is the false belief that such an imitation will remove the cause of defeat.

Nevertheless, imitation often happens in conjunction with the process of rejecting one's own image and native values, which comes as a result of an acculturation process deployed by the victor/coloniser to erase native cultures as weak, primitive and backward, and to establish its own superior culture as developed and liberal.

In other words, the dominating European culture and civilisation granted the victor the legitimacy to occupy the ground of the defeated, inferior barbaric culture. However, the French 'civilising mission' was not extended to the whole native population in order to actually and effectively bring it to the level of a civilised people who owned a 'civilised' or 'non-primitive' culture. This same process occurred in local education; after the closure of the local traditional Arabic *madrasas* and Qurʾanic schools which were indiscriminately available to all natives, the coloniser did not provide an adequate alternative and readily accessible education to all native children. The ultimate result of this closure and wiping away of the natives' schools and cultures was the creation of a vacuum as the majority of the population became both acculturated and uneducated.

One thing that Chukri Khodja could have questioned in this novel, however, is why his indigenous primitive people and locale did not benefit from the bounties of European civilisation? The author's repulsive fresco of his native dwellings brings to bear the existence of two separate and unequal worlds, one destined for the civilised, described as buoyant, and another for the uncivilised, described as mired in sweltering squalor. There is no possibility of blurring these boundaries and no prospect of modernising the natives' habitat. What we see from the novel is the rigidity of the boundary which demarcates these two worlds between which only the educated protagonist and his like can travel freely. However, since the only means for the native individual to cross over to the other world is through French education, which as it were was not accessible to all natives but only to a minute minority, there were no prospects of merging these two worlds and transforming the whole country into a uniformly civilised one. It appears that civilisation was so precious; there was not enough of it to be extended to all natives. Even those very few who were included in the civilising process have never managed to become fully redeemed, as deep inside their inner self lurked the sediments of their native upbringing and enculturation.

The protagonist's condition as a semi-primitive and semi-civilised person, ultimately results in his inner conflict as these two forces constantly quarrel within himself. On the one hand he is overwhelmed by feelings of shame and ignominy about his own people, and on the other hand he is obstinately striving to become part of the European civilised 'Self'. The more he lives in the European city, the more he distances himself from his parents and other people, considering them as belonging to a superseded epoch: 'Mon père . . . il est anachronique; il est l'être représentatif des siècles périmés: My father . . . he is anachronistic; he is the archetype of ancient centuries)'.[40] For this reason, Mamoun opts for a complete mutation regardless of his origins and beliefs. '*Il imite ses camarades français en tout, il boit du vin, il déguste volontiers les tranches de jambon que l'on pose sur la table*: He blindly emulates his French school buddies in everything they do; he drinks wine and relishes the slices of ham placed on the dinner table which he eats with no guilt.'[41] From the narrative it all looks as if Mamoun was fully redeemed from his barbarity and was well integrated into his school, yet without previous warning the reader learns about his dismissal from the school for no apparent reason. This dismissal is presented to the reader as if Mamoun was ejected from the Garden of Eden for no apparent sin since he fully complied with the school's protocol. At this stage the author/narrator intervenes to explain that his exclusion was a result of his bad performance and certainly not as a consequence of a racist act on behalf of the headteacher whom he describes as '*Un bon Français, toujours juste et sans idée préconçue, qui arrive de France pénétré de son rôle éminemment Français*: A good Frenchman, always fair and free from any preconceived views. He arrived from France imbued with his role as a remarkable French person'.[42] This categorisation goes on to confirm the contrasting image of the French who were newly arriving from France still fully believing in French republican values, and that of the European settlers who were generally viewed in a less complimentary manner, which is similar to the categorisation of the European settler community in *Zohra la femme du mineur*. Here, the French individuals coming from the metropole to work in the colony are presented as being different from the European settlers, who in turn are divided into different categories depending on whether they were French or coming from other European countries. This further confirms the existence of a class system in-built into the colonial society, and the varying levels of condescension and hatred harboured by each of these categories towards the natives.

Following his dismissal from the secure environment of his school, Mamoun does not return to his tribe, as would be expected, but decides to settle in the European city of Algiers where he occupies himself with his pursuit of the pleasures it offers. He spends his time drinking in the city's brasseries, and going to the opera house where he first meets a French woman named Madame Lili Robempierre and instantly becomes infatuated with her beauty and elegance:

> *Elle dégage un parfum si fin, fleurant si bon, qu'il semble naturellement s'échapper de ses pores; elle est angéliquement belle: yeux bleus, joues colorées, profil romain . . . séduisante.*[43]

> She gave off such a fine perfume, it was so flamboyant and delicious that it naturally seems to escape from the pores of her skin; she is angelically pretty: She has blue eyes, colourful cheeks, and a seductive Roman profile.

The author's emphasis on Lili's whiteness and allure makes her the embodiment of the ideal image of France, and at one point Lili and France become one. Having transformed himself into a white-looking man in dress and manners, Mamoun's attraction towards the white woman would bring him another step closer to total self-realisation. In *Black Skin, White Masks* Fanon theorises the attraction of the man of colour towards the white woman as an act of redemption. He posits,

> By loving me she proves that I am worthy of white love. I am loved like a white man . . . I am a white man . . . Her love takes me onto the noble road that leads to total realisation . . . I marry white culture, white beauty, white whiteness. When my restless hands caress those white breasts, they grasp white civilisation and dignity and make them mine.[44]

After a romantic chase which lasts for several days Mamoun finally manages to find Lili again and declare his love and admiration for her. Despite being a married woman he begs for her address and for allowing him to meet her another time. After much insistence Lili gives in to Mamoun's advances and eventually becomes his lover.

For a few moments in the novel the reader starts to believe in the possibility of miscegenation between Mamoun and a French woman, as should be the case following the French assimilation project which never concretised in colonial society, where such encounters were almost inexistent during the early decades of the twentieth century in the Maghreb, especially with European women from the upper strata of society.

However, we later learn that Lili is, after all, not a genuine French woman but a mere *M'tournia* (a turncoat), an epithet given to Algerian natives who converted to Christianity and therefore became naturalised. Lili's parents converted to Catholicism under the auspices of Cardinal Lavigerie, and she married a wealthy European settler, who upon discovering her adulterous relationship with Mamoun felt more offended that her lover was an Arab man than by the act of marital disloyalty. In a fit of rage he reminds her that Arabs are the worst enemies of the Christians . . . and a race of bandits and beggars. He calls Mamoun all kinds of racist appellations including '*bicôt, l'être le plus abject qui soit*: *bicôt*, the most abject person possible.'⁴⁵ Once more, as is the case in *Zohra la femme du mineur* we learn that Monsieur Robempierre is not 'un Français de souche', but a mere European settler! This explains the views held locally amongst the natives that a true Frenchman is of noble descent, holds republican values and sophisticated principles and manners which would never allow him to use such racist statements nor treat other people in such a condescending manner.

This way of idealising the French characters and distinguishing between bad and good Europeans often goes to explain and justify the infinite love and respect the authors of this early epoch of unqualified assimilation or Occidentophilia, have for France, as expressed in this instance through Lili and Mamoun who, despite their multiple setbacks and misfortunes as well as their ill-treatment at the hands of the settlers, maintain a love for their *mère-patrie* which remains unaffected; both continue to be totally infatuated with France and its universal principles. Lili proclaims: '*J'aime la France d'un amour profond*: I love France profoundly.'⁴⁶ This same unfathomable love is so anchored in Mamoun's heart that it could not be troubled even following his infinite number of setbacks and frustrations, particularly while he was looking for employment. The narrator explains that the only one to blame for Mamoun's demise and his failure to find happiness and to secure a good job, is 'his own self', not solely because he was expelled from high school but also because of his laziness and unscrupulous conduct, which made him undeserving of the status of a civilised person.

According to Mamoun's friend de Lussac, the reason why he was not totally accepted as a European was also due to his Arab looks and head-gear. Native intellectuals at the turn of the twentieth century, although they adopted European garments in lieu of their native dress, nonetheless hesitated to remove their headgear – which in this case was a fez. While this outlook was typical of the educated 'Français Musulman', as the new status of the Europeanised Algerian Muslims, it was not totally accepted by the Algerian Europeans. De Lussac tells Mamoun that his fez was the main reason for his failure to secure employment,[47] and advises him to substitute it with a felt hat which would make him look perfectly European. Were the 'Français Musulman' solely expected to relinquish all visible manifestations of their Islamic identity in order to be considered French? How about Mamoun's skin colour? And his Arab/Muslim name? Was France's assimilation project a means for the integration of the natives into a civilising scheme to elevate them to the level of civilised people, or was it merely, or at least primarily, the removal of all ocular symbols of the natives' identity as Muslims and as Maghrebis? According to de Lussac, Mamoun's fez was not just a simple identifier of the intellectual 'Français Musulman' since it also became a symbol of 'Nationalisme Musulman',[48] following the example of the young Turks and Arab nationalists in the Middle East who mostly donned a fez along with a European suit which, for de Lussac, became associated with belligerent intentions and violent projects: 'des intentions belliqueuses, des projets sanglants'.[49] Such residual Orientalist perceptions of Islam as a dangerous faith and a threat to Christianity and Christians rendered France's civilising mission impossible. This situation is comparable to the French headscarf issue experienced at the present time by Maghrebi Muslims living in France. While suppressing all religious identifiers is currently disputed as part of France's secular culture, when we compare the headscarf issue in the twenty-first century to Mamoun's fez in the twentieth century, we come to understand that the French Assimilationist project, in the same way as its *laïcité* principles, does not accept religious difference or cultural diversity. To become French implies a total self-effacement of one's looks, manners, language and even religion.

De Lussac's statement not only betrays the lack of trust between the Europeans and the local Muslim communities, including those who were Europeanised, but also proves the fallacy of the assimilationist agenda which alleged that once emancipated and educated the natives would be integrated into the European community.

Mamoun is horrified by de Lussac's unfounded suspicion, which to some extent, is symbolic of the age-old fear of Islam and everything which represents it. Deeply disappointed by his discovery he tells him,

> *Franchement; c'est bien malheureux, quand on est aussi loyalement amoureux de sa patrie d'adoption que moi, d'entendre raisonner comme ça. Je ne dis pas, il se peut faire que des indigènes dévoyés, aveuglés par le fanatisme aient des idées subversives, que tous les indigènes instruits et intelligents réprouvent, quant à les accuser de xénophobie, c'est une erreur.*⁵⁰

It is truly disheartening to hear such reasoning against those, such as myself, who are deeply in love with their adoptive nation. I cannot deny that it is possible to find some natives who are ignorant and blinded by fanaticism and therefore might have some seditious ideas, which are reprobated by all the educated and intelligent natives, but to accuse them of xenophobia is a mistake.

De Lussac's generalisations and essentialist views only reflect the views which were generally held by the European settler community towards the native population whom they never trusted and who as such they regarded as constituting a stumbling block in the natives' way to becoming assimilated into French culture and civilisation. Despite the good will of some native elements of the likes of Mamoun to build bridges between the two communities, what the novel presents is the impossibility of removing racial prejudice, but more importantly the lack of genuine intentions on the part of the Europeans to extend civilisation to all the natives even when some of them decided to totally relinquish their own native culture as in the case of Mamoun, and their religion as in the case of Lili.

Marie-Paule Ha argues that colonial assimilation was generally a fiction and that 'the belief that French colonial policy sought to transform "natives" into "Frenchmen" through pedagogic acculturation is an enduring myth.'⁵¹ While it is undeniable that French education assimilated very few native subjects to the point that they claimed and affirmed a French cultural identity, attempts by the colonised to demand inclusion using European discourses of universalism, human rights and political participation often resulted in deep disillusion. Segalla explains that when 'challenged by French-speaking colonial subjects demanding the rights of Frenchmen, colonial policy makers and especially colonial educators were then charged with the task of shepherding, preserving, and controlling the cultures and self-understandings of colonised peoples in order to prevent or stifle assimilationist demands.'[52] In the novels of this period, the figure of the French teacher or educator is almost always omnipresent and the common role played by this figure is often that of mentoring and shepherding the blind native pupils from the dark alleys of their barbarity towards the light of knowledge and civilisation. It is often the case that this relationship goes beyond the schooling years and the tendency of the native intellectual to refer to his ex-teacher/mentor for guidance is to be found in the majority of the Maghrebi Francophone novels written during the colonial period. In fact, *Mamoun: L'Ébauche d'un idéal* introduced this trend which was to continue all the way to the end of the colonial period.

Because the French teacher epitomised the vehicle of civilisation and the generous source of knowledge about how to become a civilised person, he stepped into the life of the native intellectual to occupy the place of the father or mother as a point of reference, especially since the parents were often portrayed as illiterate, ignorant and uncivilised or as belonging to a behind-the-times era.

The figure of the *Évolué* who seeks to become like the French often opts to detach himself from his roots without being able to totally re-root himself into the cultural ground of the Other to the point of looking somehow suspended between the two cultural locations, and not perfectly settling or fitting into either of the two. While the *Évolué* would reject what he knew best as retrograde and not befitting his new status as the newly civilised, he was always in need of a mentor who would instruct him on how to do things in a civilised manner, but more importantly, he was eager to demonstrate at every turn to his mentor that he was a well-disciplined pupil who learned his lessons very well.

In this circumstance the French teacher is always needed as the guiding light and is portrayed as a humanitarian character whose main role is teaching the indigenous pupil universal values. He is portrayed as kind, generous with his time and advice, which he diligently and tirelessly supplies at all times, and he is compassionate in that he understands the dilemma and the hard task of the *Évolués* in their 'evolution' process and their endeavour to become French and therefore 'civilised'.

Another symbolic role played by the French teacher, particularly when he engaged in discussions about Islam, is that he embodied the Occident and its views about the Orient and Islam. It is often the case that the pupil–teacher discussion turns into the dilemmas of Islam with modernity, the latter being embodied by the teacher who symbolised the Occident.

In *Mamoun: L'Ébauche d'un idéal* Monsieur Radomski, Mamoun's teacher from high school befits this role. Although he blames Mamoun for his failure in his education mainly due to not being an exemplary pupil, he remains compassionate and caring especially when he learns about his illness.[53] Although he is the vehicle of the French civilising mission who leads Mamoun on the path to becoming fascinated with Western civilisation as much as he became aghast at his own people's way of living, he blames him for causing grief to his father at losing him to the West, to which Mamoun replies,

> *Il y a exactement un an, je suis allé voir ma mère chérie, voir mon père, voir un peu tout le monde, mais je n'ai pu rester plus de deux jours. Rien ne me plait plus là-bas. C'est triste. Je sens bien en moi que cette situation est anormale, mais je n'y peux. Il me faut la ville, les théâtres, les brasseries, le monde européen, auquel je sens appartenir.*[54]

> It has been one year precisely since I went to see my dear mother and my father and everyone else. I could not stay there more than two days. Nothing pleased me in that place. It is sad. I do feel that this is not normal but I can do nothing about it. I need the city, the theatres, the brasseries, the European world, to which I feel I now belong.

Mamoun's unreserved attachment to the Occident ultimately resulted in his total rejection of the Orient symbolised by his own people, their barbaric customs and their mediocre heritage. His enthusiasm in immersing himself in occidental values can only correspond to his eagerness to reject his own cultural values as obsolete and barbaric. Fanon explains this phenomenon as the first phase in the *evolution* of the colonised intellectual in the period of unqualified assimilation. He says:

If we wanted to trace in the works of native writers the different phases which characterise this evolution we would find spread out before us a panorama on three levels. In the first phase, the native intellectual gives proof that he has assimilated the culture of the occupying power.[55]

Not only so, but the native intellectual idealises the Occident and attributes to it the role of the saviour almost in a celestial manner. Mamoun expresses his deep gratitude at every turn for everything that France did for him and his people. He speaks of a benefactor France for which he lines up a plethora of positive adjectives such as *couveuse* (brooder/incubator), *protectrice* (protector), *généreuse* (generous). It is she who brought civilisation and salvation to what Mamoun calls *un pays bizarre*:

> *Ce pays bizarre connait des jours heureux depuis qu'il a été assagi par une administration pondérée, je puis le dire, sans crainte de me tromper.*[56]

This bizarre country has known better days since it came under the control of a well-balanced administration, I say this knowing for sure that I cannot be wrong.

For this reason Mamoun affirms, '*La France a donc un droit sur moi*: France has therefore a right over me',[57] as a result not only did he opt for total assimilation to become fully French and to loyally love his adoptive nation, '*loyalement amoureux de sa patrie d'adoption*: devotedly in love with his adoptive nation',[58] but was furthermore ready to do anything for France in return for her taking him under her warm wing and making him a member of a great nation, that of the civilised people, in other words: the Occident. This aim, however, turned out to be a complete myth; no matter how much the native had to give from the composition of his own self, this myth remained unattainable. In the novel, Lili, who looked totally European, whose parents converted to Catholicism and became French nationals, displayed these characteristics solely as a thin veneer, because deep inside herself she was not totally European and her white husband never missed an opportunity to remind her of this reality, for according to him she was not worthy of becoming a European. Reaching the depths of despair in her identity crisis Lili chose to end her life and with it the big lie it was built around.

As to Mamoun, the novel's unhappy ending demonstrates that after everything he did to become a European, he failed to thrive under the auspices of civilisation. His father's dream to see him become a medical doctor or a lawyer through French education was totally shattered. Instead, Mamoun returns to his parents' barbaric dwellings totally ruined by the vice of civilisation and deeply devastated by disease. Ironically, on his death bed, his distraught father makes sure that, having failed to be rescued from his native status by his French education, Mamoun should at least die a Muslim. Sitting by his side he helps him to pronounce the *shahada*, the Muslim profession of faith, before he surrenders his soul as a French Muslim. Monsieur Radomski reassures Mamoun's troubled father that although his dream to see his son become a highly educated and successful man did not come true Mamoun was, at least, wholeheartedly French, '*Tranquillisez-vous, Caïd, français il le fut de tout son cœur, de toute son âme.*'[59]

Mohammed Ould Cheikh's (1906–38) *Myriem dans les Palmes* and the Romance of Two Young Algerians in the Twentieth Century

Myriem dans les Palmes is Mohammed Ould Cheikh's first novel which, according to its author, is the story of the romance of two young Algerians in the early years of the twentieth century: an emancipated Arab man (*Évolué*) and a French woman; '*C'est . . . l'idylle de deux jeunes Algériens du vingtième siècle: un Arabe évolué et une française . . .* '[60] Just as in the preceding novels of this early period, the truth about the occupation is inversed and the author deploys a tactful play with words to distort the lived reality about what he calls the Franco–Muslim rapprochement, in order to please the French readers for whom the novel was destined:

> *J'essaye tout simplement de faire plaisir aux pionniers du rapprochement franco-musulman en leur dédiant ce modeste ouvrage.*[61]
>
> I simply tried to please the pioneers about the coming together of the French and the Muslim communities by dedicating this work to them.

The author insists that France came to the Maghreb as a benefactor to save and protect its native inhabitants. It is a generous nation who brought peace and security for the Maghrebi populations and unreservedly bestowed on them the bounties of wealth, progress and civilisation, while it did not interfere with their religion but respected their faith and their local culture. Similar claims are expressed in the novels we have discussed in the previous chapters, and are presented as a shared trait of the literary works of this early period. What Ould Cheikh brings as a new element, however, is the possibility of mixed marriages and romance between the native Algerians and the Europeans. The novels presents us with the marriage of a native Arab woman and a European man, followed by the romance and marriage of a European woman and a native man, though neither a mundane Arab man nor an ordinary French woman as we will see.

Although mixed marriages could be an ideal means of miscegenation for bringing the European and the native populations together to forge 'the new Algerian people', they were extremely rare and often frowned upon in both the indigenous and the settler communities. For the former, such alliances were seen as unacceptable from the point of view of religion and culture, while for the latter they regarded the natives as an inferior race.

In *Myriem dans les Palmes,* a military man, Capitaine Léon Debussy marries Khadija, a woman from Southern Algeria. The narrator explains that Léon and Khadija were deeply in love with each other and were strongly attracted to one another. However, although Khadija's family opposed her association with a French non-Muslim man, she rebelled against her family and married the man she loved regardless of the difficulties that lay ahead of such an unconventional union,

> *Elle s'était unie au Capitaine Debussy, dans un moment de folie, sans penser aux ennuis que lui réservait la différence de leurs sentiments, de leurs goûts et de leurs croyances.*[62]

She married Captain Debussy in a moment of madness, she did not think of the troubles which would be caused to her by their differences in sentiments, tastes and beliefs.

This is mainly so because, although she loved a French man and was marrying into his culture, Khadija was not ready to change anything in her native character:

> *Bien qu'elle ait épousé un occidental, Khadija est demeurée musulmane; elle s'habille à la mauresque et pratique sa religion avec ferveur.*[63]

Despite marrying a Frenchman, Khadija remained a Muslim; she dressed in native clothes and practised her religion with dedication.

The same position is observed by Léon who, seeing that he came from a superior race and culture, was not ready to accommodate Khedija's culture or make any concessions. Ultimately, his love for Khadija wanes gradually and despite having two children with her, he continues to treat her with contempt and condescension. This brings to mind Auclert's remark on how European men in Algeria held no respect for native women and could not restrain themselves from insulting them whenever they passed by.

This same behaviour toward the native wife is also found in the couple Monsieur and Madame Robempierre in *Mamoun: L'Ébauche d'un ideal*. Lili, a native convert to Christianity whose parents opted for total naturalisation did not succeed in becoming totally French despite her European looks and her adoption of Western ways. Her husband treats her harshly and with disdain and she never feels loved or cherished which explains her attraction to Mamoun, a man from her own race.

Conversely, unlike Lili whose identity crisis and alienation led her to commit suicide, Khadija is depicted as a strong woman. First by marrying the man she loved despite opposition from her parents, and secondly for resisting Western influence and staying true to her beliefs. Khadija clings strongly to her faith and her two children Myriem and Jean-Hafid over whom she is in a constant battle with her husband as each wanted to win them over to their own culture. The names given to the daughter and the son reflect their mixed origins and show that the two parents are on an equal footing, although coming from a 'superior' culture Capitaine Léon Debussy has the upper hand in many issues concerning their upbringing. While both children studied at French schools he did not allow them to attend the Arabic school as well in order to gain Arabic language and culture alongside French. Furthermore, as a liberalist who is deeply immersed in the French ideal of *Laïcité*, he refused to give his children any form of religious affiliation whether Muslim or Christian,

> *Je ne peux pas fanatiser mes enfants, je te l'ai dit bien des fois . . . J'entends les élever comme il me plaît, cependant je ne leur apprendrai ni Catéchisme ni Coran . . . Je suis libre penseur, moi.*[64]

> I do not want to fanaticise my children, I told you this many times . . . I intend to bring them up as I please, and I will not teach them Catechism nor Qur'an . . . I am a free thinker.

To Khadija's dismay, she discovers that it was rather too late for her to radically change her French-oriented children. Myriem, for example, is depicted as an accomplished young French woman who shares nothing with her native mother; she is 'Française accomplie, instruite et cultivée.'[65] As to Jean, like his father, he is a military officer in the French army: '*La carrière militaire est la seule qu'il aime*'. Also like his father he was fighting against the Moroccan resistance in the Riff region, with his mother being very worried he would perish in the same way as his father; '*le fils finira bien comme son père par tomber dans ce Maroc maudit . . .*: The son will ultimately expire like his father in this cursed Morocco . . .'[66] Deeply concerned about her children's future, Khadija resorts to various tricks and methods to pass over her religion to them albeit in a discreet manner. This is not just for the sake of making them Muslims but for her conviction that without religion a person has no anchor and that atheism can only lead a person to their demise.

The death of Capitaine Debussy in Morocco while fighting the local resistance to French occupation signifies Khadija's redemption. She visits the local Imam to repent for her sin of marrying a non-Muslim man and asks him for his assistance to convert her children to Muslim ways.

Visiting the Imam for guidance signifies the opposite model to the native male *Évolué* who follows a French teacher as a mentor who guides him through his redemption to French civilisation. This situation enhances the view which positions native women as emblems of preserving national identity, however not in a passive manner as seen in the previous novels. After teaching Arabic language to her son and daughter, Khadija's ultimate dream is to win them over to her culture through alliances with native partners:

> *La joie de Khadija serait de marier Myriem avec un Musulman pour lui éviter les libertinages et les inconvénients du modernisme.*[67]

Khadija's dream was to marry off Myriem to a Muslim man to save her from the uncertainties and the troubles of modernism.

For this reason, Khadija, who never approved of her daughter's engagement to the Russian settler Ivan Ipatoff, works eagerly to replace him with a man from her own race and culture. Throughout the novel Ivan is portrayed not only as arrogant, racist and an opportunist, but most importantly as a coward who is undeserving of Myriem's love. On the other hand, Myriem's childhood friend Ahmed Massoudi, whom Khadija appointed to give private tuition in Arabic language to her children, is portrayed as a handsome, kind and generous man who mastered French as well as Arabic. Here again we see the appearance of the enlightened and westernised native teacher who inverses the image of the fanatical and obscurantist Arabic teacher prevalent in colonialist ideology. Ahmed Massoudi is the prototype of the native intellectual who although educated in French institutions, also acquired an Arabic and Islamic education. Portrayed as the reverse image of Ivan, Ahmed is a principled man who kept his Islamic values and dressed in his indigenous clothes with elegance and dignity.[68]

As suggested by its title, *Myriem dans les Palmes* contains a high level of exoticism, and reproduces many of the colonial tropes in terms of France's civilising mission and its redemptive aspect. These aspects are contrasted against the natives' barbarity and dangerous customs which stand as a rampart against progress and civilisation. These elements are epitomised through an Orientalist-type adventure in the Sahara desert where Myriem's aircraft crashes and she is captured by Belqacem, the tribal chief of the Oasis of Tafilalt in Morocco, who imprisones her in his harem. There Myriem experiences life among the women 'prisoners' of the harem and the medieval type of life led by the people of the Tafilalt tribe and their primitive, uncivil ways of treating women as hostages.

Jean, who goes to rescue his sister, is also captured and rendered helpless. At this stage an Arabian knight whose face is veiled comes to their rescue and, with the help and complicity of a local Berber woman called Zohra, he manages to free Myriem and Jean from Belqacem's prison. To the surprise of everyone the veiled knight happens to be no one but Ahmed Massoudi, who played his heroic act to free his beloved and her brother.

The novel ends happily with the marriage of the two couples Myriem the French woman with Ahmed the native *Évolué*, and Zohra the Berber woman from the Oasis marries Jean, the French man, in the same way as Khadija married Jean's father before her.

Through these mixed marriages, Ould Cheikh signifies the dawning of a new era in the Franco–Maghrebi/Occident–Orient relations whereby miscegenation between the two races gives birth to a new and unique race. He argues that if the generation of Khadija and Capitaine Léon Debussy could not go beyond their intolerance and hostilities towards each other despite their romantic love for each other, then at the eve of the centenary of the French intervention in the Maghreb a new generation of educated European and Maghrebi youths had managed to put aside all such prejudices and, as a result of their education in French institutions, would have learnt to live together in harmony,

> *L'éducation occidentale ayant porté ses fruits, les nouvelles générations françaises et musulmanes, contrairement aux 'anciennes' restées longtemps hostiles l'une à l'autre, commencent à se comprendre et à s'aimer.*[69]

Thanks to European education, the new French and Muslim generations, unlike their predecessors who for a very long time remained hostile to one another, have started to understand and like each other.

Conclusion

The intellectuals and the novelists of this early period in the Maghrebi encounter with the Occident expressed their deep fascination with the Occident as the bearer of civilisation and progress. Through their writings they conveyed their genuine desire to become civilised and see their own people's evolution to become part of the civilised world. For this, they worked towards building bridges between the camps of the civilised Occident and that of the uncivilised Orient in the hope that the hostilities of the conquest would be put aside and that their people would join them in their keen quest to become an assimilated part of their grand adoptive nation, France.

Their total and almost blind infatuation with the Occident has often led the young educated Maghrebis known as the *Évolués* to become ashamed of their own people and their culture to the point of self-denial. Mamoun labelled his own country as bizarre and viewed his own people, including himself, as less human because they were uncivilised.[70] In this Mamoun was looking through the lens of the French rather than through his own. It has to be highlighted, however, that the native intellectuals' commitment to becoming French was only partial as, while the national identity did not matter much at this stage, their religious identity as Muslims remained of paramount importance. They negotiated very hard to explain to France that one did not need to become Christian in order to become French. This represented an important shift in colonial ideology which led to the creation of the status of the Français Musulman/French Muslims, which helped them distinguish themselves from both Christian and Jewish French citizens. The Islam they claimed was a form of identity which distinguished them from other French citizens and which they viewed from a secular lens. A secular Islam they often compared to the way it was practised in republican Turkey and which did not prevent them from becoming totally Europeanised.

At this stage the Français Musulman presented himself as a person who adopted French looks in terms of dress and appearance, but who distinguished himself from Europeans and from French Jews by donning a red fez similar to the one worn by the young Turks and Arab Middle Eastern intellectuals of the same period.

The plea of the *Évolués* was often not well received by their own people whose suspicion about the Occident never waned but, on the contrary, they linked the French occupation to the Roman Empire which had occupied the region well before its Islamisation, and to the crusaders as major aggressors against Islam whose violence and terror was recorded in oral literature and in the peoples' subconscious thinking. Interestingly enough, this same link with the Roman Empire is evoked by the claim of the settlers' ideology that the French had come to North Africa to claim back their Roman heritage.

It is generally perceived among the *Évolués* that the Occident should not be blamed for the poverty and ignorance of the indigenous populations of the Maghreb. While they showed their social engagement through their role of bridge builders between Orient and Occident, which brought modern education and progress to the colonies, they also showed that salvation could only be achieved through the cooperation of their people, who were blinded by a fanaticism which stood in the way of their deliverance, with the help of their civilisers.

Although the three novels studied in this chapter are guided by their authors' total trust of the Occident and their unbending belief in its civilising mission and assimilationist project, the social ills they depict invite the reader to doubt this view and judge its authors as being totally blinded by the dazzling light of 'civilisation' to the point of self-denial. In lieu of identifying the colonising Occident and the ruthless European settlers as causing the poverty of the natives whose land they expropriated, they only portrayed those Europeans of non-French origins as bad characters and almost consistently portrayed characters of French origins as benefactors in every sense.

While the fundamental message in *Zohra la femme du mineur* and *Mamoun: L'Ébauche d'un idéal* is the infatuation of their authors with the Occident and their gratitude for the transformation of an uncivilised country into a civilised extension of France, calling thus for full devotion and full assimilation of all Algerians, it still remains clear that the so-called 'assimilated' characters they portrayed in their novels have not found happiness nor have they been saved from their 'barbarity'. On the contrary, whether they were fully assimilated to the point of converting to Christianity and renouncing their origins, as in the case of Lili in *Mamoun: L'Ébauche d'un idéal*, or were partially assimilated by remaining Muslims while indulging in the vice of drinking alcohol and mixing with bad Europeans, as demonstrated in *Zohra la femme du mineur*, the main characters in both novels, one way or another, meet with a tragic end.

In contrast to these two novels, however, *Myriem dans les Palmes* by Mohammed Ould Cheikh heralds a new era where, through mixed marriages and the fusion of the French and Maghrebi races, peace would reign at last, which of course was the author's wishful ideal as part of the utopia of the French civilising mission. Furthermore, this novel offers significant instances of self-exoticism and a faithful adoption of the Orientalist tropes thus providing much needed clichés to the author's targeted Occidentalist readers.

One common aspect shared by all three novels is an insistence on the role of native women as desperate guardians of native culture in the vicinity of their homes. Bearing in mind that Myriem is presented as a French Algerian, and not a Muslim native Algerian woman, the Arab and Muslim women who *are* emancipated and are actively being Europeanised do not make an appearance in the novels of the thirties or in the Maghrebi literature of this period as a whole.

5

The Occident and the Oriental Woman: Rescuing the Oriental Man's Victim?

Messieurs the Deputies, Messieurs the Senators,

I would like to call your attention to the plight of Arab women who, with France's tacit permission, are so barbarously treated.

I beg you, Messieurs to replace barbarism with civilisation on our African soil by ordering the abolition of polygamy to which Arab women are subjected by force and which is offensive to the whole female sex. I also ask you to forbid the marriage of young prepubescent girls.

The republic – *unless it contradicts its own principle* – cannot keep encouraging polygamy and marriage of prepubescent girls on one side of the Mediterranean and punish it on the other.

I hope, Messieurs that you will be inspired by civilisation's interests and will abolish the inhuman laws that govern the majority of French Africa's inhabitants.

Hubertine Auclert[1]

Introduction: Orientalist Odalisques or Booty of War?

In view of the despicable images of the French conquest which describe the extreme violence done to native Algerian women, it is tempting to think of the latter as being part of an emancipatory project under the auspices of the French civilising mission, or even as part of an exotic Orient such as depicted in the works of master Orientalist artists like Eugène Delacroix in his *Femmes d'Alger dans leur apartments,* or Étienne Dinet in his fascinating portrayals of native women in peaceful and tranquil Saharan dwellings.

The abundance of Orientalist artworks depicting Maghrebi and Middle Eastern women confirms the view that there is no other group of women in the world who were as extensively painted, portrayed and later on photographed as those of North Africa and the Middle East. In his epoch-making work *The Oriental Harem* Malek Alloula presents us with a collection of photographs of Algerian women taken by French photographers who, being defeated by the impenetrability of the harems and the veil of native women, resorted to a fictional penetration through the deployment of hired models and fictitious studios. With these tools they managed to artistically carve their way into their imagined harems to paint and photograph these women in their intimate dwellings, and enter beneath their veils to depict them unveiled and sometime even in erotic and semi-nude poses. This obsession with the female body not only symbolises the Europeans' insatiable quest for their illusory Orient, with its harems inhabited by an abundance of seductive Oriental women, but also colonial control of and penetration into the most intimate sites of the colonised subject's body and locations, rendering thus every intimate space a public domain that is open to everyone's view.[2] Alloula writes,

> History knows of no other society in which women have been photographed on such a large scale to be delivered to public view . . . Moreover, its fixation upon the woman's body leads the postcard to paint this body up, ready it, and eroticise it in order to offer it up to any and all comers from a clientele moved by the unambiguous desire of possession.[3]

However, positioning these Orientalist images next to colonial texts which describe the conquest and its extreme violence towards native women creates a perplexing site of contradictions.[4] It is often the case that the beauties of the imagined Oriental harems are at the same time referred to as war booty, as subjects whose bodies became a battlefield that bears the inscriptions of rape and mutilation. This level of violence and persecution against native women is followed, after the pacification of the country, by depictions of the same native woman as the passive victim of her barbaric and misogynist people whom the colonialists were eagerly trying to save her from. Rhetoric about and images of the victims of abominable Oriental men abound in colonialist circles and present the case of the native woman as requiring the urgent attention of the European civilisers. Starting with European images of native women and a presentation of testimonies on colonial violence against them, as reported by historians and authors from both sides of the Occidental and the Oriental divides, this chapter will swiftly move to explore the work of French feminist Hubertine Auclert (1848–1914) and the mission to save Muslim Algerian women, which in my view is the kernel of the current rhetoric about saving brown women and Muslim women from their own men. A deconstruction of her book *Les Femmes arabes en Algérie* (1900),[5] which she wrote while she sojourned in Algeria from 1888 to 1892, will be central to this discussion as a testimony of an Occidental woman's views of Oriental women in the nineteenth century, and how such views became deeply anchored in the Occidentals' mindset and became unmovable. It is therefore not astounding to find that the image of the Oriental victim of her vile men continues to persist in the twenty-first century western imagination. The discussion of Auclert's book will be juxtaposed with a reading of Fadhma Aït Mansour Amrouche's autobiography *Histoire de ma vie*,[6] as a counter-narrative and a testimony of a native woman who has undergone a full process of 'redemption' through French education and the assimilation of French language and culture, to be followed by conversion to Catholicism and embracing the Christian faith while continuing to live in the midst of her Muslim compatriots. A close reading of this narrative reveals an invaluable testimony of a woman who lived through the colonial period and thus came into close contact with a plethora of French people/'civilisers', including missionaries in the form of the White sisters and the White fathers, schoolteachers and civil administrators. This is a very rare account of an Oriental woman's encounter with the Occident between the nineteenth and twentieth centuries.

Hubertine Auclert, An Occidental Woman on a Mission to Save the Oriental Maghrebi Woman

Hubertine Auclert opens her book, *Les Femmes arabes en Algérie* with the customary description of a European author landing in Algiers for the first time. The city she describes is a site of dazzling light and impeccable purity which she calls a paradise on earth. Just like Maupassant in *Au Soleil* she promptly moves from sketching the beautiful scenery to a description of the new European settlers who have made their fortune by acquiring hundreds of hectares of land in the newly conquered colony which she designates as 'a land coveted by all nations, an African Eldorado'.[7] This image is immediately intercepted by the appearance of the veiled native women. An ugly image she depicts as a shocking contrast to the bright light and the blue sky of Algiers: 'One is immediately struck to see . . . on cobblestones sparkling like steel, shocking bundles of dirty linen,'[8] who were in reality destitute native women draped in worn-out and dirty *haiks*. Clearly shaken by what she saw, Auclert engages in an emotional description of such women as in the following excerpt:

> These bundles move toward you, and then you notice that they are held by dusty feet, topped by a head so wrinkled, worn, furrowed, and hewn that it no longer is a human face; they are statues of suffering embodying a race tortured by hunger . . . Wives of evicted landowners, famished mouths unwanted by their tribe, these poor females wander, driven away from everywhere, hunted down, brutalised, insulted in all languages by all the races that have settled on their fathers' lands.[9]

Although this emotive description perceptibly situates the author on the side of the natives, as was often the case with republican and educated French citizens newly arrived from the metropolis, Auclert does not oppose or condemn French colonialism in North Africa as the direct cause for the suffering of the women she pities, but casts her criticism on the European settlers whose prime interest was land appropriation and not the wellbeing of the native people, whom France allegedly came to civilise. In her account she repeals the common view that the natives were non-civilisable fanatics, and recognises that it was not in the interest of the materialistic European settlers to civilise them for they did not consider them as human beings worthy of civilisation. She characterises the settlers as 'vultures' and 'locusts' and blames them unreservedly for their greed, which is the direct cause of the wretchedness of the natives. As to the latter, she divides them into two distinct categories: France's allies, who are the local aristocracy of *Caïds* and *Aghas* who make a minute selfish minority, and who she criticises for partaking in the abuse and victimisation of their own people in order to safeguard their material interests and privileges. The second category is made up of the majority of the natives who are subjected to layers of abuse and exploitation. She designates them as the vulnerable subaltern group who have no political voice nor representation in their country's parliament to defend their rights.

It becomes apparent from the narrative that Auclert's empathy with the natives is mainly because she found them to be similar to French women who, at the time of writing this book (the last few years of the nineteenth century), were also the subaltern who had no political voice or rights. Furthermore Auclert argues that in this cycle of victimisation while French women were the victims of their male counterparts who deprived them of their political rights, native women were the victims of their native male victims who had no one to speak for them and fight for their rights, let alone someone who would care to ask them about their needs. According to her, native women would greatly benefit from the French assimilationist project as they would gain access to French education which would enable them to escape their fate of the victim's victim.

While we note Auclert's different and less Orientalist approach towards the natives as she does not lump them up together as one homogenous group, and as she speaks of the native women having needs no one tries to identify, she then slips into the perilous suggestion of using French women as a means to reach those areas French men could not enter, i.e., the harems and the women's worlds. She argues that because French male soldiers subjected native women to disdain and extreme violence during the wars of 'pacification', and also because most women do not leave their homes where they are sheltered from male view but especially from foreign/colonial men, that the only way to reach these women and earn their trust is through French women who, unlike French men, could gain access to their dwellings as women: 'Muslim women being invisible to men, only women could reach them.'[10] Whether intentionally or not, this is an open call to include French women in the colonial project of acculturation through penetration into the very intimate places where native women were actively preserving national culture. Auclert explains that French women could succeed where French men have failed: 'In Algeria there are many functions only women could fill. The conquerors would be ill-advised if, for lack of female officials, they neglected to strengthen their case by weighing the opinion of Arab women.'[11] This very weakness is expressed by many French Orientalists including Robert Randau who, while he criticised the impenetrability of the harem and the veil as a blockade to French acculturation, nonetheless insisted that the French civilising mission and cultural assimilation projects were not solely destined for native men but should also and more importantly, be extended to native women whom he portrays as being cloistered, forcibly veiled, subjected to polygamy and male control. Native women, therefore, should take priority as they need to be saved from the barbarity of their menfolk before one can attempt to save the latter from their own barbarity, which of course highlights the native woman's status as the victim's victim.

Based on her personal observations in the field and a good knowledge of the history books published on Algeria and its people, from which she draws substantially in her analysis, Auclert instead highlights the roles played by Algerian women in the resistance against French occupation and concludes that after all, these women have not always been passive victims secluded in harems. She sheds light on their heroic roles in battle and in encouraging their menfolk to fight the invaders. She states that these women have 'so very much helped their husbands defend their country against us every inch of the way'.[12] This remark validates the point that native women's seclusion is a result of European incursion and that excessive veiling is a result of the presence of foreign non-Muslim men in the colonial public sphere.

Native Women as Active Agents: The Defenders of the Nation

French Chronicles of the conquest include stories about the heroism of Algerian women in going to extremes in inciting their men to fight the French invaders. An example to cite here is the resistance of the Harazeli women,[13] the most famous of whom is the eighteen year old Messaouda, who, seeing that her exhausted menfolk were ready to turn their backs in battle, climbed the ramparts and faced the enemy while she spoke these words:

> Where are the men of my tribe?
> Where are my brothers?
> Where are those who used to sing songs of love to me?[14]

Thereupon the Harazeli men came running to her aid, and tradition reports that they did so while clamouring this war cry that was also a cry of love: 'Be happy, here are your brothers, here are your lovers!'[15] Similarly, in 1844 Army General Daumas reported that when he asked the Kabyle notables why they fought so ferociously against the French army under the commandment of General Bugeaud, they responded that their wives had threatened to reject them if they did not fight off the invaders.[16] As well as the valour of native women in their resistance to the occupants by inciting their husbands to fight the enemy, a tradition that goes back to Roman times, the conquering armies were surprised as well as very shocked to see women fighters in the ranks of the Algerian armed resistance. Capitaine Carette testifies that Kabyle women entered the battlefield along with their brothers and husbands whom they encouraged with their ululations. In addition to caring for the wounded and lifting the dead off the battlefield, they were also seen as combatants, right from the early years of the French conquest. He reports the following:

> In December 1834, a Kabyle woman served as a foot soldier in an attack against a cavalry charge; her body was discovered among the dead afterwards. In a military confrontation in 1835, fourteen women were killed or wounded. Finally in June 1836, I saw the widow of a Kabyle religious leader, who had been killed the day before in combat, arrive at the head of a column of Berber warriors. She remained at the site of her husband's death weeping and wailing despite the fact that bullets [from French rifles] rained about her for an hour.[17]

Such scenes totally shattered the French soldiers' and European public's preconceived images of Muslim women as the indolent beauties or passive prisoners of the harem. It was not easy for them to comprehend how such conservative communities allowed women to be part of military action, which was not always the case with European women. In his *Mémoires d'un officier d'état-major, Expédition d'Afrique*, published in 1835, only five years after the French conquest, Baron Barchou de Penhoen speaks of such women in a tone of horror and amazement.[18] Equally, while Auclert deplores the horrific acts committed by French soldiers against native women as they cut their ears and wrists in order to snip their large solid gold or silver earrings and bangles, she also goes on to describe the cruelty of native women who used incredibly ghastly methods to mutilate French soldiers.[19] On this same subject Perret, author of *Récits algériens 1848–1886*, describes a shocking scene of a battle in the Zaatcha region south of Algeria in the following terms:

> *Les femmes de Zaatcha ne tardèrent pas à se joindre aux combattants, exaltant leur courage par des cris affreux; ceux-là seuls qui ont vu au combat ces ardentes filles du désert peuvent s'en faire une idée. Ces horribles mégères ne se contentaient pas de remplir l'air de leurs vociférations, elles tenaient toutes à la main des couteaux dont elles se servaient pour achever les blessés français que la fureur de la lutte ne permettait pas d'enlever.*[20]

Zaatcha women were soon to join the male fighters exalting their courage by hideous cries [ululations]; only those who have seen these fiery girls of the desert at combat can understand this horror. These atrocious shrews did not just fill the air with their vociferous screams; they all carried daggers which they used to finish off the injured French soldiers who, because of the ferocity of the battle, could not be lifted off the battlefield.

In the same source Perret also writes about the legendary Lalla Fatma Nsoumer (1830–63),[21] the war leader who rallied the Kabyle region into an organised armed resistance against the French occupants from 1851 till 1860.[22] She headed an army of men and women and defeated the French armies under General Randau in several battles, most famous of which are the battles of Icherridène and Tachkirt in July 1854, resulting in a heavy toll for the enemy and causing them to incur 371 injured men and 800 dead, of whom 56 were officers. In his *Parole donnée*, the Orientalist Louis Massignon baptised Lalla Fatma the Algerian Jeanne d'Arc.[23] Not content with this comparison, her message was a hymn to the originality of Maghrebi women whose bravery preceded that of Jeanne d'Arc going back to the seventh century when the Berber warrior Queen Dihya (al-Kahina) led an indigenous resistance to fight the Muslim armies of the Umayyad dynasty who marched from Egypt. In 680 she defeated the Arab Muslim leader Hasan Ibn al-Nuᶜmān and resisted the Muslim incursion for another five years. In his book *Femmes D'Algérie: Légendes, Traditions, Histoire, Littérature*, Jean Déjeux devotes a whole chapter to Dihya (al-Kahina),[24] and another to other Algerian heroines, of whom he includes Messaouda of the Harazlis, Euldjia bent Bou Aziz, Lalla Zohra, the mother of the Emir Abdel-Kader and of course Lalla Fatma Nsoumer.[25]

The Native Woman as the Victim's Victim

Along with the images that show Algerian women as active agents in the defence of their invaded country, a host of narratives also portray them as victims not so much of their people but of the colonial armies. Several sources testify to the extreme violence associated with the conquest of Algeria, and, as suggested by Perret, women had to pay the price for fighting alongside their menfolk against the occupants. Referring to the women of the Zaatcha and the way they finished off the injured French soldiers, Perret explains how all native women were not to be spared as women but were treated with a mixture of disdain and suspicion:

> *Ce souvenir resta dans les cœurs, et nos soldats exaspérés jurèrent de ne plus faire de quartier aux femmes. Ce serment devait être rigoureusement tenu, et l'on verra tout à l'heure que le sentiment de vengeance provoqua d'inimaginables horreurs.*[26]

> This memory remained in the hearts, and our exasperated soldiers swore to no longer spare the women. This oath was to be strictly retained, and we will see later that the feeling of revenge caused unimaginable horrors.

In his book *Histoire de l'Algérie 1830–1878*, Dieuzaide speaks of these unimaginable horrors where entire villages were erased and their inhabitants were indiscriminately slaughtered.[27] He also describes acts of vandalism, which included killings, pillaging and burning down of the natives' homes and fields:

> *Le général en chef donna l'ordre sauvage d'incendier les magnifiques jardins qui environnaient la ville, pendant que le grand prévôt de l'armée faisait égorger dans les rues tous les habitants . . . un témoin oculaire raconte que cette boucherie dura si longtemps, qu'à la fin les soldats ne s'y prêtaient plus qu'avec une répugnance visible.*[28]

> The Commander-in-Chief made the harsh order to set fire to the delightful gardens that surrounded the city, while the Provost Marshal of the army

ordered the slaughtering in the streets of all residents ... an eyewitness states that this slaughter lasted so long, that at the end the soldiers could only continue with a visible abhorrence.

Likewise, Army General Canrobert bears witness to the disastrous effects of a terrible and barbaric war which provoked a deep sense of demoralisation amongst the French soldiers who were instructed to slit the villagers' throats, loot their possessions and rape their women.[29] Similarly, Captain Lafaye, another officer who took part in the conquest, reports that his troops burnt down a village in the Khremis, belonging to the Beni Snous tribe and did not spare the lives of the elderly, the women or the children. He states that the most hideous thing is that the women were in point of fact killed after they were dishonoured.[30] Those whose lives were spared, were captured as part of war booty, and were exchanged for horses or sold as sex slaves. Army General Montaignac writes in a letter to his mistress in Paris about the fate of the women they captured, saying:

> *Dans un paragraphe de votre lettre, vous m'avez demandé ce qu'il est advenu des femmes algériennes capturés, certaines nous les gardons comme otages et les autres sont vendues aux enchères aux hommes de troupe comme des animaux.*[31]

> In a paragraph of your letter, you asked me what has happened to captured Algerian women. Some we kept as hostages and others were sold at an auction to the soldiers like animals.

Similarly, Auclert testifies that in the early years of the conquest women were captured as spoils of war: 'Arab women kept as hostages were exchanged for horses or auctioned off like beasts of burden'.[32] Most damaging to these women, however, were acts of rape which were disseminated as acts of violence and dominance performed by a dominating coloniser on the dominated colonised women. In most cases rape was practised as a punishment against the women but most importantly against the honour of their defeated menfolk. As a result, the women who were damaged by the rape, those who lost their resources and had no male relatives to provide for them, roamed the streets as beggars, while a good number of them became prostitutes in the brothels set up in the service of the army soldiers. To protect their women and for fear of dishonour, the surviving defeated and impoverished native families resorted to excessive seclusion of women. Under these circumstances it is clear that colonial France did not come to civilise women or to rescue them from the dominance of their own people. The colonial presence brought poverty to the natives, increased the veiling and seclusion of women as measures to safeguard their honour and intensified the unequal treatment of women often as a reaction against colonial rule and Western ways.

Seeing their suffering as a direct consequence of French colonial presence it becomes difficult to reconcile the natives, men and women with their colonisers who claim to have come to civilise them by assimilating them.

Nonetheless, as a republican woman who deeply believed that France came to Africa to civilise its barbaric people, Auclert, like most European women who arrived in the colony either as settlers or visitors, did not question the civilizing mission's political ideology of domination. She argues that the only way to bestow the bounties of civilisation on the natives was through their total assimilation. She advances the view that because the atrocities of the conquest were committed by French men, French women were better positioned to gain the trust of native people in general and native women in particular. Speaking from a European woman's position she believed that unlike native men, native women would be in favour of French assimilation: 'How delighted they would be to express their support for assimilation!'[33] Furthermore, speaking from her position as a civilised and free French woman, she argues that native women yearn to resemble European women. She declares that

> The dream of Muslim women whose lives are lived in inner courts and windowless houses is to be assimilated to French women and thereby escape the life of a recluse. They envy the European women's lot as caged birds envy the life of birds free to fly in the sky.[34]

This statement not only betrays Auclert's paternalistic position, which assumed that European women were superior to and better off than native women simply because they were not 'secluded', but also demonstrates that she was not cognisant of native women's needs and that with regard to the French occupants they shared the same position as their male counterparts. What seems to have escaped Auclert's understanding of native women is that their needs and 'dreams' were far removed from those of European women. Furthermore, the dreams of a colonised person cannot be similar to those of their coloniser; while native women were steadfastly safeguarding their national culture and identity, Auclert writes about their dream to resemble French women and become assimilated to French ways. If any Algerian person, regardless of their gender, had been asked about their dream by Auclert they would all have said that their dream would be to see their country liberated from the colonialism which shattered their lives.

Nevertheless, when one closely reads Auclert's claims it becomes apparent that her support for the assimilation of native women was not so much for their own benefits after all. She explains how the benefits of assimilating Arab women are manyfold, greater than those of assimilating Arab men for obvious social and political reasons. She also expounds the view that girls assimilate right away whereas boys take much longer and therefore, that their assimilation comes at a much higher cost.

Furthermore, Auclert blames the French authorities and the European settlers for contributing to the victimisation of native women not only by augmenting the barbarism of native men, by which she means their control of women and therefore the worsening of their condition, but also by subjecting them to sexual violence at the hands of the soldiers of the conquest and to continuous humiliation by European settlers and civil servants who never spare an opportunity to demean them and insult them. She says: 'one would believe that Algerian civil servants cannot walk past an Arab woman without insulting her,'[35] and, she 'is insulted in all languages by all the races that have settled on their fathers' lands'.[36] Similar attitudes towards native women by French soldiers were recorded by ʿAbd al-Rahman al-Jabarti in his book *Tārikh muddat al-firansī bi misr*,[37] where he describes at length how the lax moral behaviour of the French soldiers in Cairo made them renowned for their bad behaviour towards women, whom they insulted in the streets and sometimes even physically abused them. Such behaviour subjected Egyptian women to seclusion and intense veiling to protect their honour and that of their families, which in turn promulgated the view of the harem and the veil as two strongholds of European fantasies. However, in addition to the 'barbarism' of the native men and their 'barbarous customs' of veiling and secluding women, Auclert also casts the blame on French authorities in the colony who did not try to save the helpless native women from their misogynist religion by allowing Muslim communities to retain religious courts with jurisdiction over matters relating to family affairs, including marriage, divorce and inheritance, while French law was applied to all other sectors in the Maghreb. According to her, it is under such laws that many injustices were committed against native women especially child marriages and polygamy, which although not permitted in France were perfectly legal in the French departments in Algeria and the protectorates of Morocco and Tunisia. She asks, 'Will French law always give in to the Koran? Won't the republic give assistance to the young victims of Muslim debauchery?'[38] by which she means polygamy and child marriages. Adherance to Muslim laws, according to Auclert, is in outright contradiction with French republican ideals. Moving to political action as the spokesperson of the 'voiceless' native Algerian women, she wrote petition upon petition to the president of the Chambers of the Deputies asking for a radical change in native women's juridical and social conditions, the abolition of polygamy and improved education. Here is an excerpt from one such letter:

> We have permitted the Arabs to keep their laws, their mores, and their language for too long. Don't you think it is urgent to make them children of the Republic, to educate them, and to assimilate them to the French? . . . The Republic – unless it contradicts its own principle – cannot keep encouraging polygamy and marriage of prepubescent girls on one side of the Mediterranean and punish it on the other.[39]

The president of the Chambers of Deputies answered her saying that 'the Arab woman's situation could not be improved without altering the Muslim personal and inheritance status that has always been respected by the Algerian legislation'.[40] Auclert found this response totally unconvincing and rather hypocritical. Well aware of Arab and Muslim women's aspirations for change across the Middle East where Muslim men had begun to call for the emancipation of Muslim women, a move which is not deemed to be in contradiction with Islam, Auclert rejected the response of the Deputies as ungrounded. To substantiate her argument she cites the example of Egypt and the work of Qasim Amin who championed the cause of Egyptian women through his calls for reforms to educate and emancipate them. She explains that native Algerian women were sacrificed for France's political ends,

> France, under the cover of its civilising mission, has dispossessed Arabs of Algeria's territory, and now it claims its respect for the barbarism of the vanquished in order to keep them outside the very civilisation in the name of which it conquered them! This is unimaginable![41]

Auclert saw this as a deep fault line in the colonialist ideal of assimilation and civilisation. It is hardly possible to call for the assimilation of the natives when their personal status law, which draws its articles from local tribal customs as well as from the Qurʾan, remains unchanged.

Acting out of a moral duty to elevate the status of native women and make it possible for them to be treated on a par with French women, Auclert paralleled French male prejudice against women in France with the racial prejudice they held against the colonised in Algeria, ultimately resulting in the double victimisation of native women who were, unlike their male peers who suffered from racial prejudice under colonial rule, subjected to both racial and gender discrimination.

Speaking in all good faith and from a humanist and a feminist standpoint Auclert, while criticising the position of the settlers and the French authorities on the ground, neither of whom were in favour of any form of racial rapprochement through the assimilation of the natives to French ways, was militating for the benefit of native women to liberate them from their victimhood without fully understanding their actual needs.

It is interesting to note here that this trope of the Muslim woman as needing saving by the West albeit after bloody wars of conquest, and this ongoing tendency by Western feminists to save the Muslim woman from her own people, has its roots in the nineteenth century and continues to manifest itself in the very same manner in the twenty-first century.[42] Likewise, applying Shariʿa-based patrimonial laws to Muslim women who live in some European countries in the twenty-first century, while they are citizens of these countries, poses the question of whether Muslim women are genuinely saved from their people's 'outdated' laws and customs even when they live in the West far from their countries of origin. In her reaction to claims made by First Lady Laura Bush in a radio address to the nation on 17 November 2001, justifying US intervention in Afghanistan on the pretext of saving Afghan women, Lila Abu-Lughod argued that before one can speak about saving Muslim women one needs to develop a serious appreciation of the differences that exist between women across the globe as products of different histories, expressions of different circumstances and manifestations of differently structured desires.

Likewise, the same tropes about the dangerous yet sensuous and lazy Oriental man produced in nineteenth century Orientalist representations also continue to manifest themselves in the present day. In Auclert's work there is a clear demarcation between the lazy, tyrannical and sensual Arab man whom she describes as a polygamous person whose sexuality is uncontainable, 'the barbarian who does nothing but gaze at his navel,'[43] and his victim, the Arab woman as the prisoner of the harem and the veil who is inhumanely exploited on all fronts. This lifestyle is sustained by a misogynist religion, which she perceives as fanatical and, most importantly, as an iron barrier to progress and civilization. Therefore, her blame is not solely cast on the settlers and colonial authorities who failed to save the Muslim woman, but also on native men and Islam itself, which she often misunderstood with regard to the rights of women as for example when she believes that forced marriages are dictated by Islam: 'According to Koranic law, no woman can refuse marriage.'[44] Furthermore, Auclert also failed to understand that the Muslim woman did not exist as a separate entity from her menfolk and that, much like any other society, Algerian society could not be divided on the basis of its genders. It is logically difficult to understand how it would be possible to assimilate native women as a separate group from native men who happen to be their very own people. More importantly, it is either the case that Auclert missed the fact that it was the female victims, who she considers better targets for assimilation, who kept national culture and memory alive in the safety of their homes and in the face of a fierce colonial campaign of acculturation, or it is precisely because native women played this key role that they represented obstacles to acculturation and assimilation and therefore they should be singled out as the first target of any assimilationist project. Moreover, though perhaps unintentionally, Auclert's book on Arab women in Algeria was hailed as a further justification for French occupation, because it highlighted the perceived degraded condition of Arab women as the victims of their people whom the civilised French needed to rescue. Oftentimes she highlighted the urgency for France to lead a genuine campaign of assimilation if it wanted to keep a stronghold in its colonies. On this, Marnia Lazreg remarks that Auclert's feminism '[. . .] fell prey to her commitment to the colonial order, no matter how imperfect and problematic she knew it was.'[45] As things stood, during colonial times native Maghrebi women did not perceive themselves as victims of anything other than French colonialism. In the domestic realm, they maintained an identity strongly resistant to colonial influence and, while they became the guardians of tradition and cultural values, they had no intention to become agents of French assimilation from which they guarded their children and husbands. On the other hand, in stark contrast to the colonised and brutally Europeanised public sphere, the home became a place of safety, a refuge where men and children, constantly undermined by colonialism, could regain their pride and identity.

In her study 'The Colonial Gaze: Islam, Gender, and Identities in the Making of French Algeria',[46] Julia Clancy-Smith argues that in her criticism of the negative influence of French colonialism on Algerian women, Auclert is similar to contemporary British feminists in using a discourse of a 'universal sisterhood' that was oxymoronically imperial and hierarchical, to save the native women. She argues that although Auclert cast her criticism towards a French administration who, through the maintaining of the native's customary laws in family matters both maintained and worsened the 'barbarism' of native men, much of her rhetoric to advocate for the rights of native women still portrayed them as victims of their barbaric customs and misogynist religion and not of the colonial order. Furthermore, portraying these women in need of saving and as the victims of their male folk stripped them from all forms of agency and condemned them to the status of the helpless victims who are incapable of defending themselves and are therefore in dire need of being saved.

French Feminists and the Mission to Save Muslim Women through French Education

Girls' education in colonial Algeria was held hostage to the natives' resistance to expose their girls to European influence and to the settlers' constant interference with any venture destined for the education of the natives in general and native girls in particular. This is confirmed by Auclert, who clearly demonstrates that the French project for native girls' education was not solely opposed by the 'fanatical' natives during the nineteenth and early twentieth centuries but also by the European settlers who interrupted any project to open schools for native girls. Oftentimes they went as far as diverting their allocated budgets. She says:

> In its session of 1861, the conseil général of Algiers took away the allowance intended for Arab girls' schools, asserting that pedagogical teaching did not suit the women's condition in Muslim society and that it could not be reconciled with the duties and mores imposed on women by Muslims. Educating them would therefore do young girls a disservice.[47]

In the same vein, Lazreg argues that the colonial administration in the nineteenth century did not see any profit from educating native girls: 'While they were concerned about the creation of a group of French-educated Algerian men to serve as their links with the native population, colonial leaders evinced no such interest in women.'[48] She then remarks that this was expected as they had yet to recognise the principle of equality between men and women in their own society, let alone in the country they had just colonised. As such, girls' education in Algeria during the nineteenth century was not seen as a priority and the few individual attempts made in the 1850s by some French women to launch girls' schools were not taken seriously and were often sabotaged by the settlers. Not only this, but the reputation of these women was also often attacked and they were exposed as dubious by angry colonialist opponents as with the case of Mme Eugénie Allix Luce (1804–82), a young French woman who cohabited with Mr Luce before they were actually married:

> Her reputation is doubtful among Europeans as well as natives who find her repulsive. Her school is attended by girls from the poorest families only because of the fifteen-centime stipend allocated to each one of them daily.[49]

In addition to this, rumours were spreading about her loose morals. Rebecca Rogers explains how the whiff of immorality that had plagued Mme Allix Luce from her early dealings with colonial officials heightened in the late 1850s soon began to spread to her students:

> Administrative reports suggested that her students were not raising the moral tone of Muslim families; rather, they were becoming concubines

for Europeans or were prostitutes. Journalists dwelt on the dangers of *déclassement*: too much education pulled young women from their social milieu, making them unattractive marriage prospects, an argument used throughout France to limit educational achievements for low-class French women.[50]

This same view is expressed by the natives whose representatives conveyed the message to the authorities. Lazreg reports one such case in the following excerpt: '"Never", said a native member of the General Council during its 1860 session, "would a self-respecting Muslim send his daughter to the school or choose his wife among her pupils."'[51]

This terrible campaign was in fact an alibi to put an end to girls' academic education in Algeria which, at this stage, was not seen as either useful or necessary. Instead, an official decree was issued in 1861 to transform these schools into vocational workshops, *ouvroirs* where native girls were taught handcrafts such as weaving and embroidery. Then again these workshops were also severely criticised for their purely vocational nature and for not training the native girls in academic subjects. Not only so, but despite their young age the girls were exposed to long hours at the loom which made many parents withdraw their daughters from school 'for fear that the emphasis on weaving, which required the use of relatively heavy metal tools, and long hours spent sitting in the same position, might stunt their growth.'[52] Furthermore, Mme Allix Luce was criticised for exploiting the girls' poverty for her own ambitions. Lazreg quotes her as saying, 'Misery and hunger are my real helpers,'[53] as fifteen out of her seventeen pupils came from very poor backgrounds, resulting in the labelling of her school as a charitable organisation rather than a school, which is not far from the truth. Although Mme Allix Luce claims that by training these girls she helped divert them from prostitution and taught them a skill that would help them earn an honourable living, she profited from their crafts more than they ever did. She understood the market value of 'Oriental goods' within an imperial economy that extended well beyond France. According to Roggers, she used her workshop and the embroideries produced by her pupils to attract foreign visitors and to seek foreign sales.[54]

Auclert, whose feminist trajectory in Algeria seems to build on the work of Mme Allix Luce, expresses her admiration of her courage and dexterity. She regrets that her great efforts to promote girls' education in Algeria as a service to the French empire were not appreciated because she was well ahead of her time. She explains how she was forced by the *conseil général* to transform her school into an *ouvroir*, where she taught young native girls to create original embroidery. However, Auclert elucidates, thanks to her clairvoyance she managed to find a way to instil French culture into the minds of her pupils through the French language. Auclert praises her saying:

> [...] opening her pupils' minds as well as directing their hands. While exposing them to the refinements of artistic embroidery and teaching them to follow or trace a drawing, a figure, or a cabalistic sign, she secretly teaches them to speak and write in French ... This teaching gave so much to art and the French motherland. Foreign winter residents pay good money for this embroidery which they carry away as souvenirs of African industry.[55]

It is surprising that Auclert did not see any harm in the exploitation of the young girls who did not benefit from the profits made from their labour. On the contrary, she writes, 'Arab thick-pile carpets ... are so much in demand that a native vocational school was created in Algiers by Mme Delfau to manufacture them.'[56]

Likewise Mme Allix Luce, who sought out the company of British feminists wintering in Algiers, succeeded in carving out for herself the image of a benefactor and a feminist who devoted her life to helping native women and saving them from poverty and prostitution. Instead, she exploited their labour and trained them to become good wives and excellent mothers.[57]

Fadhma Aït Mansour Amrouche, *Histoire de ma vie* or the Odyssey of a Kabyle Woman Convert

The question this section asks is whether the campaign to save native women through French education in the nineteenth century was successful, and whether the project of converting them to French ways through the medium of education has saved them from their status of victims and has resulted in the creation of a generation of well-educated and fully emancipated native women.

The first native Maghrebi woman to have witnessed and recorded a full process of assimilation through French education followed by conversion to Catholicism is Fadhma Aït Mansour Amrouche who also happens to be the first Maghrebi woman to have written the story of her life in French. The author did not keep a regular diary where she recorded her life happenings as a day-to-day account, but instead resorted to memory to help extract the events that marked her life after she was asked by her son, the poet Jean Amrouche, to bear witness to a remarkable trajectory that should be recorded and shared. She started the writing process in 1946 while she and her family lived in exile in Tunis.

The life story that Fadhma narrates is not just a personal account but the story of a whole region whose women, being in their vast majority totally illiterate, were largely unable to record their own stories. In a way the story of Fadhma's life is therefore not only a testimony of a whole generation, but also a native woman's account about the civilising mission and its effect on herself and her contemporaries. Its importance grows even larger because it reports on the early beginnings of French education in the Kabyle region and bears witness to the work of the Christian missionaries in the same region. On this latter subject close to nothing was written from the perspective of the natives. Searching the Maghrebi literature of the colonial period the only mention of the Kabyle Christians appears in one novel by Mouloud Feraoun, namely *Les Chemins qui montent*, where the author puts as central protagonists two hybrid characters: Amer, son of a French Christian mother and a Kabyle Muslim father, and Dehbia, daughter of a Kabyle Muslim mother and a Kabyle Christian father from the Aït-Ouadhou (Ouadhias), the very village where Fadhma Amrouche had encountered the White Sisters which she describes in her autobiography.

Feraoun terms the Ouadhias 'Aït-Ouadhou', the name it had before it was changed to Ouadhias by the French. He presents it as a Kabyle region whose inhabitants had been converted to Christianity. In the same fashion he introduces the nine year old female protagonist Dehbia as the Christian girl who landed in her mother's all-Muslim village following the death of her Christian father; '*une étrangère, une chrétienne, une malheureuse*: A stranger, a Christian, a doomed girl.'[58]

This fate of the wretched stranger is also that of Fadhma Amrouche as she describes it in her autobiography. She says, 'In the village ... certain women would look at me pityingly and I would overhear them saying, "May God's curse be upon Kaci [Fadhma's biological father]; it's his fault that such a pretty child is destined to be an outcast!" ... I bore an indelible mark engraved on my forehead.'[59] There is a huge resemblance between the fictional character Dehbia and that of Fadhma Amrouche, to the point where one wonders whether Mouloud Feraoun had met her and been inspired by her story. However a close reading of his non-fictional works such as *Lettres à ses amis*,[60] where he speaks about his novels, suggests that he did not encounter the Amrouche family of authors and did not exchange letters with them.

It is important to note that central to Fadhma's autobiography are the encounters she has with the Occident, offering very rare instances of a native woman's account and impressions of the Occidentals as missionaries as well as secular educators, all the way from the nineteenth through to the twentieth century. This rare account not only offers a counter narrative which juxtaposes against Auclert's book on the women of Algeria and other accounts by French/European women about native women, but also brings up names of people and places referred to by both authors. It is interesting to see how the two women present the same events and personalities through the coloniser's and colonised's lenses.

Born in 1882 as the illegitimate child of a young widow who lost her husband at the age of twenty-two, Fadhma was rejected by her co-villagers as a child of sin who, like her sinning mother, Aïni, did not deserve to live. Although the narrative exposes the reader from the onset to the harsh Kabyle customs it also very quickly shatters the image of the weak native woman, or 'the bundles of dirty linen' described by Auclert. Fadhma's mother, like all women in rural Kabylia, was not a prisoner of the harem but a woman who worked in the fields and did not wear a *haïk*. This image reverses the stereotype of native women being 'all exactly alike'[61] and the tendency to homogenise them as being veiled and needing to be freed from their veils and their seclusion.

Furthermore, although Kabyle customs are harsh, 'when a woman transgresses she must disappear',[62] this does not mean that women helplessly gave in to such customs but that they also ferociously resisted them.

Aïni is portrayed as a resilient and powerful woman who defied traditions and withstood the threats of her brothers and her in-laws in equal measure.

As a young widow with two sons from her late husband and a daughter born out of wedlock she stood her ground and refused the protection of any male relative. Instead of bowing to the commands of her in-laws to leave her sons with their late father's family and return to her parents' home to live under the wing of her brothers, she decided to stay put in her deceased husband's house, farm her land and provide for her family from her own labour.

Likewise, when Aïni entered into a relationship with her neighbour and became pregnant, his family did not allow him to marry her. When Fadhma was born, she lodged a complaint with the public prosecutor against Fadhma's father, asking him to acknowledge her as his daughter. She harassed the colonial magistrates for three years but, since the law at that time forbade the establishment of paternity, Fadhma was condemned to live as the child of sin: 'the seal of shame was branded on my forehead.'[63] Instead, Fadhma's father was sentenced to pay the sum of 300 francs as damages to her mother. Proud and defiant, Aïni turned down the money. Fadhma quotes her mother saying in all boldness 'The tattooing on my chin is worth more than a man's beard!'[64]

Aïni worked indoors and outdoors, day and night to singlehandedly provide for her three children. All along she also battled against those who wanted to cause harm to her and to her illegitimate daughter. Fearing for her safety, she entrusted her to the Catholic nuns, known as the White Sisters of the convent in the Ouadhia village, at the age of three where she stayed for one year (1885–1986). This event in the autobiography links with the work of the Christian missionaries in the Kabyle region discussed above in chapter three.

Fadhma's memories of this phase are unhappy and only include episodes of ill-treatment and severe punishment, such as when the nuns flogged her till she bled which made her mother take her home. Angry and disenchanted, she told the nuns,

> 'Was it for this that I entrusted my daughter to you? Give her back to me!'
> The nun undressed me, even stripping me of my chemise. My mother took off her headscarf, knotted two corners together over my shoulder, pinned the material together on the other shoulder with a large thorn, by way of a clasp, untied her wide woollen girdle . . . and lifted me on her back.[65]

The effect of the whip was so traumatic that Fadhma associates her mind image of her first encounter with the nuns to a whip being part of their attire, 'I have very little memory of this period of my life. Pictures, nothing but pictures. First, that of a very tall woman, dressed all in white, with black beads. Another object made of knotted rope hung next to the rosary – probably a whip.'[66]

The next station in Fadhma's life story is the Taddert-ou-Fella orphanage, which also operated as a girls' school. It was founded between 1882 and 1884, a period when the first French schools for boys were opened in the Kabyle region, while 1850 was the year when such schools were opened in major cities such as Algiers, Oran and Constantine.

Fadhma Amrouche went to school in 1887. Her autobiography provides significant first-hand knowledge and vital eye-witness discernments into the workings of such schools from the perspective of one of their native pupils. As such her story is a rare testimony in the whole of the Maghreb and the only hitherto known text which conveys a native Maghrebi woman's account about her encounter with the Occident during the nineteenth century yet brought to light.

Fadhma speaks about the circumstances which surrounded the launch of the Taddert-ou-Fella village school. Her description of the recruitment of the pupils resonates with Auclert's advice on how to recruit pupils for colonial schools. Disappointed about the low numbers of native children who attended French schools she advised that 'the French . . . would do well to imitate Egypt's viceroy Mahomed Ali who had children picked up in the streets and public squares to take them to school.'[67] It is interesting to see that this same method was used to recruit children for the newly opened school in Taddert-ou-Fella in Kabylie. Fadhma reports,

> He (M. Sabatier) summoned all the *kaïds* (Caïds), cavalrymen and rural police in his area and asked them to ride through the *douars* (villages) and collect as many girls as possible. The *kaïds* and the horsemen set off, with the rural police, who set the example by bringing their own daughters.[68]

The result of this launch is a mixed bag of destitute orphans, children whose impoverished parents could not provide for them and the well to-do daughters of the Caïds. There were also some European girls, but they had a separate dining room and a separate dormitory – showing the segregation between the living conditions of the European and the native girls. Fadhma describes the poor sleeping conditions in the icy dormitory as well as the poor quality of the food they ate: 'black coffee for breakfast, with a piece of bread; for our midday meal, lentils full of grit, haricot beans, rice or split peas.'[69]

Nevertheless, despite being a poor boarding school with harsh living conditions, Fadhma kept fond memories about the ten years she spent there from 1887 to 1897. Unlike the *ouvroirs* (workshops), her school taught a good array of academic subjects such as French language, history, geography and biology in addition to which they did crafts as a supplementary subject once a week. She recounts with pride how she fully engaged with some subjects while she did not like some others, which is quite revealing. For example, while she could never remember all the Departments and Districts in France, which were both unknown to her and far removed from her Kabyle environment, she loved the French language dearly. However, even then she failed to understand French proverbs and maxims because they were not accessible to her culturally despite the huge efforts that were deployed to Frenchify all the pupils, not just through teaching them subjects that did not take their own native culture into account but also by Gallicising their first names: 'We had all been given French names, as there were too many Fadhmas, Tassadits and Dahbias.'[70] While Fadhma, who was given the name Marguerite at school, did not think much of this practice, Lazreg saw it as France's way to assimilate native women and as a means to Frenchify Algeria. She refers to the work of Camille Sabatier, a former judge in the city of Tizi Ouzou in the Grande Kabylie who in 1882 prohibited Kabyle women from tattooing their faces as tattoos were repugnant to Frenchmen. Furthermore, 'To make Kabyle women more attractive to his compatriots, Sabatier proposed that the governor of Algeria issue a decree permitting the Gallicization of Kabyle women's first names'[71] which would facilitate the unions between these elite women and young Frenchmen in Algeria. This said, and as much as such unions were sought after by the advocates of assimilation, marriages between Kabyle women and European men in the nineteenth century were unheard of while marriages between Kabyle men and French women started to take place in the twentieth century following their economic migration to France from 1910 onward. Despite the Kabyle Myth theory that promoted the view that Kabyle people were similar to Europeans and more accepting of assimilation, facts on the ground proved that they were much attached to their customs and very reluctant to accept French ways. They resisted French education and schooling in the same way as all Algerians, be they Arab or Berber.

Although Amrouche recounts that her school was seen as a success story and therefore a show-place visited by tourists, and a succession of members of the French government, including Jules Ferry, this success was down to the devotion and hard work of its headmistress, Mme Malaval, who dedicated herself wholeheartedly to girls' education in colonial Algeria. Despite numerous difficulties, her school succeeded in pushing the girls to study for their *certificat d'études* and to become schoolteachers although success rates were extremely low among the native girls. However, this realisation was short-lived as the authorities quickly turned against Mme Malaval and decided to close her school.

Deeply disillusioned, Fadhma Amrouche reports that while people started to demand the emancipation of Muslim women across the Muslim world, girls' schools in Algeria were scarce and were not taken seriously. Although she had hoped that the colonial administrator, M. Masselot, who came to visit her school, should have intervened in favour of the hardworking girls, she was shocked to learn that he supported its imminent closure: 'He had us stand in rows and said, "I can't help you. If you were men I'd issue you with a burnouse and give you a job in the police or the horse regiment, but you are girls . . ." And he added nonchalantly, "*they're pretty, they'll get married . . .* !"'[72] M. Masselot's statement resonates with the motivation behind the vocational workshops for native girls, according to which the only role girls' education should play was to prepare them to become good housewives. The girls at the school rebelled and were very angry with Masselot's verdict. Fadhma describes their vain attempts to seek help by writing to various authorities including 'the English women to ask if they would take them, but they got no reply.'[73] While it is not clear who these English women were, Dorothy Blair suggests it may be the women of the Methodist mission who were at that time operating in the Kabyle region.

Not happy with Masselot's verdict, Mme Malaval kept the school going for six months out of her own savings. Fadhma Amrouche speaks of her genuine dedication to the education of native girls and her battle to keep the girls' school running despite government's decision to cut its budget and opposition from the local authorities. She says, 'Mme Malaval ... moved heaven and earth, writing to members of the government and any influential persons who might help her. Eventually she got her way in 1893. It was decided that the Taddert-ou-Fella Orphanage should be taken over by the state and renamed "the Taddert-ou-Fella Normal School".'[74] This, however, did not give it stability for too long as two years later the girls were yet again sent home. Having tried very hard Mme Malaval understood that she had fallen out of favour with the authorities because she believed in training native girls academically to become schoolteachers, while the norm was in favour of training them in crafts and housewifery. After much pressure Mme Malaval had to step down from her position and Mme Sahuc, a more conforming headmistress, took her place. With much sadness Fadhma concludes: '[. . .] we were not to be educated in the same way any longer: we were not to be trained to become primary schoolteachers',[75] instead Mme Sahuc brought in bales of wool so that the girls could learn to spin and weave. Fadhma disliked weaving and felt very disillusioned. At the end of the year the school had to close for good and the girls were sent home.

Deeply disillusioned and feeling rejected by her 'civilisers' Fadhma decided to rid herself of the veneer of civilisation that she had acquired at school and not even think about French education any more. She says, 'Since the *Roumis* had rejected us, I resolved to become a Kabyle again.'[76]

Her time back home was a learning process in becoming a Kabyle woman, and at this stage she asked her mother to teach her everything she knew in order to second her in every task she performed. Through this process she not only delved into Kabyle heritage, crafts and culture, but most importantly she reconnected with her mother and strengthened her bond with her. Not only did Fadhma learn about her native culture, which she describes in detail thus providing valuable ethnographic knowledge about nineteenth century Kabyle life, but she also got to understand why she was the only girl in the village to be sent to the 'Christians', therefore gaining awareness of her social status as an outcast. It became clear to her that being the 'child of sin' and having been sent to the White Sisters, and subsequently to the school of the French, compromised her prospects of finding a suitable husband as advised by M. Masselot when he sent her home after the closure of her school. In fact her interrupted education, if anything, had only made it even more difficult for her to find a Kabyle husband, 'The inspector who has said, "They're not bad-looking, they'll get married," did not know that the Kabyle man instinctively mistrusted an educated woman.'[77] Seeing her vulnerability as an 'orphan' the nuns had sent for her to join their mission in the Aït Mengueleth hospital where she was employed in the linen room. Having studied at a secular school she found the religious aura that reigned in her new environment rather overwhelming: 'Everyone kept talking about God, everything had to be done for the love of God, but you felt you were spied upon, everything you said was judged and reported to the Mother Superior.'[78]

Ending up as the linen girl in a missionary hospital living in a gruesome environment and in dreadful conditions was far from an enviable position for a girl whose French education could have destined her for a better future.

Conclusion

This chapter's main aim is to challenge the perceived and much circulated view of native women as the Muslim men's victims whom the Occident was set to save. It began with a discussion of the early accounts of the conquest which brought to the fore images of native women both as active agents in the defence of their conquered nation and as passive victims of their religion and culture. A culture these women–victims were actively safeguarding in the face of a violent campaign of acculturation which targeted the very essence of the natives' existence as a group of people who were culturally dissimilar to their Occidental occupants.

Central to this chapter was the work of Hubertine Auclert, *Arab Women in Algeria*, as an interesting and important document which contributes to the understanding of the workings of Occidental culture and perceptions of native women and how the mission to save them was understood by prominent French feminists in the nineteenth century. The chapter then brought into the discussion their work and efforts to use French education as a means to save native women from their oppressive people and culture. As we saw through the discussion, this mission was caught up in a web of difficulties: partly due to the natives' resistance to French education, which they identified as a means to destroy their cultural identity, and also due to the colonial administration, which did not take girls' education in the nineteenth century seriously. Instead of academic schools with the prospect of preparing the girls for respectable professions that would then save them from the precarity of their lives, colonial authorities opted for the notorious *ouvroirs* which provided vocational training for native girls whose labour was then often exploited for a growing market demand for indigenous handcrafts.

In the course of this investigation it was rather thought-provoking to consider how native Algerian women became victims of France's anti-feminist positions, and how the denigration of women in France during the nineteenth century was even more intense in its colonies. Native women, as demonstrated by Auclert herself, were not respected but were insulted by European men in the streets. They were homogenised as Moorish and 'Fatmas' who were perceived either as maids or prostitutes.

The women headteachers of the likes of Mme Allix Luce and Mme Malaval were not portrayed as respected either. They were battling against a stiff colonial culture which often caused them personal harm leading them to give up their missions to 'save native girls'.

Looking closely at the case of Fadhma Amrouche gave us an intimate account of the workings of this mission from the perspective of a native girl. Having experienced a mix of religious missionaries and secular school encounters her account is that of a long suffering which knew no end. At the end of her autobiography she wrote, 'I have always remained "the Kabyle woman"; never, in spite of my basically French education, never have I been able to become a close friend of any French people . . . I remain for ever the eternal exile, the woman who has never felt at home anywhere.'[79]

Her mother, on the other hand is illiterate and not exposed to Occidental influence. She is portrayed as a much happier woman. She is a strong and full agent who said no to customs and male control. With much pride, she took charge of herself as a young widow with small children whom she raised singlehandedly. She never suffered from hunger but reaped the fruit of her labour and looked after her home as well as her fields. In her old age, she turned to religion, as is the way among the Kabyles, and led a pious life. Aïni is barely in need of being saved from anything or by anyone; she defended herself against her in-laws and brothers, and went to the authorities when she needed to sue her daughter's biological father. She told off the nuns for ill-treating her daughter and made a decision on the spot to take her away from them. She also made the decision to send her to school and gave her the choice on whether to go and work in the hospital or accept a marriage proposal and settle in her village. What is most important in all this is that Aïni is content and self-sufficient.

In contrast, the case of her daughter Fadhma demonstrates that although she was put right in the midst of missions that were supposedly destined to save native women, she was not saved in any way, but more than the girls who were not exposed to the Occident she suffered endlessly from a plethora of setbacks in addition to the pains of dire poverty, exclusion and exile.

Does the ongoing mission to save native women in the twentieth century offer a better story? This remains to be investigated in the next chapter.

6

The New Maghrebi Woman and the Occident: From Occidentophilia to Ambivalence

En Algérie, une objection pourrait être soulevée par les Musulmans: l'évolution dans le cadre occidental n'a pas toujours donné d'heureux résultats . . . et nos filles et nos femmes n'ont retiré de cette évolution aucun avantage moral. La Musulmane algérienne réclame de la collectivité (et particulièrement de la grande famille musulmane) une protection et une aide qu'elle lui a jusqu'à ce jour refusés. Elle demande aussi à l'État de la guider dans son contact avec la vie moderne.

In Algeria, an objection could be raised by the Muslim community: evolution in the Western context has not always given positive results . . . our women as well as our girls have gained no moral advantage from Occidental civilisation. The Muslim Algerian woman demands of the Community (and especially the great Muslim family) the protection and assistance that it has so far denied to her. She also asks the [French] government to guide her in her encounter with modern life.

Djamila Débêche[1]

Introduction

By the turn of the twentieth century the emancipation of native women through the medium of French education had become the subject of talk in both native and European circles. Newspaper articles were published in both the French and the Arabic press generating conflicting views on the roles native women should play in their society. Should parents educate their girls in French schools or in the Arab *madrasas* that had started to open in some major cities? And when sent to school how much schooling should they receive? Would their French education not divert them from their prime role as the guardians of national culture? Would too much Occidental culture not contaminate them and alienate them from their own people? Would exposure to French ways not incite them to rebel against their traditions and customs? In other words *how much* exposure should they be permitted?

These concerns were raised in juxtaposition to, and as a reaction against, the move by European women who openly started to campaign for saving the native woman–victim from her own people. They spoke about the opportunities that were denied to her by her male kin, and therefore made saving her the first priority of the French civilising mission. The irony in this is that, in their vast majority, women were unaffected by the attention accorded to them. Lazreg argues that, 'the majority of women could neither read nor write Arabic and/or French, and therefore had no access to what was said about them.'[2] However, while this was generally the case during the nineteenth century, in the 1940s new voices and images of native women started to make their appearance not only through the medium of literature but also through women's press. Articles published in *Dialogues, Méditerranée, L'Action* and *Al Manar* started a new wave of discussions by native Algerian authors who debated the status of women in colonial Algeria.

It is important to note that the Young Algerians group who started speaking to the Occident in the nineteenth century were all men and they did not single out the native woman as needing 'saving' or in need of the Occident's help. Their demands focused on the emancipation of the natives in general without specifying any gender differences. It seems that the native men's interest in native women's rights and improvement of their social status only occurred as a reaction to the French feminists' demands to save the native man's victim.

This chapter proposes to study the work of Djamila Débêche, and it will begin by analysing *Leila, Jeune fille d'Algérie* as the first Maghrebi feminist novel which represents the voice of the Algerian woman as part of the pre-1950s literature and heralds the emergence of a new French-educated native Algerian woman; a woman active in the public sphere who, like the Algerian male intellectual, also speaks to and engages with the Occident.

As well as depicting the first appearance of woman's literature in the twentieth century, which denotes a total shift from the image of the silent and secluded native woman whose main positive role is the safeguarding of national culture and identity, this novel presents us with an interesting mix of educated and non-educated women and their various reactions to Occidental culture and the so-called 'mission to save native women'.

Djamila Débêche's second novel *Aziza*, while it denotes the double sense of alienation experienced by native women who were leading a dual battle against patriarchy and colonialism, also signifies the somewhat shocking shift from the period when the Occident represented a pole of attraction and fascination to the period when it shocked, baffled and as a result alienated its neophyte followers by its contradicting positions: especially manifested during the massacres of 8 May 1945.

In order to gain a better understanding of these novels and explore the motivations underpinning their author's engagement with feminism as a movement that promotes women's rights in order to save women from their inferior status, I will situate them in their feminist context and interrogate whether French feminism had an impact on their author's opinions. Furthermore, seeing that these novels constitute a voice which emanates directly from the Algerian feminist movement, in which Djamila Débêche played an important role through her publications and social work of which very little is known, this chapter will both introduce this movement and situate it in its socio-political context.

Feminism and Imperialism in Algeria

Hubertine Auclert's years in Algeria made her one of the first French thinkers to engage theoretically with empire from a feminist perspective, thus resulting in a strong sense of imperial feminism.[3] Echoing the work of other feminists such as Madame Allix Luce, she positioned herself as the saviour of native women working under the aegis of the French civilising mission destined to rescue the colonised from their barbarity. Auclert demonstrated that among the uncivilised natives women were in dire need of rescuing from their men who prevent them from receiving the bounties of the French civilisation. As a far-sighted person Auclert was aware that by assimilating Algerian women France could assimilate the whole nation. On this basis she laid the foundations for the interwar French feminists, both through her use of a metropolitan-based Journal *La citoyenne*, which she launched in 1888, and through her book *Arab Women in Algeria* wherein she expressed her views and succinctly passed the message to the colonial administration that unless it adhered to its republican values and its assimilationist ideals it risked losing its African Eldorado.

In her article 'La citoyenne in the World: Hubertine Auclert and Feminist Imperialism', Carolyn J. Eichner explains how *La citoyenne* emerged not only as France's first suffragist newspaper but also as its first feminist periodical to address imperialism. Eichner elucidates,

> Shaped by her understandings of civilization, history, and race, Auclert's republican universalism and Franco-assimilationism ultimately undervalued Arab women's experiences, voices, and culture. Although she strove to ameliorate their conditions, she nonetheless appropriated their oppression to further her primary goal of French women's full citizenship.[4]

As a great admirer of the work of Mme Allix Luce and her colossal efforts to promote girls' education in Algeria as a service to the French Empire, through her book and articles Auclert echoed her views and developed them with more depth and vision. See for example the following statement made by Madame Allix Luce as she harassed the authorities to provide her with funding to support her girls' school project:

> As you well know, Mr. Minister, in Africa as well as in Europe, women are the most powerful force. If you convert [sic] to our civilisation 100,000 native girls of all classes and races in the regency [that is Algeria], they will, given the circumstances, have the privilege of becoming the wives of the most notable men of their class, thereby guaranteeing for ever *the subjection of this country to ours*, and setting into motion the irreversible process of its future assimilation. (My emphasis.) [5]

Auclert explains that the opposition and animosity shown by the colonial administration to Mme Allix Luce was mainly because she was well ahead of her time and therefore her intentions were not understood. Although the same level of hostility was also shown to Auclert by the European settlers, who opposed any form of genuine emancipation for the native population, she tried to bypass their reactions and to speak directly to the authorities by warning them about the shortfalls of their efforts to educate and assimilate native men while their women were continuing to safeguard national culture – thus rendering all assimilationist efforts insignificant. It is the women before the men that one should target if one wants to acculturate and assimilate a nation. By assimilating the women one would not only stop them in the first instance from interposing themselves into the acculturation process but, once assimilated, they would bring up a new generation of totally conformed individuals.

Therefore, many decades after Auclert's writings, and having identified native women as the repositories of the Islamic and cultural values of Algeria and the axis around which the whole society revolved, and having given up hopes of assimilating Algeria through its men, the French colonial administration deployed inordinate efforts for the assimilation of native women. With the rise of Algerian nationalism during the interwar period this mission became even more urgent, not only in Algeria but also in neighbouring Maghrebi countries. In Morocco, for example, the Frenchwoman Aline Réveillaud de Lens, known as an orientalist artist and novelist whose oeuvre focused on the Moroccan harem, wrote to her mother-in-law saying:

> Like the Young Algerians, Young Egyptians, etc., the Young Fassis [from Fes] have ideas of independence, but these are still early, and they see it very far in the future. For now, their greatest concern is to reform the religion . . . You see, they have interesting ideas, about education, about improving women's status . . . I am able to study them and get to know them. I think that if we influence them, *we could render the greatest service to France* by preventing them from turning against her.[6] (My emphasis.)

Unlike the often hostile reactions of the colonial authorities in Algeria to French feminists, De Lens's ease of access to the Moroccan harems led the protectorate administration to recruit her as an ethnographic researcher and a facilitator between the authorities and the women in the harems.

However, it also has to be highlighted that the direct and sustained contact that Aline de Lens had established with Moroccan women, avoiding any maternalistic sense of superiority, could not be found anywhere in

Algeria. Testimony to that is Fadhma Amrouche's statement that 'never, in spite of my basically French education, never have I been able to become a close friend of any French people.'[7]

Auclert, her contemporary French feminists and educators, as well as French feminists in the first half of the twentieth century who also embraced the view of rescuing native women from their own people, were under the influence of the colonial rhetoric of civilising the uncivilised natives and were therefore speaking from a patronising position of superiority.

Furthermore, they negotiated with French authorities to obtain their suffrage rights in exchange for helping the colonial administration to conquer native women. In 1933 French suffrage-seeker Jeanne Bottini-Houot indicated that: 'in our Algerian colonial domain, another sphere of activity is opening up to our feminist groups. This activity can be carried out in indigenous homes, where women have not yet lived in contact with European civilisation.'[8] This demand was emphasised through the pages of *La Française*, a feminist newspaper established in 1906, which between 1924 and 1939 was heavily drawn to colonial matters. Although, like Auclert's *La Citoyenne*, the contributors of *La Française* portrayed Muslim women as needing French women's help to free them from the harem and the veil, they showed a less superficial understanding of Islam: 'several authors argued that the Quran did not force women to wear the veil, while it did grant them considerable financial and legal autonomy.'[9] They, however, blamed their male kin, the native men, for having deprived them from an education which in turn prevented them from understanding their rights as Muslim women. Interestingly, however, they also blamed French men for allowing native men to keep their laws, a claim also made by Auclert forty years earlier.

During the same period the French feminist and politician Cécile Brunschvicg believed, like Auclert, '[. . .] that France was defaulting in its civilising mission by allowing the indigenous to continue to oppress their women when these women were supposedly protected by French Laws.'[10] French feminists found it difficult to comprehend why the French Empire did not interfere with Muslim personal laws in its colonies while it imposed French Laws on all other domains. In his article 'The Colonial "Emancipation" of Algerian Women, the Marriage Law of 1959 and the Failure of Legislation on Women's Rights in the Post-Independence Era', Neil MacMaster elaborates on the reasons which made Muslim personal status Laws a no-go-zone for the colonial authorities:

> Until 1957 the Algerian government, advised by its own administrators and experts in Islamic law and customs, had hesitated to interfere with the sensitive issue of marriage or family legislation, particularly as there continued to exist, since the great anti-French revolts of the nineteenth and early twentieth century, a fear of stirring up insurrection guided by 'fanatical' jihadists, religious confraternities or pan-Arabic militants.[11]

In view of this, the rights and emancipation of native Maghrebi women were compromised to avoid potential rebellions on the part of the natives, which in a way explains why the colonial authorities had waited until 1957, right in the midst of the Algerian War of Independence, to introduce new measures to interfere with Muslim family law in Algeria in order to emancipate native women. Here again, women's emancipation was used as counter-insurgency and a desperate act to win over the native women. While the colonial administration publicised the case of the oppressed native woman, as the victim who they wanted to save from her own men, this move was, in reality, a desperate eleventh-hour decision to divide Algerian society and to isolate the liberation army fighters who relied heavily on the work of native women.[12]

Here, as advised by Auclert and promoted by subsequent French feminists, it was now the French women who, willing to serve the Empire as at all times, highlighted through the pages of *La Française* the potential for French women to enter the domains which were closed to French men and therefore to succeed where the latter had failed. In return, they maintained, the Republic should grant them suffrage rights, which much later than many European countries, French women only obtained in 1947. This self-serving goal of suffrage in return for serving the Empire, and not questioning the ethics of the latter's colonial endeavours, compromised the feminist and humanistic missions of French feminism vis-à-vis colonised women in general, and native Algerian women in particular.

This provided confirmation of the suspicion raised by nationalist male elites and theorists with regard to the education of native girls in French schools or the inclusion of native women in charitable actions. Frantz Fanon wrote extensively about this imperial aspect of French feminism, explaining this state of affairs as follows,

> The colonial administration could then define a precise political doctrine: 'if we want to hit the Algerian society in its deep contexture, in its resistance strategies, we must start to conquer the women; we must go and find them behind the veils under which they conceal themselves and in the houses where the men hide them'.[13]

According to Fanon, to go and find these women in order to 'liberate' them, in the view of French feminists, and conquer them by acculturating them, demonstrates the French view of these women as the passive victims of their menfolk from whom they were to be rescued, and the nationalists' view of them as active agents who have always resisted Western acculturation and contamination.

While this dichotomy of opinions seems logical, it did not escape the French colonial administration's attention that native women were in real fact working tenaciously to preserve and maintain their national identity and cultural memory. As such, they exploited the idea of rescuing them as proposed by French feminists not for any good intention but as a means to destroy their cultural resistance.

Fanon explains how assimilation is equivalent to acculturation and, therefore, how the more the French tried to assimilate the Algerians the more the latter resorted to their cultural values – central to which were the veil and the seclusion of women as a reaction to the French project to culturally dominate Algerian society through targeting its women. This project was often openly expressed by the colonial administration whose excessive attacks on the native women's veil signified a direct assault on Algerian national identity.

Having said this, the European settlers continued to oppose any project for the benefit of the native population whom they did not see as anything but a cheap labour force they feared to lose. Despite changes in the political scene from the nineteenth to the twentieth century, their colonial ideology and mindset did not evolve but remained static and uncompromising. This gave rise to conflicting views and positions between metropolitan French politicians and thinkers who truly believed in France's republican ideals and the European settlers residing in the colony who mocked the naivety of the

French from the metropole, who believed all the while that the natives did not deserve education or civilisation. This ultimately resulted in the ambiguous and inconsistent positions of the colonial administration towards the natives in general and native women in particular.

At the turn of the twentieth century Algerians increasingly felt that their identity and integrity were becoming dangerously threatened by the imposition of Western culture and values, and as a result the meaning of the veil took on new dimensions: it evolved from its old meaning of modesty, and increasingly began to primarily communicate 'Algerianity' rather than religiosity *per se*. Maghrebi literature from the colonial period expressed in many different ways how dress codes are signifiers of identity, and while the Young Algerians who called for the status of the 'French Muslims' created a new look for themselves by adopting European dress (to express their Frenchness) while donning a fez (to express their Muslimness), they were hesitant to accept native Algerian women in European attire. As the repositories of national culture they did everything to protect their female compatriots from European influence. In terms of appearance, they preferred to see them clad in traditional dress, and draped in their *haiks* when outdoors in urban areas in order to be protected from foreign gaze. More than the Frenchification of the native Algerian man that of the native woman was seen as highly political.

The Birth of the Algerian Feminist Movement

The open campaign to save native women from their own people during the interwar period resulted in the 'woman question' becoming central to many cultural and political debates among the native population but especially among the members of the nationalist movement attracting therefore the attention of the Algerian nationalist parties such as the PPA (the Party of the Algerian People) and the MTLD (the Movement for the Triumph of Democratic Freedoms).

While male nationalist elites had initially believed that there was no genuine women's question for as long as Algeria was under French occupation, and it was generally seen as almost indecent to speak about the rights of women and their emancipation while their nation was colonised and the prime concern of all was to join forces in order to fight colonialism, the aggressive colonial campaign to save native women from their own people had alerted them to the woman question as part and parcel of any nationalist movement. While the male nationalists acknowledged women's roles as the guardians of national culture as being vital to the resistance against acculturation, they saw French moves to rescue native women from native men not only as culturally and politically dangerous but also as targeting the native man's honour by exposing him as a barbarian and a misogynist.

The Union of Algerian Women (Union des Femmes d'Algérie: UFA) was thus created in 1943 under the aegis of the Algerian Communist Party (Parti Communiste Algérien: PCA), as the first Algerian political party to believe in the equality of the sexes. In its first congress in 1944 the PCA deplored the miserable condition of Algerian women as a direct consequence of colonialism, and set up an agenda to make women aware of their condition, identifying education among rural and urban girls as the main key to their emancipation. Between 1944 and 1951 the UFA gathered some 10,000 to 15,000 members, and issued its own journal known as *Femmes d'Algérie*.[14] The demonstrations of 8 May 1945 saw women from all ranks and backgrounds, for the first time in modern Algerian history, leave their homes in huge numbers to participate in political demonstrations. They moved to the forefront of the nationalist opposition to French colonialism and showed political awareness and engagement in the nationalist movement.

On the social level women showed to their male compatriots that their roles should not be constrained to the safeguarding of national culture in the home but should be extended to the nationalist struggle against colonialism. While women were counted among the dead just like men, they spontaneously jumped to action to tend to the sick and the wounded. The women of the UFA organised a relief action; they distributed clothes and food to the needy and helped the families of the victims in the days that followed the massacre. On the political level, believing in the roles they could play in an armed national struggle, several nationalist parties welcomed the membership of women.[15] This work, however, also attracted the attention of the French colonists who saw a unified people demonstrating as one huge and threatening crowd made of men as well as women. Having exhausted the ethnic division between Arabs and Berbers through the Kabyle myth, which had proved largely unsuccessful, the division of the Algerian society along gender lines was quickly deployed in order to disrupt the rise of Algerian nationalism in the 1940s and was used with more intensity during the War of Independence at a time when women were fully engaged in the war on all fronts. Being in total denial of Algerian women's new roles as members of the national liberation army the French intensified the rhetoric of the native woman as the victim they urgently needed to save. The most scandalous action however was the orchestrated scene of public unveiling of native women by French women on 16 May 1958 as a sign of loyalty to France. Lazreg comments on this event saying that:

> Rounding up Algerians and bringing them to demonstrations of loyalty to France was not in itself an unusual act during the colonial era. But to unveil women at a well-choreographed ceremony added to the event a symbolic dimension that dramatized the one constant feature of the Algerian occupation by France: its obsession with women.[16]

While I agree with Lazreg on France's obsession with native women, who they wanted to control and possess rather than save, I would add that this position is a result of colonialism being another patriarchy that strives to control women's bodies. Whether imposing veiling on women or exposing their bodies via the mediums of Orientalist art and colonial photography, both are analogous acts of control of women by men who see these bodies as their possessions. The women who were brought for the orchestrated unveiling scene did not perform unveiling by their own will or as a conscious political act; they were brought to the place of the demonstration by French Generals as part of a crowd forcibly gathered to demonstrate to the Metropolis the Algerians' loyalty to France. To this day these women remain anonymous; according to some 'they were the all-around maids of the General Government [the colonial government] as well as boarders of whorehouses,'[17] and to some others they were 'Servants on the threat of being fired, poor women dragged from their homes, prostitutes.'[18] Regardless of their identity, staging an unveiling event of Algerian women when in reality these same women had taken to the bush as fighters and had been central to the Battle of Algiers (1956–7), only serves to depict colonial France's stuborn and unchanging views and mindset about native women who they could not envision as other than 'Fatmas' and victims who needed saving, which is correspondent to the general patriarchal view of protecting women.

With regard to whether the women in question perceived themselves as needing saving and as victims of the veil and prisoners of the harem, their views diverged according to their social status and their level of education. For illiterate women, the veil was not seen as a shackle and the harem was not seen as a prison. On the contrary, they both offered them protection and sanctuary, as I have demonstrated in Chapter 4. For the rural Kabyle women the veil was not observed in Kabylie where women worked in the fields, therefore they did not need saving from veils or harems. For working women in urban areas the veil was worn as a coat or a uniform which they put on in the public sphere and then removed in the private sphere regardless of whether men were present or not. This shows the difference between cultural veiling and Islamic veiling, the latter of which women should wear at all times in the presence of men who are not blood relatives. As to the newly educated women, since they were educated in French schools it was generally conceived that they did not need to veil while they dressed in European clothes as part of being educated.

If this was the case, then what did women need to be saved from? Here again women's needs diverged according to the rural/urban divide and the level of education of the women in question. For the uneducated women they believed the only thing they needed to be saved from was colonialism, while for the educated women, they believed they were subjected to a double patriarchy, colonial and indigenous. In 1953 Fadhila Ahmed wrote: 'we, the women of Algeria, have two gaolers: colonialism ... and the apathetic creatures who cling on to customs and traditions inherited not from Islam but from their ignorant fathers. The second gaoler is worse than the first'.[19] The outbreak of the Algerian War of Independence on 1 November 1954 was the occasion women seized to rebel against both gaolers.

Djamila Débêche's *Leila, Jeune fille d'Algérie*, as the first Algerian Feminist Novel

The publication of *Leila, Jeune fille d'Algérie*[20] in 1947 signals the beginning of women's novel writing in the Maghreb, thus making Djamila Débêche (1926–)[21] the first Maghrebi woman author writing in French. Studying this rare text, which was never reprinted after its first edition, allows us to gain a good understanding of the encounter of the first generation of Maghrebi female intellectuals with the Occident. Like the male novelists of the pre-1950 period who specifically wrote their works with the French readers in mind, Débêche also addresses the French readership right from the onset of the novel; '*C'est en pensant à vous, femmes de France, que j'ai écrit ces pages*: It is with you in mind, women of France, that I write these lines.'²² But, more specifically she is addressing the French women and most certainly she is engaging in a writing back process to the French feminists who made the saving of native women their own mission:

> *Dans la Métropole comme dans la France d'Outre-Mer, un magnifique effort est fait par l'élément féminin. En Algérie, des femmes se groupent aussi; elles apportent leur bonne volonté et leur dévouement intégral à la grande œuvre de régénération sociale en préparation.*²³

> In the Metropolis as in France Overseas, magnificent efforts are being made by the feminine element. In Algeria, women are organising too; they bring their goodwill and full dedication to the ongoing inordinate struggle for social regeneration.

It is clear that Djamila Débêche is sending a message to French feminists assuring them that a feminist movement is in full sway in the colony too and that native women are both organising and participating in social development. Here she may also be referring to her own work and feminist activism. In 1947 she launched *L'Action*, a feminist review in which she published most of her feminist writings and established a forum to discuss issues relating to the evolution of her female counterparts. She also published *Les Musulmans algériens et la scolarisation* (Muslim Algerians and Education) in 1950 and *L'Enseignement de la langue arabe en Algérie et le droit de vote aux femmes algériennes* (The Teaching of Arabic in Algeria and Algerian Women's Suffrage Rights) in 1951, two volumes of essays on the importance of education for native Algerian girls and on suffrage and other political rights for Algerian women.

Furthermore, like the male novelists of the pre-1950 period, Débêche begins her novel with an expression of her gratitude for all the efforts made by the Occident to civilise the Orient under the auspices of the French civilising mission:

Dans ce pays ou l'œuvre française s'est inscrite sur les routes, dans les villes, aux sommets des montagnes et dans les douars les plus reculés, un peuple commence à se former; il est en pleine évolution et celle-ci retient l'attention de la France.[24]

In this country, where the good work of France is inscribed on the roads, in the cities, on mountain tops and in the most remote villages, a new people is being born; it is in full evolution and this is thanks to France.

This paragraph sets the tone for the whole novel which, despite the expression of a civilising ideology with distinct racist overtones on the part of its French protagonists, does not show any doubts its author might have had about the demeaning fashion used by the French to describe the native Algerians as uncivilised yet undergoing an evolutionary process to become civilised.

Throughout the novel the author persists in using this same manner to portray her own people as if she is well above their level and does not actually belong to them. This novel makes it very clear that there are three distinct factions in the society it describes: the uneducated and therefore uncivilised natives, the civilised Europeans, and between these two factions we find the educated natives who are undergoing a process of becoming civilised and playing the role of the go-between the two groups.

As such, a clear string of binaries dominates *Leila, Jeune fille d'Algérie* from start to finish. These are especially prominent in the description of Leila's indigenous family in juxtaposition to the European family of her French friend Madeleine Lormont, highlighting Leila as the one person who knows both worlds and is well positioned to highlight these differences. Leila contrasts the destructive feelings of hatred and jealousy which reign in her family with those of love and compassion in Madeleine's, and, whilst Leila's uncle and guardian after the death of her father is portrayed as sly, rude, greedy and conservative, Madeleine's father is depicted as kind, courteous, generous and open-minded. Likewise, Leila's step mother is ugly, authoritarian and spiteful just as Madeleine's mother is gracious, compassionate and amiable, and so on.[25] For these strong divergences Leila opts to repudiate her own family and seeks the protection of the Lormont family, symbolising her rejection of her own people, the uncivilised Orientals, for the camps of the civilised Occidentals. This move befits the prevailing view of white Europeans saving brown Muslim women from their own people. Like the protagonist of *Mamoun: L'Ébauche d'un idéal* and most of the young Maghrebis who were educated in French schools in the first three decades of the twentieth century, Leila is the daughter of a wealthy man who believed in the benefits of French education not only for boys but also for girls. This reflects the mood among some native enlightened men and their call to extend French education to native girls. In his newspaper *Le Mobashir* (Al-Mubashshir) Mohammed Kamal was forcefully demanding education for native girls.[26] Likewise, Leila's father, Sheikh Ibrahim ignored the indignation of his tribesmen when he decided to send his daughter to Algiers to study in a French school. For them, French education alters the moral fabric of those who receive it to the point of becoming estranged from their own culture and way of life. Therefore, when Leila returned to her tribe she was nicknamed a renegade '*Mtournia*',[27] while her educated male cousin Hamza was welcomed back as the pride of his tribe. To better understand this position we need to situate Leila as an educated woman in the context of her time. When French education for native children was introduced in colonial Algeria, it was solely made available to male children. Lazreg remarks that a striking aspect of the period 1880–1930 is the absence of women from the first generation of French-educated natives. She explains that while colonial authorities were concerned about the creation of a group of French-educated Algerian men to serve as their links with the native population, they showed no interest in girls' education. Statistical data demonstrates that at the eve of the 1954 revolution there were only 81,448 native girls attending schools in comparison to 225,289 boys.[28] In my view, this is mainly due to two factors: firstly, the promise not to interfere in the religion and the personal status legislation of the natives, to whom women were seen as central, and secondly because the colonial administration did not see the use of women beyond their domestic roles. Again two factors shaped this view, one is the demeaning stand vis-à-vis native women in general, who the French lumped up together as 'Fatmas', and the second is because at that time the French authorities were yet to recognise the rights of women in France let alone in the colony, as demonstrated by Auclert in her book *Arab Women in Algeria*. In fact, the view of targeting women as the repositories of national culture came much later in the day, almost four decades after the publication of Auclert's book, and especially following insistent demands in the twentieth century by Algerian intellectuals for girls' education. Being educated themselves they could not find educated native women to marry, and therefore often this first generation of native intellectuals tended to marry European women, as for example with Ferhat Abbas and many others.

Unlike that of Fadhma Amrouche, Leila's education was not a traumatic experience. As a daughter of a distinguished man, her father entrusted her to the Institut Marie, a well renowned girls' boarding school in Algiers, to make of her the most educated girl in her tribe although he insisted that, despite being educated in a French school, she should remain faithful to her Islamic teachings, reflecting the general trend of the *Évolués*,[29] who were happy to become Frenchified while remaining good Muslims. Leila's experience in the boarding school, which is predominantly attended by European girls, is one of the happiest in her life; she was loved, respected and well treated. The boarding school is described not only as a place of acquiring an education but mainly as a nursery where French civilisation is cultivated and inculcated by French teachers, and well received and highly appreciated by their pupils. The enthralment of Leila with everything in the school, including its strict disciplinary rules, cannot be dissimulated. In fact, Leila is even fascinated by her own self-image when dressed in European attire and genuinely sees herself as being lucky to inhabit a unique location whose doors were only reachable by the chosen few. Leila's beautiful dream, however, was interrupted by the death of her father and her ultimate return to her native tribe, Ouled Djellal, for the summer vacation.

As soon as she arrived home she was told by her uncle: '*Pas d'évolution féminine ici. Je la briserai*: No women's emancipation here. I will crash it.'[30] He and Leila's stepmother, Lalla Mesaouda, the epitome of the evil native woman, set up a plan to redeem and cure her from Occidental contamination at which they looked with suspicion. They instructed her to wear traditional tribal clothes and not to be seen again in her European outfits, they confiscated her books and advised her to put her emancipatory dreams aside, to conform to tribal ways and prepare herself to become the wife of her cousin Hamza as a means of keeping her inheritance in the family. Leila reports,

> *Dès mon arrivée, elle m'a signifié sa volonté de me voir abandonner toutes les habitudes occidentales prises à Alger et son désir de me voir vivre suivant les*

coutumes ancestrales. Messaouda s'est attaquée à mes plus intimes et chères habitudes. Mes costumes et mes lectures ont retenu son attention et ont, aussitôt disparu.[31]

As soon as I arrived home she ordered me to give up the Western ways I learnt in Algiers and urged me to live according to our ancestral customs. Messaouda targeted my most intimate and cherished possessions. My European outfits and my books caught her attention and they disappeared without delay.

While these actions by Lalla Messaouda can be interpreted as a means of returning Leila to her native culture, from the viewpoint of Leila, who is seeing through the Western lens, she is described as an uncivilised and evil woman. Clearly Frenchified and in total self-denial Leila rebels and rejects the plans and practices of her family as archaic and belonging to a bygone era. She writes to her French best friend Madeleine and tells her about her ordeal – imploring her to come to her rescue.

As soon as she receives Leila's letter Madeleine mobilises her entire family to go to the rescue of her friend who they call '*La jeune Musulmane* (the young Muslim girl)'. This situation legitimises the rescuing efforts put forth by French feminists of the likes of Auclert to save native women. It is very much the case that native women in this instance are imploring their French civilisers to rescue them from the barbarity of their own people. What needs to be specified here though is that it is only the type of Leila who had undergone a Frenchification process in her school that could see the West as her saviour from what had become her barbaric people. Having become totally alienated from her native culture she began to see it through Occidental eyes.

After having thought well about the consequences of his intervention, M. Lormont decides to bear the 'white man's burden', to rescue Leila from her tribe and adopt her as his second daughter. On route to her new home she changes into European clothes, as she deemed her Oriental outfit unsuitable for travel. This physical cross over from the south of the country to its north also symbolises her shift from Orient to Occident as she extracts herself with the help of her rescuer from the world of her barbaric people to seek adoption in the world of the civilised European Other, where she feels more accomplished as an educated and emancipated woman.

The Lormont family greet Leila as one of theirs and bestow on her the love she was denied by her own family. She settles down very well as an adopted daughter and is soon to join forces with her adoptive family to contribute to the economic development of her country.

M. Lormont is a second-generation French settler who invested in industry and became famous for expanding the industrial sector in northern Algeria. In a conversation with his daughter he highlights with pride the great oeuvre of the settlers in Algeria. He explains that while his father's generation (the first settlers) conquered the land and worked in agriculture, his own generation turned to the industrial sector. As to her generation (third generation), they would dedicate themselves to social services as a third phase in the European mission of civilising and modernising the Maghreb.[32] As if to endorse and pay tribute to the hard work of the European settlers in modernising the country, M. Lormont highlights the suffering and sacrifices of the settlers to modernise Algeria: rhetoric which is very similar to that of the colonialist Louis Bertrand. M. Lormont recounts,

> *Nous avons lutté, peiné, souffert et travaillé ensemble; nous avons bien souvent pleuré et connu des heures de découragement. Mais ces jours sont oubliés puisque, par nos efforts, nous avons pu acquérir la plus belle des récompenses : la réussite pour nos enfants et le bonheur de ces êtres jeunes qui continueront notre œuvre.*[33]

> We have fought hard, we toiled, suffered and joined forces; we have sometimes cried as we encountered unbreakable obstacles. But those days are now behind us because, thanks to our efforts, we made great achievements: our success is for the sake of our children and the happiness of these young people who will for sure extend our realisation.

To enhance these traits, the author puts emphasis on the almost ideal pattern of life the Lormont family revels in and the esteem they earned in their community for all their good work in developing the industrial sector in their region, which ultimately brought employment and wellbeing to the native populations. Not only so, but M. Lormont is kind to his employees and treats them humanely, which of course subverts the common view among the natives regarding the greed and inhumanity of the European settlers.

This is once more contrasted with the type of repressive atmosphere which reigns amongst the members of Leila's family, who are not only depicted as being a nuisance to each other but do not do any useful work which may contribute to the development of their own country. On the contrary, their actions are destructive and go against any form of progress. Her uncle is renowned for his arrogance and greed while his son Hamza is despised by all for his ruthless attitudes towards others.

Well aware of the rift which exists between herself and her family Leila understands that this is mainly due to their ignorance: '... *tout le mal vient du fait que j'ai évolué, alors qu'elle vit encore en marge de la vie actuelle*: This is all because I am emancipated while my family continues to live in the margins of current times',[34] and also because of their feelings of jealousy due to the fact she is an educated woman whilst they are not. Her sister points out to her that ever since she learnt to read and write in French she saw herself as superior to the other women: '*Tu te croies supérieure à nous toutes, depuis que tu as appris à écrire et à lire en français!*: Ever since you learnt to read and write in French, you begun to think you have become superior to all of us.'[35] Feeling unaccepted and misunderstood, Leila realised that her dream to play the role of the bridge builder between the two communities is a mission impossible. Instead, she resorts to prayers asking God to help her people understand the benefits of civilisation and to enable them to put aside their misconceptions about modernity and Western ways: '*Mon Dieu! disait la jeune fille, faites que les miens comprennent et ne persiste pas dans leurs fausses conceptions*: My God! Said the young girl, may my people understand and may they not persist in their misconceptions.'[36] To further demonstrate that her people's fears and misgivings towards the Occident are not justified the author shows the respect held by the French people towards the natives' customs and religion, especially in the course of M. Lormont's response to his daughter's plea to rescue Leila from her family. However, despite his awareness that colonial authorities promised the natives not to interfere in their cultural and religious practices, he tells Madeleine that the women's issue is a very important one and necessitates the careful attention of all: '*En Afrique du Nord, le problème le plus important se trouve être justement, à l'heure actuelle, l'émancipation de la femme musulmane*: In North Africa, the most important problem at the present is that of the emancipation of the Muslim woman.'[37] This depicts the centrality of targeting native women and rescuing them from their own people; a view that goes in tandem with those expressed by Auclert in *Arab Women in Algeria* as well as in subsequent feminist writings during the interwar period. This whole idea, however, creates a division between the emancipated woman and her own people as we have seen here in the case of Leila. While it is true that this same division also occurs between emancipated native male intellectuals and their people, unlike their native female counterparts they are not portrayed as victims who are in need of saving to the point of being forcibly removed from their own people. This state of affairs further victimises the native woman as she is portrayed as being unable to save herself. Perhaps a more positive plot would be for Leila to save herself rather than call on the help of her French friend.

M. Lormont reassures his daughter of his optimism that as long as there are some good people in both camps who are ready to cooperate for the good of everyone, things would eventually change: '*Allons! dit-il, il y a de braves gens dans ce pays et l'on arrivera bien un jour, entre bons musulmans et bons français, à s'entendre parfaitement*: Come on! He said, there are still some good people in this country, and one day good Muslims and good French people will manage to perfectly understand each other.'[38] This statement insinuates that the local Muslim people and the French settlers do not live in harmony and that this remains the dream of a certain elite: that of the Maghrebi *Évolués* and a very select minority of European settlers, whose attitude is otherwise generally known to be hostile to the natives who they only see as a source of cheap labour that should never aspire for a better life – let alone to be on the same social level as the Europeans. In fact, M. Lormont is an idealised image of a European settler who perhaps was to be found nowhere in the colony. It is more probable that Djamila Débêche created him for the sake of her novel in order to show her European readers the prototype of settlers who would have the good of their community at heart and therefore win the trust of the natives who would then cooperate with them for the common good of their shared country. As such, Leila is portrayed as the diligent native who deeply believes in the noble mission of her rescuer who also has the key to the salvation of her own people from their miserable condition. She argues that by approximating their efforts to those of the likes of M. Lormont some wellbeing will eventually enter many a native peoples' household. Like Leila, M. Lormont is also confident that despite the natives' resistance to Western civilisation the young educated Maghrebis well understand that salvation lays in cooperation between Orient and Occident. According to Leila,

> *Notre Afrique du Nord parait également sortir de sa torpeur. A la croisée des chemins, la veille civilisation orientale a rencontré la jeune civilisation occidentale et, pour que naisse un monde meilleur, il faut qu'elles s'appuient l'une sur l'autre.*[39]

Our Maghreb [North Africa] seems to be leaving its indolence. At the cross roads, the ancient Oriental civilisation has encountered the young Western civilisation, and for the sake of a better world they should benefit from each other.

Beyond her work in the Lormont enterprises, Leila becomes very sensitive to the social problems encountered by her people. Well aware of the stumbling blocks in their way to redemption, she works tenaciously to explain their case to various colonial authorities in the hope that they will speed-up reforms and bring some wellbeing to their existence. In her numerous letters to the Occident, exemplified here by French officials and important French personalities, Leila works persistently to challenge the view held in the colony that, by dint of their religion, Muslim women should not have an education or aspire to become emancipated. She cites examples of powerful women from Islamic history, beginning with Khadija and Aisha and the important roles they played in the life of Prophet Mohammed, and a host of Muslim women known for their erudition and strong character during the Umayyad and the Abbasid eras. She then moves to modern times and cites the emancipation of Turkish and Egyptian women as examples to be emulated across the Muslim world.

In a letter to a French minister who came from the Metropolis on an official visit to the colony, she tries to make him aware of the malaise of the Algerian people, meaning the native Algerians, but especially the condition of native women. Going into a meticulous analysis of this malaise she highlights the centrality of women to the progress and prosperity of any society, and emphasises that without educating women and opening opportunities for them, the civilising mission of France would not succeed – which resonates with the views of the French feminists.

Furthermore, Leila explains that a form of emancipation which takes into account these women's religion and culture, should be established for them to be integrated into the progress of their society. Her views and endeavour are in fact emblematic of the Maghrebi *Évolués* in general and the views of the Young Algerians in particular. Their attempts were made the subject of many publications and letters addressed to the Occident, in the form of the French authorities, asking them to speed up reforms for the wellbeing of their destitute people and making them aware of the urgency of the situation.

In his book *Les Jeunes Algériens: Correspondences et rapports*, Mahfoud Smati includes a plethora of such letters which were written by various young native intellectuals to French authorities including one addressed to the Governor general of Algiers by Ahmed Tounsi,[40] and another by Mejdoub ben Khalfat, a teacher in a French High school, which he addresses to the Occident reminding France of its duties towards its colonies and its promises to save its subjects from their barbarity. He says,

> *Il est donc du devoir de la République d'améliorer, intellectuellement et moralement, la race vaincue, c'est la une dette que la France a contractée, le jour où elle a mis le pied en Algérie.*[41]

It is therefore, the duty of the French republic to improve the intellectual and mental levels of the vanquished race. This is a debt contracted by France the day it set foot in Algeria.

Deeply believing in the promises of the French civilising mission Mejdoub ben Khalfat ends his letter with a plea to both the Orient and Occident to join forces for the common good of their joint country, as in the following extract:

> *Mettons-nous donc la main dans la main et aidons-nous mutuellement dans cette œuvre Française et patriotique, afin de faciliter le rôle civilisateur de la France dans notre Afrique du Nord.*[42]

Hand in hand, let us work together for the realisation of this French patriotic mission which would facilitate the civilising role of France in our Maghreb.

Leila's report on *Le malaise du peuple Algérien*,[43] contains similar concerns to those expressed in the many reports sent by the Young Algerians to French authorities, in which the authors oftentimes plead with the Occident, again embodied by the French government, to save their own people from dire economic conditions often exacerbated by the inhumane conduct of the European settlers who ruthlessly exploit them. At the same time these reports offer their services as the bridge builders and the intermediaries between their people and their civilisers. Writing to the high authorities in Paris not only symbolises the need for dialogue with the Occident but at the same time it denotes the urgent attention that the French government was supposed to pay to the inhabitants of its colonies. This is seen, as explained by Mejdoub ben Khalfat above, as a moral duty of France since it became the new ruler of the country.

In *Leila, Jeune fille d'Algérie*, Leila's social engagement is reflected in her deep sadness over the case of the street children, the *yaouleds*, who work as bootblacks running after the wealthy settlers to shine their shoes. She would have liked to see such children going to school instead of working at such a young age to alleviate the poverty endured by their families.

Although these issues are explicitly exposed in Leila's letter to the French minister, and consequently in the novel, Leila (and Djamila Débêche) do not accuse or blame France for this condition; Leila says, 'Mais ne cherchons pas les responsables de cette situation et essayons plutôt de trouver, en toute bonne foi, les solutions',[44] in other words let us not look for who is responsible for this condition but let us work in good faith to find the right solutions. The finger is never pointed directly at the Europeans even though they were the direct cause of the impoverishment of the native Algerians. Instead, Leila blames her own people for their fanaticism, mistrust and lack of cooperation with their civilisers, which has resulted in their destitution.

Djamila Débêche's *Aziza*: From the Dream of Emancipation to the Dilemma of the Native Woman's Double Sense of Alienation

The positive tone and the optimistic outlooks which are expressed in *Leila, Jeune fille d'Algérie* will not be found in Djamila Débêche's second novel, *Aziza* (1955), where the blind love for the Occident (Occidentophilia) expressed in the first novel turns into a more ambivalent position towards an Occident which is also ambivalent in its political positions towards the natives.

Although, like Leila, the main protagonist, Aziza, is portrayed as an accomplished French-educated young Algerian woman, she is also portrayed as being disorientated and at a loss as she fails to find the peace and harmony ostensibly achieved by Leila. Unable to identify either with the Occident or with the Orient she is the archetype of the alienated native intellectual whose female gender has subjected her to an additional layer of alienation. From the first pages of the novel Aziza is presented as a character that struggles to define her own identity. Standing in a queue with her native compatriots while she is dressed in European attire, she attracts the attention of the French security agent who asks her to move 'to the other side' and join the European queue. While this scene describes the segregation which exists between the two communities of Europeans and natives/Occidentals and Orientals, it also puts into the limelight the character of the Europeanised native whose hybrid location is indeed very complex. Unable to identify with either group, '*Ni dans un groupe, ni dans l'autre, je n'étais à ma place*: My place was in neither of the two groups,'[45] the likes of Aziza suggest the creation of a third queue; in other words, a third cultural location for those who opted for full assimilation. When the queues were organised, Aziza based on her identity certificate which she would have to present at the counter, decided to join the queue of the native people. However, because of her physical appearance both in dress and looks she did not blend with her non-assimilated natives who were dressed in indigenous clothes. Had she joined the queue of the Europeans she would not have stood out from the crowd and would not have attracted the attention of the agent who asked her whether she was in the wrong queue.

> *Parmi les miens, on me regarda avec surprise, sans sympathie. Une gêne m'envahit.*[46]

> My compatriots scrutinised me but, with great surprise rather than sympathy; I was overwhelmed by a strong feeling of embarrassment.

Memmi delves with depth into the intricacies of this condition. According to him it is not enough for the colonised to fully imitate the coloniser because, regardless of their level of assimilation, at the end of the process the coloniser will never fully grant them access to their world: 'All that the colonized has done to emulate the colonizer has met with disdain from the colonial masters. They explain to the colonized that those efforts are in vain, that he only acquires thereby an additional trait, that of being ridiculous.'[47] Aziza's condition of embarrassment and her failure to merge into the group she worked so hard to imitate indicates the illusory aspect of the assimilation project which remains a mere discourse that cannot be realised because the coloniser is not prepared to relinquish his privileges as the master for the benefit of the colonised subject.

The complexity of this position is even more accentuated among the category of Maghrebis whose Mediterranean or European looks, when dressed in European attire, made them pass for Europeans, especially under the colonial condition where the two communities were severely segregated. One thing that escaped the proponents of the project of assimilation is perhaps whether the Europeans would have been content to be imitated in such manner in a colonial society whose main essence was racial ghettoization? In fact, such level of imitation would not make the coloniser content but would irritate him. According to Memmi '. . . he will say the colonized is an ape. The shrewder the ape, the better he imitates, and the more the colonizer becomes irritated'.[48] Here Fanon's theory in *Black Skin, White Masks* becomes rather disorientating as while it explains the complexity of the coloured native aspiring to look like white Europeans by adopting their dress and manners, it does not reflect on the category of the natives whose looks are European or Mediterranean. Their barrier is not in the way they look but in the colonial administration that does not put the assimilation project into practice. The assimilated native may totally transform their looks but they cannot change their identity. Memmi explains how 'Everything is mobilized so that the colonized cannot cross the doorstep, so that he understands and admits that this path is dead and assimilation is impossible.'[49] Débêche explains how in order to overcome this condition some assimilated individuals went as far as camouflaging their origins by changing their names as in the case of Aziza's friend Fakia Brahil, who became Francine Brahil:

> *Fakia avait donc opté pour l'Occident et de façon excessive. Toujours élégamment vêtue, à la dernière mode de Paris, elle avait abandonnée toutes les*

coutumes musulmanes et avait même rompu avec les familles arabes qu'elle connaissait jusque-là. Elle se souciait peu des commentaires.[50]

Fakia, on the other hand, had opted for the Occident and in excess. Always dressed to the nines and sporting the latest in Parisian styles, she discarded all her Muslim customs and severed all her ties with the Arab families whom she knew thus far. She was not very concerned with what people would say about her.

Introducing the character of Fakia/Francine in juxtaposition with Aziza indicates the levels of Europeanisation that existed in the colonial society. The difference is that while the former completely detached herself from her own people and did not pay heed to what they thought of her, the latter did not wish to do so and as a result found herself in an in-between location both physically and mentally.

As such, *Aziza* signals a shift in the seemingly harmonious relation with the Occident enjoyed in the pre-1950 Maghrebi novels, and enters an era wherein the novelists and their protagonists are battling with their overwhelming feelings of disorientation and alienation. Not only so, but the tone of the novel has also changed; while in the earlier novels the authors' criticism was always directed to their own people for not adhering to their civilisers' mission to bring them out of their backward condition and never to the Occident, *Aziza* shows more sympathy towards the difficult condition of being a native in a colonial society and more criticism of the disdainful and often unsympathetic Europeans. While it sheds light on the latter's racism and arrogance, it also casts doubt on the authenticity of their civilising mission and the French assimilationist project whose shortcomings resulted in the rise of Algerian nationalism as the ultimate result of the many setbacks experienced by native intellectuals who, for several decades prior to the 8 May massacres, used to sing the glories of the Occident. Through *Aziza* Débêche introduces the character of the fervent male nationalist and sends clear messages about the irreparable gap, which separates the two communities of Orientals and Occidentals.

The story in this novel begins with a reunion between Aziza, a Europeanised young Algerian female intellectual who works in a press agency, with her childhood sweetheart Ali Kemal, a solicitor at the Bar of Algiers. They meet at a soirée organised by Laura Berthier, the wife of a senior French civil servant who has newly arrived to the colony. The attraction between Ali and Aziza is almost spontaneous and they immediately stand as a good match between two Europeanised natives who not only shared childhood memories in their common tribe of the Beni Ahmed, but a French education and a privileged social status. Their encounter soon turns into a love relationship. Nevertheless, because Aziza is too westernised Ali's parents and his zealous nationalist friends oppose their union. They often tell her that she is not fit to marry a Muslim man. Their position as educated and ostensibly Europeanised natives, and their ambivalent reaction to Aziza's situation as their native female counterpart, reflects the position of the Algerian male nationalists, who while they fully opted for their own Europeanisation continued to see native women as the eternal guardians of national culture and heritage and as a result feared their Europeanisation. Both perplexed and disappointed about the native male's selfishness, and his lack of support for educated native women, Aziza explains her difficult position:

> *A l'agence parmi mes confrères, figuraient plusieurs compatriotes. En général, ils ne me témoignaient aucune sympathie et me créaient de nombreux soucis. J'entendais leurs sarcasmes à propos de l'évolution de la femme musulmane attirée par le monde occidental; on ne se gênait plus pour faire devant moi des réflexions sur les filles dévoilées qu'il faudrait 'renvoyer à leurs fourneaux.'*[51]

> At the Press Agency there were several compatriots among my colleagues. In general, they did not show me sympathy but caused me much heartache. I could hear their sarcasm about the evolution of the Muslim woman who is attracted to the Western world; They were not at all worried to make known their criticisms of emancipated native girls who no longer wore the veil, and to say that they 'should be sent back to their kitchens'.

Although these views were also shared by Ali, he still marries Aziza but in secret and hides her in their native tribe, the Beni Ahmed, in the hope that her return to the roots would redeem her back to her original status and make her a 'native' woman again. He tells her:

> *Tu sais bien . . . que ma carrière serait entravée si l'on connaissait notre mariage. Tu es devenue trop occidentale. C'est la raison pour laquelle je voulais te voir rester aux Beni Ahmed.*[52]

You know well that my career would be hampered if people discover we are married. You've become too westernised. This is the reason why I wanted you to stay in the Beni Ahmed.

Deeply in love, Aziza accepts to leave her career, becomes Ali's wife and lives with him in their common tribe. However, she soon discovers that he only took her there in order to win her back to native culture, which she often saw through Western eyes as both primitive and outdated. Deeply disillusioned and unable to conform to a lifestyle totally alien to her, she decides to leave the tribe and return home to Algiers at which point Ali rejects her on the grounds that she is too Westernised to be his wife: '*Tu ne vis pas comme les femmes de chez nous et tout ce que tu fais est en contradiction avec nos doctrine*: You do not live like our women and all you do is in contradiction with our principles.'[53] In fact 'contradiction' and ambivalence are both traits of the native male intellectual's position vis-à-vis the Occident. While he himself opted for the Occident and adopted the manners and looks of its people, he was not prepared to see native women doing so. What deepens this contradiction is the tendency among native intellectuals to marry European women as part of their cultural emancipation, when at the same time they hesitated to marry Europeanised and educated native women whom they often rejected as too westernised. While Memmi considers mixed marriages as an extreme expression of the audacious leap towards the culture of the coloniser,[54] Fanon conjectures that the attraction to the white European woman was part of the attraction to European culture and that the white European woman became the medium that helps the native male to be admitted to the realms of the civilised people. Being accepted and loved by a White European woman symbolised being accepted by European civilisation and fully entering the realm of civilised people. Therefore, not conceding to marry a native woman who is educated and has adopted European traits, fundamentally contradicts the justification many native intellectuals presented to their families for marrying European women because their own illiterate women were not at their level of intellect. In the case of the Maghreb, marriages of the intellectual male elite with European women during the colonial period were frequent – especially among nationalist leaders such as Habib Bourguiba, Messali El-Hadj and Ferhat Abbas who all married French women while they led the nationalist cause against French colonialism.⁵⁵ Although these mixed marriages were generally seen as identity changers, as argued by Claude Liauzu in his book *Passeurs de Rives: Changements d'identité dans le Maghreb Colonial*, in most cases it is the European wives who were fully accepted and well integrated into their husbands' community but not the reverse.

Furthermore, while the marriage of native men with European women was tolerated and seen as a privilege, this was not the case with the rare native women who married Europeans regardless of their position towards the natives' nationalist cause. A good example is that of Djamila Bouhired who married Jacques Vergès, the French lawyer who defended her in court when she was given a life sentence.⁵⁶ In *Aziza* we are shown that while native women acquired the same intellectual level as their native male counterparts, which would position them as adequate wives, their position as native women did not grant their partners entrance to the world of the civilised Europeans. Having Aziza as his partner Ali Kemal symbolically escapes from the European soirée where he met her, on the pretext that such environment was not their own: '*Que faisons-nous? Ce milieu n'est pas pour nous. Voulez-vous que nous partions tout de suite. Nous parlerons de notre enfance*: What are we doing here? This is not our milieu. Shall we leave now? We will talk about our childhood.'⁵⁷ The symbolic return to the Beni Ahmed through childhood memories is Ali's way to extract Aziza from her present as an emancipated native woman who mingles with Europeans to send her back to the past when she was a child in their common tribe which symbolises a pure environment, uncontaminated by European civilisation. When they agreed to get married, Ali, beyond the symbolic act, also physically removes Aziza from the European city and its surroundings and takes her back to the tribe for full cultural redemption. The contradiction occurs when, whilst he subjects her to performing and living according to their ancestral rules, he himself does not join her in this redemptive process but commutes to the city where he continues his life as an emancipated male intellectual. Furthermore, this ease of moving between ancestral and European cultures enjoyed by Ali as he symbolically moves with ease between the two locations is denied to Aziza. When she leaves the tribe, Ali leaves her too: '*Tu vois que tu n'es plus une musulmane, que tu veux vivre comme les femmes d'Europe*: You see you are no longer a Muslim woman, you want to live like European women.'⁵⁸

And when she attempts to return to her European friends their rejection was radical: '*Comment voulez-vous que l'on vous fasse confiance, désormais? Votre conduite est sans excuse*: How do you want us to trust you any longer? Your demeanour is unforgivable.'[59] The outcome is a double rejection from both parties thus resulting in a double sense of alienation from European as well as from ancestral/native culture: '*Pour les musulmans, j'étais bien devenue une occidentale . . . Quant aux européens, je m'étais placée dans une situation sans excuse*: For the Muslims, I have become a true Occidental woman. For the Europeans, I have put myself in an unforgivable situation.'[60] Therefore, *Aziza* reflects a paradoxical condition in which the Algerian men who were struggling against racial segregation also opposed their countrywomen's struggle against gender segregation. At the same time, Débêche conveys a clear picture of the double sense of alienation experienced by native Algerian women, whose quest for emancipation confronted two patriarchies in the form of colonialism and native customs.

This state of affairs is also reflected in the lack of support of the nationalist parties for the Algerian feminist movement prior to the 8 May 1945 massacres. Apart from the communist party, who were the first to welcome women into its ranks, they otherwise unanimously believed that there was no 'Woman question' for as long as the nation was colonised. Women's contribution to the 8 May 1945 demonstrations and their social work in the aftermath of the massacres convinced the nationalists that there could be no national independence if women were not included in the nationalist movement. Likewise, on a symbolic level, at the end of the novel Aziza is presented with two choices: either to escape her alienation by leaving her society and immigrating to the Occident, or to remain in her country and engage in social activism. She opts for the latter choice, which symbolises women's engagement with the nationalist cause in the aftermath of the May 1945 massacres and subsequently in the liberation struggle in 1954 as a means to revolt against the two patriarchies – colonialism and local customs.

Conclusion

While the novel *Leila, Jeune fille d'Algérie* subscribes to the Occidentophilic literature written by the pre-1950 generation of Algerian intellectuals and authors, whose works expressed their deep infatuation with Occidental culture and civilisation, it also introduces another layer of Occidental influence in the form of French feminism. Through this novel along with her scholarly publications Débêche played the role of a feminist activist who militated for the wellbeing of her own people in general and the emancipation of Algerian women in particular. At this stage, while she is well cognisant about the problems experienced by her own people she deeply believed in the French as a superior nation who came to civilise the uncivilised people of Africa. She therefore adopted the position of the go-between or mediator who could only see salvation coming from the French.

Like most of the Algerian novels published in the pre-1950 period, *Leila, Jeune fille d'Algérie* makes it clear that the role of the new generation of French-educated Algerians was vital for facilitating the crossover of their country from its primitive state to entering the world of civilised people. In the same way as they tried to speak to the Occident to help improve the condition of their people, the Occident expected them to play the role of the go-between and explain the benefits of embracing French civilisation to their people,

> *C'est avec de nouveaux éléments jeunes et sains comme ceux-là que nous construirons ici, sur des bases nouvelles, une maison neuve dans laquelle régnera un climat de confiance et de fraternité.*[61]
>
> It is with these [the young Algerians] new, young and vital elements that we will lay new foundations to build on this land a new house where an environment of trust and fraternity would reign.

Leila, Jeune fille d'Algérie tells the success story of an educated native girl whose French education has opened for her a world of opportunities from which her backward family tried to remove her in order to win her back to her native culture. However, thanks to Mr Lormont and his daughter Madeleine, Leila was rescued from the world of the uncivilised natives and granted a place in the world of the civilised Occident. Telling this successful story creates a positive atmosphere in the novel and conveys the reality about the trust the Young Algerians placed in their *mère-patrie* France, and its civilising mission. In addition to the concerns which preoccupied the male Young Algerians, *Leila, Jeune fille d'Algérie* contributes a female voice and discusses the emancipation of the Algerian woman for the first time in the history of Algerian literature, which puts the character of Leila on the same battlefield as that of the male intellectuals but with the additional issue of the 'woman's question'.

This novel, as well as other feminist publications by Djamila Débêche, demonstrates the influence French feminists have had on Algerian intellectuals in general and Algerian feminism in particular. The feminism Débêche promotes, however, is a combination of French feminism and Arab–Muslim feminism. While she refers to Egyptian and Turkish women in the same way as the Young Algerians refer to the Young Turks and the Egyptians of the Young Egypt party, and cites them as good examples that Algerian women should emulate, she also refers to early Islamic history and the women who played important roles in the life of Prophet Mohammed. Not only this but she also brings up the names of prominent Muslim women who played significant roles in the Islamic Empire both under the Abbasids and in Al-Andalus. While this can be seen as a way to empower her female compatriots by referring to Muslim as well as to Occidental role models, she does so while addressing the Occident and telling its women that Muslim/Oriental women have not always been passive victims of their cultures, but have throughout history played important roles in their societies. While she reminds her addressee (a prominent French woman) about this state of affairs she also suggests that one should not forget that the Orient has had its glory days and that its 'old' civilisation should now fuse with the 'young' Occidental civilisation in order for the two to benefit from each other,

> *À la croisée des chemins, la vielle civilisation orientale a rencontré la jeune civilisation occidentale et, pour que naisse un monde meilleur, il faut qu'elles s'appuient l'une sur l'autre.*[62]

> At the crossroads, the old Oriental civilisation met the young Occidental civilisation, and to create a better world, they should rely on one another.

While on the social level *Leila, Jeune fille d'Algérie* depicts a compliant society where the natives live in harmony with their civilisers, *Aziza* describes a society in flux where the atmosphere had become electrified and the air filled with anger and disillusion as a result of the 8 May 1945 massacres. The gap between the two communities of natives and Europeans has started to deepen and the trust the natives might have had in their civilisers has started to wane. For this reason *Aziza*, published in 1955 eight years after *Leila, Jeune fille d'Algérie*, heralds the birth of the feminist intellectual who is alienated and at war with all those around her be they Oriental or Occidental. This position makes her relationship with the Occident rather ambivalent and, therefore, the harmony achieved by Leila is contrasted against Aziza's feelings of anxiety and loss. Unable to identify or be accepted by the Orient or the Occident, she is in a desperate search for a new location. She describes herself as follows,

> *Je me sentais condamnée . . . rejetée d'une communauté qui était malgré tout la mienne. J'étais celle qui avait rompu tous les liens avec les siens.*[63]
>
> I felt doomed . . . rejected by a community that was after all my own. I was the one who had broken all ties with my own people.

Like her male compatriots she is experiencing a reversal of all the beliefs she thought were immovable and she assumed as absolute truths. Discussions among native intellectuals no longer sing the praises of the civilisers, who have now dropped their masks and made the native intellectuals question all their certainties:

> *C'est en vertu de cette civilisation pleine de déceptions pour l'humanité que l'on juge aujourd'hui, en criminels des hommes qui sont en réalité des victimes.*[64]
>
> It is under this civilisation full of disappointments for humanity that today those who are actually victims are judged as criminals.

The criminals and the victims she is referring to here are the native people who believed in France's promises of reward for fighting against its enemies once the war had ended, but who were instead indiscriminately killed for celebrating the Armistice Day.

While the theme of alienation of the native male intellectual became the focus of the literature of the 1950s period, which saw and reflected the national liberation of Tunisia and Morocco in 1956 and the Algerian War of Independence (1954–62), the merit of *Aziza* is its focus on the dilemma of the native female intellectual and her odyssey to try to find acceptance among her own people. More importantly it sheds light on the reaction of the male intellectuals and nationalists to the emancipation of the native woman.

In conclusion, Djamila Débêche's *Leila, Jeune fille d'Algérie*, is a groundbreaking novel which heralded the birth of the woman's voice in modern Maghrebi literature and the birth of Algerian feminist literature as well as the birth of feminist Press in the Maghreb. Yétiv Isaac describes her work as follows:

> *Cette thèse plaça Djamila Débêche à l'avant-garde de la croisade féministe de sa génération et en fit le porte-drapeau de la lutte pour la promotion de la femme musulmane en Afrique du nord, pour sa libération des carcans qui la contraignaient à un statut de mineur et la réduisaient à un objet dont pouvaient disposer à leur gré le père ou le mari.*[65]

This thesis positioned Djamila Débêche at the forefront of the feminist crusade of her generation and made her the leading figure of the struggle for the advancement of the rights of the Muslim woman in North Africa, militating for her release from the shackles that constrained her to a minor status and reduced her to an object at the disposal of the father or the husband.

As a final point, although the woman's issue is central to Débêche's oeuvre, with her first novel *Leila, Jeune fille d'Algérie* the author also positioned herself as part of a literary current whose authors, while they did not point the finger at the colonisers as the cause of their people's suffering, played the role of intermediaries and pleaded to the Occident to improve the Orientals' social and economic conditions. These works expressed their authors' unwavering belief and trust in the Occident and its noble mission to civilise the uncivilised people of the Orient. While this generation of early authors totally disappeared in the aftermath of the May 1945 massacres, Débêche is the sole author to have managed to straddle the two periods by shifting positions in her second novel *Aziza* through which she joined the new generation of authors whose tone towards the Occident is ambivalent and at times Occidentophobic.

7

The End of the Chimera: Disillusion, Alienation and Ambivalence

I am a French author. I represent to a high degree of perfection the prototype of the assimilated native. But I am not, I am no longer, and for a long time an adherent of assimilation. That is because the Algerian tragedy is not taking place on a stage that is remote from me. The battlefield is within me: there is no piece of my mind and my soul that does not belong both to the two warrying camps. I am Algerian, yet I feel fully French. France is the spirit of my soul, yet Algeria is the soul of this spirit.

Jean El-Mouhouv Amrouche[1]

The massacre of 8 May 1945, which was the direct impetus behind the 1954 Algerian War of Independence, was a major game changer in the rapport between the Algerian intelligentsia and the Occident. The demonstrations which began as peaceful marches to celebrate Victory in Europe Day on 8 May 1945 quickly degenerated into a series of massacres in the cities of Guelma, Setif and Karrata, East of Algeria, resulting in the indiscriminate killing of innocent civilians and a death toll which, according to nationalist sources, had reached 45,000 native Algerians and 103 European settlers.[2] On this day and for a few days thereafter, the demonstrators witnessed horrifying savagery and hatred – but not civilisation.[3] Arrests of intellectuals, summary executions of civilians and random shootings continued for several days. Furthermore, 'Villages were bombed by the air force, and the navy fired on the coast.'[4] What had dismayed the population the most was the betrayal and treachery of the promises made by General De Gaulle on 12 December

1943 in a speech he delivered in Constantine. In gratitude to the thousands of native Maghrebis fighting for France against its enemies, and the hundreds who died in foreign lands to save Europe from Nazism, he promised reforms and citizenship rights for native Algerians on a wide scale. Instead, the joyous demonstrators were faced with fire and the spilling of more native blood. Benjamin Stora writes:

> In Algeria, nothing could ever be as it had been before May 8, 1945. The rift had widened between the majority of Muslim Algerians and the European minority. Plebeians from the cities (the underclass, the unemployed), the proletariat, and the Algerian peasantry had experienced the power of collective action; a new generation was making its entrance, one that would make the armed struggle an absolute principle.[5]

As a result, the idea of the Occident as a site of human rights and justice crumbled away to reveal what was behind the façade: the ugly face of colonialism, that of an Occident that lies and never keeps its promises and an Occident which, while it promotes republican ideals of *Liberté, Egalité* and *Fraternité*, only applies them for its own people and not for the subjects in its colonies. Jean Amrouche explains how his people unfailingly defended their *mère-patrie* with their own lives; from the Franco-Prussian War in 1870, to the First World War and the Second World War, they have always furnished the French army with brave soldiers who were not rewarded by their adoptive nation with the rights of its citizens for having performed their duty towards it, nor did it treat them as citizens while they were fighting for a cause they mistakenly thought was their own. Jean Amrouche explains:

> *De génération en génération ils ont payé sur tous les champs de bataille au poids du sang de la fidélité, le prix de la liberté, de l'égalité et de la fraternité française.*
>
> From generation to generation they [the natives] have paid on all the battlefields with the blood of their fidelity the price of the *liberté, égalité,* and *fraternité* of the French.

The crux of the matter is the fact that regardless of the natives' fidelity and their sacrifices for their *mère-patrie*, in the colonial mindset the colonised subject was never considered human and in consequence did not deserve respect. Memmi explains how the coloniser tends to strip the colonised of their humanity:

> He is hardly a human being. He tends rapidly towards becoming an object. As an end, in the colonizer's supreme ambition, he should exist only as a function of the needs of the colonizer, i.e., be transformed into a pure colonized. The extraordinary efficiency of this operation is obvious. One does not have a serious obligation toward an animal or an object. It is then easily understood that the colonizer can indulge in such shocking attitudes and opinions.[6]

In view of this dehumanisation of the colonised it did not matter for the colonisers whether they kept the promises they made to their subjects, the colonised. More importantly, now that the Second World War had ended the coloniser would not tolerate seeing the colonised rewarded for their war effort while fighting side-by-side against Nazism, and therefore being elevated to the level of citizens who would enjoy the same rights as their masters. To disrupt this dream, that was nurtured in the mind of the colonised by De Gaulle's speech of 1943, the most efficient means was the iron fist which would show the natives that in the colony things never change and the settler always exists as the master. This explains the extreme violence shown to the demonstrating natives by the settlers and the colonial police who joined them, but most importantly its normalised aspect. Memmi theorises that, 'a machine-gun burst into a crowd of colonized causes him [the coloniser] merely to shrug his shoulders.'[7] Accounts and testimonies of the 8 May massacre demonstrate that the savagery shown by the settlers is a manifestation of power to stub out the native's dreams of becoming French citizens. In an article he published in *Le Figaro* following the horrifying events of the massacre Jean Amrouche resolutely speaks of two Frances: Metropolitan France, which he calls La France d' Europe, and Colonial France, which he calls *La France d'Afrique*. He explains:

> *Ce n'est pas à partir de l'émeute qu'il faut poser le problème mais à partir de la répression. De la haine on aboutit au désespoir et si la France ignore les frontières des races, des couleurs et des religions, il n'en est pas de même pour les Français d'Algérie chez qui le racisme constitue plus qu'une doctrine: un instinct, une conviction enracinée.*[8]

The problem should not be posed from the riots but from the repression it was faced with. Hatred leads to agitation, and if Metropolitan France tends to ignore the boundaries of race, colour and religion, this is not the case with the French of Algeria for whom racism is more than a mere doctrine: it is an instinct, a rooted conviction.

Therefore, for those natives who have never seen *La France d' Europe* all they have been exposed to is a barbarian and unscrupulous France whose image is one of horror and hatred, thus resulting in a general setback for those who thus far deeply believed in its civilising mission, and a profound crisis for those who threw themselves unreservedly into its camp while they sometimes severed their ties with their own people.

It is no surprise, therefore, to see the Occidentophilic novelists who wrote their novels in the pre-1945 period enter into a dilemma and consequently sink into literary silence and cease to produce literary works which sang the praises of a faultless and unstinting Occident. The novels written after May 1945 will, henceforth expose the deep sense of alienation experienced by Algerian intellectuals at their encounter with the other face of the Occident; *La France d'Afrique,* an Occident that arbitrarily kills unarmed demonstrators in their thousands, and most importantly an Occident that does not keep its promises and callously betrays its admirers.

The Aftermath of the 8 May Massacre and the Malaise of the Native Population: The End of the Chimera?

Discussions and forums about *Le malaise du peuple Algérien* also known as *Le problème Algérien*, which began at the turn of the twentieth century among the Young Algerians, who beseeched France to alleviate the misery of their own people, intensified in the aftermath of the May massacre. However, the tone was no longer the same. New rules of the game had to be created as the Occident, who had formerly denoted a source of hope while it was still trusted as the party that possessed the solution to the native populations' problems, now became seen as the source of all its problems.

Whereas colonial authorities and settlers were confident that the repression was necessary in order to discipline the natives, they failed to realise that while their own colonial mindset was rigid and unmovable, that of the natives, whom they had always figured as static, had actually evolved. The natives' sacrifices along the years, together with the unfulfilled promises of progress and civilisation, were strong indicators that they should no longer rely on France, especially *La France d'Afrique*, for their salvation. Moreover, that from now on they should only rely on their own efforts in order to change their own destiny.

This state of affairs created an impasse not only for the assimilated native intelligentsia, who felt totally disoriented and severely betrayed, but also for the Algerian-born European intellectuals who became aware that the severe repression of the 8 May 1945 demonstrations was bound to bear severe effects for the future of French Algeria and their own future as Europeans who were born in Algeria, who considered themselves 'Algerians', and to whom Metropolitan France was a remote location. They too felt alienated by the new situation and experienced the fear of an uncertain future which in turn resulted in an identity crisis voiced in works of the likes of Camus' (1913–61) *L'Étranger* (1942),[9] a novel often explained as expressing the alienation of Camus who was himself the stranger both in Metropolitan France and in Algeria, his country of birth. Ill at ease and often totally disoriented, these left-wing European intellectuals engaged in lengthy discussions with their native Algerian counterparts in the hope of finding a solution to the ensuing political crisis and the loss of trust between the two communities of natives and Europeans. Reading their articles, which were published in progressivist journals such as *L'Arche* and *Combat*, and listening to radiophonic recordings of their discussions, which were aired on French Metropolitan radio stations,[10] offers a dynamic representation of a generation at a time of deep crisis which is ill at ease with itself and desperately trying to hold onto France as a civilised and civilising nation – when for them is has become a decaying fortress standing on unsteady ground. Much more than any time before the massacres native intellectuals found themselves in an embarrassing situation vis-à-vis their own people, who emphasised time and again that the Occident, who invaded their country, ruthlessly killed their own people and deprived them of their land, could not possibly claim to have come to civilise them. Feeling deeply duped by their *mère-patrie* for whom they rejected their own nation, they made a radical departure from the camp of their civilisers and a definitive return to that of their own people who, despite their illiteracy, were after all right to not trust the colonialists.

In February 1936 Ferhat Abbas, while he made public his belief in France as his own nation and denied the existence of Algeria as a separate nation, forewarned France of the consequences of not genuinely extending the bounties of its civilisation to all the natives. He wrote:

> If I had discovered the 'Algerian nation', I would be nationalist and I would not blush at that as if it were a crime. Men who have died for the national ideal are daily honoured and respected. My life is not worth more than theirs. But I will not make this sacrifice. The Algerian *patrie* is a myth. I have not found it. I have questioned history, I have questioned the living and the dead, I have visited the cemeteries – no one has spoken to me of it. Of course, I have found 'the Arab empire', 'the Muslim empire', which do honour to Islam and to our race, but these empires are extinguished ... Should a Muslim Algerian seriously dream of building his future with the dust of the past? Don Quixote is not a man of our times. One does not build on the wind. We have brushed aside once and for all [such] daydreams and illusions to tie our future definitively to that of the work of France in this land ... Six million Muslims live in this land which has been French for a hundred years, living in shacks, barefoot, without clothing and without bread. Of this famished multitude, we want to make a modern society through the school, the defence of [the rights of] man, that this society should be French ... *Without the emancipation of the indigènes, French Algeria cannot endure.* (My emphasis.)[11]

Abbas' assimilationist stand went as far as divorcing his native Algerian wife and instead marrying a French woman from the European community of settlers. He blindly threw himself into the arms of the Occident with full faith in its universal principles to the extent of conscripting in the French army to fight against Nazism. The experience of the War, however, taught him that even in the battlefield native soldiers were not treated in the same way as European soldiers. Deeply disillusioned, he published *Le Manifeste du Peuple Algérien* (A Manifesto of the Algerian People) in 1943, in which he made a definitive break with the assimilationist ideology he had hitherto adopted, and called for an autonomous Algeria with its own constitution and a government allied with and supported by France.

Although at this stage Abbas did not call for complete independence from France, he nevertheless was accused of organising the May 1945 popular demonstrations and was as a consequence arrested and kept in prison for eleven months without trial along with many Algerian intellectuals who were in deep shock at seeing their 'civilisers' act in the most barbaric and ruthless manner in the way they spread death and terror amongst innocent civilians. As if that was not enough, they were incarcerated almost as a way to punish them for their blind siding with their civilisers and, ironically, also for having rejected their own people.

The events of 8 May 1945 changed everything in the encounter between the Occident and the Orient, signalling a deep crack in the relationship between native intellectuals and their European 'civilisers' and as a consequence in the set of beliefs they acquired as a result of their French education. Memmi argues: '[. . .] by obvious logic, at the very moment when the colonized best adjusts himself to his fate, he rejects himself with most tenacity. That is to say that he rejects, in another way, the colonial situation.'[12] Voices from both sides of the divide now believed in the failure of France's assimilationist project, which they all saw as a mere illusion. What seemed to be a fixed reality, however, was the colonialist view that the colonised is not worthy of European civilisation.

Rather indignant, Albert Camus, who had in 1936 deplored the miserable living conditions of the natives and called for urgent action to alleviate their suffering, expressed his anger at the way the authorities handled the demonstrations which he saw as heralding the end of the utopic dream of seeing the two communities coming together as one nation, but more importantly the utopia of an Algeria who would be an integral part of France. Bitter and disillusioned he wished history had taken a different course and things had not occured in the way they did. Angry, and at the same time genuinely worried, about the consequences of incarcerating native intellectuals who devoted colossal efforts as intermediaries between their people and their civilisers, he wrote:

> *Ce n'est pas en envoyant les intellectuels au bagne qu'on peut faire triompher une politique d'assimilation . . . On a préféré y répondre par la prison et la répression. C'est une pure et simple stupidité.*[13]

It is not by sending intellectuals to prison that one can make triumph a policy of assimilation ... They preferred to answer by detention and law enforcement, which is pure and simple stupidity.

Likewise, in a letter to his friend Jean Amrouche, Jules Roy wrote, *Nous sommes au fond du puits, et je ne sais si un miracle nous permettra d'en sortir.* We are at the bottom of the well, and I am not sure whether a miracle will allow us to resurface.'[14] Unlike European intellectuals who could see the precariousness of the future of their 'French Algeria' as a direct result of the continuing injustice of the colonial order, the colonialist settlers were engrossed in the notion that their existence as colonisers was eternal in the same way as that of the natives as colonised was also eternal. This dialectic relation is called by Memmi 'colonizability' and a form of 'dependency complex', which is somehow anchored in the colonialist mindset. He explains:

> There undoubtedly exists – at some point in its evolution – a certain adherence of the colonized to colonization. However, this adherence is the result of colonization and not its cause. It arises after and not before colonial occupation. In order for the colonizer to be the complete master, it is not enough for him to be so in actual fact, but he must also believe in its legitimacy. In order for that legitimacy to be complete, it is not enough for the colonized to be a slave, he must accept this role.[15]

For this reason, the colonialist settlers were adamant that the severe repression of the 8 May 1945 demonstrations was a necessary action with the purpose of restoring order and to show the natives that they should obey their masters and should never rebel. What had escaped them, though, was that the natives of 1945 were not those of the years that preceded the Second World War. The Orientalist notion of the native Algerian population as possessing atavistic characteristics, which rendered them stagnant and incapable of evolution, traits that warranted France's continued domination, had become obsolete. In fact, the long process of colonisation has rendered 'stagnation' a condition of the settler's mindset that has become mired in his own dated colonialist beliefs. The natives, on the other hand, had evolved and as a result of colonial injustice, nationalism had taken root among the masses. Therefore, while the settlers' instinctive reaction was to safeguard their interests and protect their privileged position by the use of extreme violence, the destitute natives had nothing left for them to lose – including their dignity as human beings. Pondering the comportment of the European settlers and their stagnant colonialist attitudes and mindset Jean Amrouche wrote with a tone of anger:

> *Inutile de raisonner, d'argumenter de faire appel à l'Histoire, à la Sociologie, à la Religion même: l'infériorité essentielle, naturelle, congénitale, incurable de l'indigène est un dogme plus rigide, plus inébranlable que les dogmes religieux les plus absolus. Telle est je l'affirme en pesant mes mots la manière de sentir et de penser qui commande le comportement de l'immense majorité des Français d'Algérie à quelque niveau social qu'ils appartiennent.*[16]

> It is pointless to reason, to argue, to make an appeal to history, sociology, or even religion: the essential, natural, congenital and incurable inferiority of the native is a dogma that is more rigid, more unfaltering than the more absolutist religious dogmas. This is, and I say this while weighing my words, the way of feeling and thinking that controls the behaviour of the vast majority of the French of Algeria regardless of their social level.

As to the native intellectuals who played the role of intermediaries between their people and their 'civilisers', they had encountered the abyss. Jean Amrouche, who describes himself as '*Algérien autochtone-Français, aussi pleinement assimilé qu'on peut l'être*: Native French Algerian, as fully assimilated as one can be',[17] admits that after the May massacres he ceased to believe in France's assimilationist project. More crucially he also confesses that his position as an assimilated individual, although he now rejects the assimilationist ideology of colonial France, is indeed a difficult one. It is the condition of the alienated individual whose alienation can only end by suppressing its causes, i.e., colonialism. Memmi argues: 'in order to witness the colonized's complete cure, his alienation must cease. We must await the complete disappearance of colonization, including the period of revolt.'[18] Putting an end to colonialism, while it poses itself as the only solution to end the condition of the European as coloniser and of the native as colonised, signifies putting an end to the likes of Abbas and Amrouche but also to the likes of Camus and Roblès whose souls were dramatically divided between: Orient and Occident; Algeria and France; the nation and the *mère-patrie*.

When the Algerian War of Independence was in full swing, Jean Amrouche, while fully siding with his native people whose defence he voiced in his various publications, eloquently described himself as a battlefield where the fighting between the two warring factions was taking place:

> *Le champ de bataille est en moi: nulle parcelle de mon esprit et de mon âme qui n'appartienne à la fois aux deux camps qui s'entretuent. Je suis algérien, je crois être pleinement français. La France est l'esprit de mon âme, mais l'Algérie est l'âme de cet esprit.*[19]

> The battlefield is within me: there is no piece of my mind and my soul that does not belong to both warring camps. I am Algerian, yet I feel fully French. France is the spirit of my soul, but Algeria is the soul of this spirit.

As to Ferhat Abbas, who became one of the historical leaders of the Algerian War of Independence (1954–62), he declared that after all that: '*L'Afrique est si loin de la France et les Algériens si différent des Européens!*': Africa is so far away from France and the Algerians are so different from Europeans!'[20] This, in a way justifies the definitive divorce between the two nations.

A Literature of the Oppressed: May the Voice of the Subaltern be Heard?

Just like the ideological shift experienced by the Algerian intelligentsia in the aftermath of the 8 May 1945 massacres, a major turn took place in the style of the novel; new literary voices emerged with a new tempo which totally differed from that of the earlier novels studied thus far, they are the voices of the oppressed people who did not belong to any privileged social categories.

Literary historians of the likes of Jean Dejeux, Charles Bonn and Jaqueline Arnauld tend to mark this new wave with the publication of Mouloud Feraoun's novel *Le Fils du pauvre* (The Poor Man's Son),[21] which was hailed upon its publication in 1950 as the birth of a genuine literature of the Maghrebi masses. This was because it brought a totally new tone to Maghrebi literature in general and Algerian literature in particular. Unlike the authors of the pre-1945 period Feraoun, just like the main protagonist of his novel, Fouroulou, was the son of poor people. Delving into Fouroulou's world and putting into action his fellow villagers is an act of giving voice to the downtrodden categories of colonised society, those who were severely ignored by the Occident and its civilising mission. Feraoun describes his village as a place cut off from civilisation, it has no roads, no hospitals and no amenities bar the tiny village school, which has two classrooms and was run by two native teachers. The absence of markers of 'civilisation' also means the absence of Europeans in the village setting of this novel. What is worthy of note here is that while the novel totally excludes the presence of the French from the reality of the villagers, whose lives were totally unaffected by France's *mission civilisatrice*, it sends a strong accusatory message to the French readers that the natives whom they came to civilise have not been reached by their civilisation. Feraoun's constant concern which he expressed in his letters to his French friends, later published in a book titled *Lettres à ses amis*, is the fact that the two communities of natives and Europeans lead different lives and live in two rigidly separated worlds both in the physical and the emotional sense. Each community ignored the other and in a way each wished the other did not exist. In fact, the impetus behind writing this novel in the manner he did was as a reaction to French Algerian writers of the likes of Emanuel Roblès and Albert Camus who excluded the native community from their literary works despite being set in Algeria. Seeing that Oran is the setting of Camus' novel *La Peste* Feraoun wrote to him to reproach him, albeit in a gentle manner, regarding this tendency of wiping out the native population from its locale:

> *J'ai lu* La Peste *et j'ai eu l'impression d'avoir compris votre livre comme je n'en avais jamais compris d'autres. J'avais regretté que parmi tous ces personnages il n'y eut aucun indigène et qu'Oran ne fut à vos yeux qu'une banale préfecture française. Oh! Ce n'est pas un reproche. J'ai pensé simplement que, s'il n'y avait pas ce fossé entre nous, vous nous auriez mieux connus, vous vous seriez senti capable de parler de nous avec la même générosité dont bénéficient tous les autres. Je regrette toujours, de tout mon cœur, que vous ne nous connaissiez pas suffisamment et que nous n'ayons personne pour nous comprendre, nous faire comprendre et nous aider à nous connaitre nous-mêmes.*[22]

I have read *La Peste* (The Plague) and I have the impression of having understood your book as I have never understood any other. I have regretted, however, that there are no natives among its characters and that Oran is in your eyes nothing more than an ordinary French prefecture. Oh! This isn't a complaint. I simply thought that, *had there not been this gap between us*, you would perhaps have known us better; you would have been better placed to speak about us with the same way accorded to all the others [the Europeans]. Still, I regret from the bottom of my heart, that you do not know enough about us and that we have no one to understand us, to make the others understand us and help us to know each other. (My emphasis.)

Feraoun's regret about the wide gap that separated the two communities from each other is another way to express regret for the failure of the French Algerian project; the dream of many assimilated native intellectuals, who had hoped that the French were there to genuinely bring the bounties of their civilisation to the natives and that their project to assimilate them was a reality and not a mere utopia.

In an explicit accusatory tone Feraoun describes the miserable living conditions of his people, the stark reality of French education for the natives, and the constant feeling of hunger that almost becomes a malicious tyrant tormenting the lives of the native characters not only in Feraoun's *Le Fils du pauvre* but also in subsequent Algerian novels published during the 1950s.

Mohammed Dib's (1920–2003) first novel, *La Grande maison* (The Big House) (1952) opens with the sentence '*Un peu de ce que tu manges?*: Can I have a bit of what you are eating?'[23] Just like the rural inhabitants of the remote mountain village where the events of *Le Fils du pauvre* take place, the urban inhabitants of *La Grande maison,* a big house, which symbolises colonised Algeria, spend their time wrestling with their hunger. Often novelists would stage hallucinating scenes whereby their characters would speak to their hunger and sing it to sleep, and when they become so desperate they end up quarrelling between themselves for futile whys and wherefores, showing thus a society at the edge of ignition. Mouloud Mammeri (1917–89) also describes similar conditions in his novel *La Colline Oubliée* (The Forgotten Hill) (1952),[24] a hill forgotten by civilisation and progress where people are also on edge. More than just the act of writing back to the colonial authors and telling them 'this is who we are and this is how things are for us', as written by Feraoun in a letter to his friend Roblès,[25] according to Wadi Bouzar and Andrea Page the success of these novels lies in their authors' ability to describe '[. . .] from the inside what it was like to live in a society that was held in check by the colonial regime, these novels denounced its inherent iniquities as well as the temptation, the difficulty, or the impossibility of becoming fully assimilated into the Occidental universe.'[26] All three novels depicted native people living in a separate world from that of the Europeans and marked the remoteness, if not the total absence, of European characters from their settings. The emphasis on the suffering and the poverty of the natives is in many ways accusatory of the French whose civilising mission did not reach the inhabitants of the three different locations depicted in these novels. However, by presenting characters such as Fouroulou and Omar, who attend school and aspire for a better future that they hope to attain thanks to their education and despite the dire poverty of their parents, these novels contain within their lines a glimmer of optimism. Possibly the hopefulness still held by their authors at this stage before the outbreak of the Algerian War of Independence when many native intellectuals believed that salvation was still possible. Despite the major shock brought by the May massacres, they continued to talk to the Occident in the hope that their conscience would awaken and they would as a result try to save the situation. As if sending a last warning to the French, Jean Amrouche wrote in *Le Figaro* expressing these same hopes:

> *On ne demande pas au Français d'être grand mais d'être juste, on ne lui demande pas d'avoir du génie, on lui demande seulement de ne pas démentir ses discours par ses actes, on ne lui demande plus d'être charitable mais d'avoir le respect de l'homme. Parce que s'il ne respecte pas ce contrat sur lequel est fondée l'autorité de la France, sa défaillance ne porte pas préjudice à lui seul mais elle atteint à travers lui la France universelle.*[27]

We are not asking the French to be great but to be fair, we do not ask them to have genius we only ask them not to go against the universal ideals expressed in words by their actions. We no longer ask them to be charitable but to have respect for other human beings. Because if they do not respect this contract upon which is based the authority of France, their failure does not prejudice them alone but it reaches through them as French people the Universal France.

A Literature of the Alienated: Self-redemption and Rebellion

While *Le Fils du pauvre* and *La Grande maison* portrayed their protagonists' primary school experiences where they were put into contact with Europe through their education, *La Colline Oubliée* is the first Maghrebi novel to depict a group of French-educated young men on the eve of the Second World War. Although in a subtle manner, the novel moves the malaise of its young characters to centre stage and signals the discomfort of a young French-educated generation who, while they were still at this stage, a well-integrated part of their people, had their eyes opened to new truths about two separate and unequal worlds by their education: the world of the Europeans, who live in comfort and enjoy the bounties of their civilisation along with the bounties of the land of the colonised; and the world of their own people, with all the opportunities that were denied to them while they continue to live in a forgotten hill resolutely named by Mammeri as *La Colline Oubliée*.

The irony of this condition is that, while this village is totally forgotten by the French *mission civilisatrice*, its educated youth straddle the two worlds and were called upon by their *mère-patrie* to go to Europe and fight against the Germans. Their mobilisation and departure brought the Second World War home to the point of becoming the talk of everyone. Everywhere in the village the villagers while they dreaded seeing their youth embark on a journey to unknown destinations and not sure of returning home, all hoped the War might change their monotonous lives at last:

> *Enfin un grand évènement, essential, puisqu'on y laissait la vie, général, puisqu'il affectait tout le monde, allait briser la monotonie de vivre.*[28]

A great event at last, it is essential since many are giving their lives. It is general, since it affects everyone, it will certainly change this monotonous lifestyle.

Anxious and as if wrestling with some mysterious elements the only hope of the inhabitants of the forgotten hill, is to see the war come to an end and to see their mobilised men return home safe and sound, although at the same time they all suffer from anxiety as they are uncertain about what the end of the Second World War could bring.

Just as Ferhat Abbas experienced and described, on the war front the conscribed young men, although initially enthusiastic to fight for their *mère-patrie* for a cause that was not their own, were soon shown that the demarcation between coloniser and colonised was also applicable on the battlefield in Europe. As indigenous people they were not fed in the same way as the Europeans and were not given the positions they deserved as educated people. As such, beyond the ideals they constructed through their French education, they encountered racism and ill-treatment. Alienated and profoundly disillusioned they decided that after their demobilisation they would not return to their universities for they had taught them nothing but packs of lies, and would definitively sever their ties with a civiliser who only sold them utopic dreams.

In his second novel *Le Sommeil du juste* (Slumber of the Just) (1955) Mammeri further dramatises this feeling of alienation by putting under the limelight the trajectory of his main protagonist Arezki, who represents the prototype of the Fanonian assimilated native intellectual. Deeply infatuated by everything he learnt at school about the universal values of the French revolution and the principles of the French civilising mission, he rejects his own people as uncivilised and uncivilisable, and throws himself avidly into the arms of European civilisation guided by his French teacher Monsieur Poiré who becomes a point of reference for him in lieu of his backward father.

After escaping his family and his village, his journey leads him all the way to Europe to fight against the Nazis. However, regardless of his status as an *Évolué*, he was exposed to unfair treatment in the same way as all the native soldiers of the many African regiments conscripted to fight along with the European allies. Arezki remarks that even at the same rank the indigenous officer should obey his European counterpart: '*à grade égal, le gradé indigène doit obeissance au gradé Européen*: Native officers should obey orders from European officers of the same rank.'[29] Every time he tried to rebel he was reminded of his condition as an IMANN (Indigène Musulman Algérien Non Naturalisé (Non-naturalised native Algerian)). Jean Amrouche theorises:

> *L'indigène, le vaincu ne doit jamais oublier sa condition de vaincu et reconnaître qu'il s'agit là d'un fait irréversible, il est un sous homme. La charité du*

> *maître, sa fraternité protectrice prétend s'organiser sans contrôle. Elle ne reconnaît ni droit ni justice pour l'indigène que dans le cadre des rapports établis une fois pour toutes entre maîtres et serviteurs. Il y a en Algérie une légion d'honneur à titre indigène, c'est à dire dévaluée.*[30]

> The defeated native must never forget his condition of the defeated and he must admit that this is an irreversible condition; he is a sub-human. The charitable character of the master and his protective brotherhood although they may appear as natural traits, they do not discern rights or justice for the natives apart from what has always been the norm between masters and servants. In Algeria, although a Legion of Honour for the natives exists, it is devalued.

In fact, Amrouche put forth the above statement to explain the causes that led to the outbreak of the Algerian War of Independence. Likewise, Mammeri explains that the way Arezki and his likes were treated by the French was what led them to make a radical return to their people and to fully embrace their cause for decolonisation.

Angry and regretful of his earlier conduct towards his father Arezki turns to the Algerian nationalist party in the hope of redeeming himself, 'Il faudrait que je me retrouve: I must redeem myself.'[31] In a dramatic act of retribution, he piles up all his books like a heap of lies, sets them ablaze and symbolically urinates on them as if to rescind their lure.[32] Fanon explains this fundamental shift as follows:

> In order to ensure his salvation and to escape from the supremacy of the white man's culture the native feels the need to turn backwards towards his unknown roots and to lose himself at whatever cost in his own barbarous people. Because he feels he is becoming estranged, that is to say because he feels that he is the living haunt of the contradictions which run the risk of becoming insurmountable, the native tears himself away from the swamp that may suck him down and accepts everything, decides to take all for granted and confirms everything even though he may lose body and soul.[33]

In Mammeri's next novel *L'Opium et le baton* (Opium and the Baton) (1965)[34] the central character, Bashir, a medical doctor who represents a continuation and a natural evolution of the character Arezki, completes the cycle: he tears himself away from the city and his European environment to join the War of Independence as a freedom fighter, signalling therefore the definitive redemption of the native intellectual from his alienation and his ultimate divorce with the Occident. Fanon explains how 'this tearing away, painful and difficult though it may be, is, however, necessary. If it is not accomplished there will be serious psycho-affective injuries and the result will be individuals without an anchor, without a horizon, colourless, stateless, rootless – a race of angels.'[35] Through the pages of this novel Mammeri exposes his readers to yet another face of the Occident through the French army with its savage war alongside its hideous methods of torture and ruthless bombings of villages. Simone de Beauvoir describes the barbarity of this war in the following terms: 'Men and women, old folk and children, have been machine-gunned during "mopping-up operations" [*ratis-sages*], burnt alive in their villages, had their throats slit or their bellies ripped open, died countless sorts of martyrs' deaths.'[36] Such exposure is one definitive manner of uncovering and re-evaluating the universal principles of the French civilising mission. For 132 years of French presence in Algeria the colonisers have used the *Opium and the Baton,* as expressed in the title of this novel, in an alternate manner. In other words, 'the carrot and the stick' typified by the rule of every coloniser in their policies and treatment of the colonised natives.

A Definitive Divorce? Decolonisation and the Post-independence Intellectuals

The savagery of the Algerian War of Independence left an indelible mark on the literature of the era written by Algerian authors of both European and native origins. At the same time as the war was tearing the two nations apart in order to give birth to an independent Algeria, these authors were experiencing deep psychological rifts as they strove to change positions from coloniser and colonised to ex-coloniser and independent people. As is the norm, the end of colonialism brought the end of the coloniser as well as that of the colonised, and both groups therefore needed to recreate themselves and find new ways and new means to retrieve as well as accept their new identities.

This identity quest, however, can be a torturous and an uneasy process, which in turn creates new dilemmas in the rapport between Orient and Occident. Albert Memmi contends: 'the colonizer is a disease of the European, from which he must be completely cured and protected'.[37] After a long history of colonisation is it possible for the Occident to unlearn its accumulated prejudices and stereotypes about the ex-colonised people? Would it be a swift process to change one's position vis-à-vis the newly independent people who are no longer the subjects of the Occident but the masters of their land and in charge of their own destiny? How arduous had it been for the coloniser to accept its new identity as a disinherited settler who, having left all the privileges of a master in the ex-colony behind, returned to the metropole to become an ordinary French citizen in a totally alien environment? For some settlers they had never set foot in Europe before Algeria's independence while for some others France was not even the land of their ancestors. Although in processes of decolonisation one tends to pay more attention to the newly independent state and its people, according to Memmi it would be absurd and unjust to ignore or underestimate the drama of the colonisers whose 'cure involves difficult and painful treatment, extraction and reshaping of present conditions of existence'.[38] This drama did not escape the native intellectuals who forewarned the coloniser about the implications of their immutable colonialist attitudes on both the coloniser and the colonised natives. According to Ferhat Abbas, who after a long odyssey during which he devoted immense efforts to bringing the two communities together, he was exasperated by the settlers' inflexible stand and irreversible colonialist outlooks. Although the War of Independence was the last option and the ultimate solution to end colonial injustice it was nevertheless a painful process for people of Abbas' category too. He told Jean Amrouche in a radio interview recorded in 1947:

> *Voyez-vous* . . . je suis un homme malheureux *qui connaissant un mal subjectivement et objectivement, veut le guérir. Je connais une médication, que je crois seule efficace. C'est la médication* . . . pour mettre fin au régime colonial.[39]
>
> You see, *I'm an unhappy man* who knows the illness both subjectively and objectively, and wants to cure it. I know a remedy, which I think is the only cure. It is the medication . . . *to put an end to the colonial regime.* (My emphasis.)

In the same manner Amrouche, whose soul was split between France and Algeria, agonisingly expressed his dilemma – stating that although the independence of Algeria was a historical necessity to put an end to colonial domination and injustice, it was also tearing him apart in the most painful manner because for him France and Algeria could not be separated since one was the spirit of his soul and the other the soul of his spirit.

The tragic deaths of Camus in 1960, followed by that of Amrouche in 1961 and the assassination of Feraoun a few months before the independence of Algeria in March 1962 symbolised the end of an era which had presented the possibility of a French Algeria, and the birth of a new era where the two nations were painfully torn apart and where cultural hybrids had no place.

Decolonisation between the Political and the Cultural

The end of the Algerian War of Independence and the liberation of Algeria, which also meant the liberation of the whole Maghreb, heralded a new era for the ex-colonised which brought with it new dilemmas. How can one unlearn one hundred and thirty-two years (1830–1962) of domination and subjugation and learn to become a free individual? Decolonisation on the individual and the cultural levels proved far more complicated than political decolonisation and posed more dilemmas than the newly liberated individual had ever anticipated.

After what Abbas calls a long colonial night in his book *La Nuit Coloniale* (The Colonial Night) Algerians did not know what it meant to be free from colonial domination. No one in Algeria had experienced freedom before 1962 and what France had left behind was a people that was not only deeply acculturated, illiterate in its huge majority and deeply traumatised by a savage war of independence that had lasted eight years, and claimed an extremely high number of martyrs, but also a country whose resources were laid to waste and whose internal politics in shambles.

On the eve of the War of Independence all political tendencies and social movements, including the feminist movement, joined forces under the FLN (National Liberation Front) to lead a national war against French colonialism. As a result all other political and social activities in the country came to a halt, and any Algerian who did not rally around the nationalist cause was considered a traitor and was punished accordingly.

Although the FLN worked unabatedly towards the building of a national identity based on the people's values, traditions and customs, religion, culture and language it solely followed the revivalist route adopted by the Algerian Muslim *ʿUlama* as expressed in their slogan of cultural nationalism claiming: 'Arabic is our language, Islam is our religion, Algeria is our country', overstating, therefore, that all Algerians were Muslims and that their sole language was Arabic. While in reality, this slogan ignored two vital elements: that not all Algerians were Muslims, and that Arabic was not the sole language spoken in the country. Such ideological confusion was not identified by the people, who, while experiencing a brutal war of independence had no choice but to hope for the imminent liberation of their country to end their suffering. Helie-Lucas explains,

> We did not recognise the implications of such ideological confusion. We, too, were afraid to betray the people, the revolution and the nation. At no point did we see that a power structure ... was being built on our mental confusion. Obedience, morality and conformity were necessary to the revolution. In a struggle where secrecy is the basis for action, one cannot question the decisions of the comrades in charge.[40]

The Algerian War of Languages

Immediately after independence the FLN saw the generalised Arabisation of Algeria as a means to confirm Algeria's affiliation to the Arab nations. However, by declaring Arabic the only official and national language, the FLN disregarded vital constituents of the Algerian identity, namely that 20–30 per cent of the population were Berbers who did not speak Arabic. Furthermore, even the Arabic-speaking population, which was illiterate in its majority, only spoke various versions of colloquial Arabic depending on their geographical region. Needless to say the French language as the legacy of colonialism was officially relegated to backstage at a time when Algeria's intellectuals in their vast majority could only read and write in French.

At a time when successive Algerian governments aimed to decolonise Algeria and solve its identity crisis,[41] they worked towards the creation of new cultural and identity conflicts that led to riots and the loss of life not only among the Berber populations, who staged popular demonstrations in the 1980s to safeguard their endangered language as a major signifier of their cultural identity, but also during the decade of terrorist violence in the 1990s known as the Black Decade (1991–2001). What the governments of Algeria seem to have ignored is that regardless of the French language being the conqueror's legacy, Algeria, much like its neighbour Morocco, as theorised by Sadiqi,[42] has always been a culturally and linguistically complex speech community. In her book *Algeria in Others' Languages*, Anne-Emmanuelle Berger provides an interesting and lively forum on the language question in Algeria. She explains how in spite of the nationalist rhetoric for adopting Arabisation as a tool to retrieve Algeria's 'true personality', 'the process entailed the teaching and generalised use of an Arabic foreign to the speakers of dialectal Arabic . . . who therefore were not considered "Arabophones". The question was then: which Arabic should the Algerians be taught in order for them to become proper Arabophone speakers and hence legitimate citizens of the new Algerian nation?'[43] While the intention of these governments was to create a nation 'unified by a language', the wholesale Arabisation project alienated the Algerian population and widened the gap between the people and their rulers, as incomprehension often reigned in political, institutional and administrative relations. Often the people never understood the language of their rulers and the irony is that they wondered whether the rulers knew the content of their written speech, which they often read with obvious exertion.[44]

To Write or Not to Write? Decolonisation and the Post-colonial Algerian Novel

This linguistic war soon spread to every aspect of life in Algeria. Not only did it ignite the Berber Cultural Movement for the safeguarding of Berber identity, but infiltrated into cultural milieus and ignited a heated debate between the Francophone and the Arabophone intellectuals, with the latter accusing the former of being followers of the Occident and enthusiasts of neocolonialism.

While some Francophone writers continued to write in French regardless of it being the legacy of colonial France, some others decided to stop writing altogether. The most famous contribution to this controversy was made by Malek Haddad (1927–78), who wrote four novellas in as many years between 1958 and 1962 when,[45] immediately after independence, he decided to reject the French language, a medium in which he had expressed himself prior to independence, and withdrew into literary silence since he believed the use of French was inappropriate in a liberated Algeria. In his long essay titled *Les Zéros tournent en rond*,⁴⁶ he incited other Francophone Algerian writers to reject French in order to complete the process of national independence through cultural liberation. He openly declared that the French language alienated him and that he felt less separated from his homeland by the Mediterranean Sea than by the French language.⁴⁷ As if by repudiating the French language he would become closer to his homeland, and unable to write in Arabic, a language he did not master, Haddad preferred literary silence to continuing to be an 'orphan of genuine readers'. In other words, the genuine readers Haddad was hoping for were not the French readers who were the first audience of the Francophone novel, but readers from his homeland, his own people.

Instead of a total silence other authors, who knew all too well that an illiterate people would not be able to read in any language even if this language was their mother tongue, switched from the written word to colloquial Arabic, as the language understood by the vastly illiterate population, and from the genre of the novel to that of live theatrical performance. A good example is the work of Kateb Yacine (1929–89), who, unable to reach his people through the medium of the Francophone novel, turned to popular drama, which not only celebrated the language of the masses but revived elements of popular culture and included the audience in the performance as the most efficient means of giving voice to the illiterate voiceless masses. With his popular drama, Kateb Yacine was met by a public thirsty for an entertainment they could interact with, unlike the forms of classical drama in standard Arabic promoted by the government, which they found both incomprehensible and alienating.

Despite the enormous popularity of this medium, the government persisted in its Arabisation programme and called upon teachers, writers, artists and intellectuals to express the Arabness of the nation in classical Arabic. This call was consolidated by the emergence of the Arabic novel in Algeria almost a decade after independence. Arabophone novelists of the likes of Abdelhamid Benhadouga (1925–96), author of *Rīh al-janūb* (Wind from the South) (1971) known as the first Algerian novel written in Arabic, and Tahar Wattar (1936–2010) received all necessary support and propaganda moving them thus to centre stage while their Francophone counterparts were pushed to the periphery.

A good example of this process is that of the prominent Francophone novelist Rachid Boudjedra (1941–). After his first novel *La Répudiation* (The Repudiation),(1969), through which he gained notoriety for his explicit language and frontal assault on patriarchy and outdated customs, he published many successful novels in the post-colonial period and established himself as a precursor of a new movement of experimental fiction. In his novel *L'Escargot entêté* (The Stubborn Snail) (1977) he exposes the obstinate bureaucrats whom he calls 'the snails' and satirises their mediocre life and values, while also accusing them of sabotaging their newly-born nation. Critics hailed this novel as a critique of the Algerian revolution, which, while it had brought political independence to the country, had failed to liberate the minds of its people. In 1979 Boudjedra published *Les 1001 Années de la Nostalgie*, a satire of a Saharan village whose inhabitants were shaken to the core of their cultural values by cultural imperialism – embodied by an American film company which was built in the desert.

In 1982 Boudjedra surprised his readers by publishing his novel *The Dismantling* in two languages: in French as *Le Démantèlement*,[48] and in Arabic as *Al-tafakuk*. While the Arabic text was celebrated as a political statement of this shift from the language of the coloniser to that of the liberated nation, Boudjedra's style was much more rigorous in French than in Arabic: a fact that he must have noticed himself, especially because he had returned to writing in French in the 1990s, embracing it once again not as the language of colonialism and imperialism but as a tool he used with great proficiency. Other authors such as Mohamed Sari (1958–), having mastered both French and Arabic, would write their novels in one or the other language and then translate them by themselves.

Pondering on this situation Hafid Gafaïti explains how, while Arabic became the hostage of nationalism and was held as a tool of decolonisation, the Arabisation policy quickly cut off the Berberophone and the Francophone Algerians from their fellow citizens. Moreover, 'In the late 1970s and 1980s, the "Islamization" that followed the policy of systematic and authoritarian "Arabization" further separated even progressive or secular Arabophones from other Algerians. These developments have contributed substantially to the violence of recent times'.⁴⁹ As to Assia Djebar, who recorded women's participation in the War of Independence in two important novels namely *Les Enfants du nouveau monde*⁵⁰ (*Children of the New World*) and *Les Allouettes naïve*,⁵¹ (*The Naïve Larks*) published in 1962 and 1967 respectively, she too observed a decade of self-imposed literary silence during which she set up on a three year journey to investigate the many silences of her women compatriots. However, and most importantly, she searched for their silenced voices about their major contribution to the liberation of their nation. Having spent a long period of time in her mother's village in Mont Chenoua listening and recording women's testimonies about the war, she decided to eternalise their voices in a film documentary titled *La Nouba des femmes du Mont Chenoua* (1978), which set out to record the subaltern voices of her female compatriots who due to their illiteracy could not write their stories about the War of Independence which, as Djebar makes sure to note, was not just the achievement of men but also of women. She writes,

> In my films, I have experimented with the different versions of the Arabic language in Algeria. I had an Arabic sound track and a French soundtrack for *Nouba*. I lived immersed in the language of the hinterland, an experience that ran quite contrary to the current efforts to impose a version of classical Arabic upon the land.⁵²

This linguistic and cultural immersion convinced Djebar that in the postcolonial period, the French language is no longer a colonising tool and on the contrary it has become 'the booty of the colonial war' which Algerians obtained after they won the war of liberation. In a 1985 newspaper article, she went as far as to call the French language a liberating tool.⁵³ This idea was initiated by Kateb Yacine, who declared in the midst of the Algerian War of Independence, that:

> The French language, which was introduced into Algeria as a means of depersonalisation, has become, with a certain poetic justice, a powerful megaphone broadcasting a chorus of real voices in a country of a thousand faces, which is attaining its unity by the shortest route, one which opens up the knowledge of its last conquerors. One does not use a universal language to humiliate a people in its very soul without consequences. Sooner or later,

the people seize that language and culture for themselves, and it helps them a great deal on their way towards freedom.[54]

The language Yacine is speaking about is not the language of the French armies who in Djebar's words 'they came, they killed, they conquered. They write, and kill as they write – in the act of writing',[55] but the language of French culture, that of its great authors and humanists, a language laden with the republic's universal principles of *Liberté, Égalité, Fraternité*. At the same time as the leaders of post-independence Algeria were actively operating a total divorce from the legacy of colonialism as a means to redeem national identity, Djebar claims her Algerianness through the medium of the language of the ex-colonisers. For this, Clarisse Zimra describes her as being 'unusual in her defiant embrace of the French language as an instrument of self-liberation'.[56] After her decade-long literary silence Djebar has taken charge of her writing and used the French language as the most efficient tool that enabled her to do so to the point of speaking about looting it and feminising it. Confident and linguistically proficient she is simultaneously appropriating the oppositional tradition and turning it on its head. In Djebar's hands the French language has become subject to many alterations, additions, cadences and images unfamiliar to the coloniser's French language and culture. She skilfully weaves into the language turns of phrases and syntax that result in a stylistic signature typical of the Djebarian text. In consequence Djebar is doing violence to the French language, in other words she is counter-colonising it and at the same time she is enriching it. She writes: 'I know today that one can write in a foreign language, integrate it to one's imaginary without having to renounce one's origins.'[57] Decolonisation proves to be more fundamental than just rejecting the language of the ex-coloniser.

It needs to be highlighted, however, that this difference of registers of French Language used by French authors and by Francophone authors was highlighted by Mouloud Feraoun, who while he was writing his first novel, *Le Fils du Pauvre,* he became aware that although his mission was to write about his own people in order to make them known to his French readers, a novel written by a Francophone author such as himself was bound to display the mark of the environment that produced it using thus a different linguistic register to that of French authors. Regardless of their language of writing,

Algerian authors have succeeded in reaching wider audiences and attracting considerable attention to the themes they engaged with, from their search for a national identity beyond the colonial era, or the truth about their people's struggle for self-realisation, they continue to speak to the Occident not as subjects but as agents, sometimes expressing fascination about occidental culture while at other times they hold the Occident to account for its atrocities during the colonial period as did Leïla Sebbar (1941–) in her novel *La Seine était rouge*.[58] Published in 1999, this novel revisits the massacre of the pacific demonstration held in Paris on 17 October 1961 by 30,000 unarmed Algerian immigrants who protested about the curfew imposed on them by the French authorities as well as the atrocities committed by France in Algeria during the war. The brutal repression of the demonstrators resulted in a widescale massacre with many victims being thrown into the Seine rendering its waters red from their blood. Revisiting the site of these events commemorates them while reminding the Occident of the ugly face of colonialism and the wounds of the past, so that future generations do not forget the causes of the brutal divorce between Algeria and France.

Conclusion

The 8 May 1945 massacre changed the course of the encounter between native Algerians and colonial France. Nine years after this landmark event the Algerian revolution began as the ultimate divorce between France and Algeria. This political divorce engendered an important volume of literature as a vehicle through which authors expressed their views and anguish as one nation painfully tore itself away from the domination of another.

From disillusion with the false promises of their *mère-patrie* to the joys of becoming liberated, the novels of this period documented the evolution of the Algerian person from the status of the colonised to that of the decolonised. Decolonisation proved to be a difficult process confronting the newly-liberated Algerians with often very severe growing pains. Caught between the traumas of yesterday's long colonial night, and the uncertainties of tomorrow, the expression of this dilemma and anxieties in literature produced accounts of high value which remain severely understudied.

Mainly written in two languages: French and Arabic, in addition to Berber and English in recent years, the post-colonial Algerian novel presents a wealth of themes and subject matter. From a narrative of alienation, and a rebellion against colonial injustice it swiftly progressed to a testimony to history, a questioning of decolonisation and imperialism, a revolt against social prejudice, a mark of insubordination toward authority and most importantly an endless search for identity, and an account of the East–West encounter based on the relationship between the self and the other. From the above discussion it can easily be concluded that the other of the Maghrebi novel is the Occident and that its Occident mainly revolves around France, its ex-coloniser.

Having shared a long history of colonisation during which the relation between the Occident and the Maghreb evolves from infatuation/Occidentophilia, which resulted in blind imitation of the Occident, to an ambivalent phase during which the Maghreb still hoped for repair, and again to the stage of the ultimate divorce brought about by the means of a political struggle in the cases of Morocco and Tunisia (1956), and a bloody war for independence in the case of Algeria (1962).

After independence this position tended to lose its intensity as, while decolonisation often meant a repudiation of everything that was brought by the ex-coloniser including its language, the ex-colonised came to realise the eternal dichotomy between two Occidents: the Occident as a colonial power which is now defeated and no longer in existence, and the Occident as a culture and a civilisation which continues to captivate and enchant the Maghrebi person.

Dorra Bouzid, a Tunisian writer, activist and artist told Julia Clancy Smith in an interview about her cultural and political relationship with France, that: 'we were opposed to racism and colonialism, not to Europe or the West'.[59] Likewise Ferhat Abbas after a long struggle against colonialism, he explains that the liberated Algerian people are not the enemy of the French people but the enemy of colonialism.

> *Le peuple algérien n'est pas un ennemi-né du peuple français. Le colonialism aboli, rien n'empêchera plus les deux peuples de coopérer, de s'entraider et d'harmoniser leurs intérêts. Il n'est pas interdit de penser que Marseille restera un grand port pour la production algérienne et Paris une grande université pour notre jeunesse. Ce qui compte pour nous, dans ce domaine, c'est de*

conserver les mains libres pour planifier et sortir notre peuple de la misère, de l'analphabétisme et du taudis.[60]

The Algerian people are not born enemies of the French people. Now that colonialism is abolished, nothing will prevent the two peoples from cooperating and helping each other to harmonise their common interests. It is not prohibited to think that Marseille will remain a major port for Algerian goods and Paris a great University for our youth. What counts for us, is to keep our integrity and freedom of action to find ways to save our people from poverty, illiteracy and the slums.

Afterword

> Truth is a thing of this world: it is produced only by virtue of multiple forms of constraint. And it induces regular effects of power. Each society has its régime of truth, its 'general politics' of truth: that is, the types of discourse which it accepts and makes function as true; the mechanisms and instances which enable one to distinguish true and false statements, the means by which each is sanctioned, the techniques and procedures accorded value in the acquisition of truth; the status of those who are charged with saying what counts as true.
>
> Michel Foucault[1]

The initial project of this book aimed to cover the literary Maghrebi representations of the East–West Encounter from their first manifestations at the turn of the twentieth century all the way to the present, with equal depth. While collecting data for this research it became clear that the early period of this encounter is still seriously understudied and yet at the same time it represents an important link without which a full understanding of many major issues which continue to perturb this relationship down to the present cannot be gained.

The major issues which are today central to the East–West encounter have their roots deeply anchored in the history of the colonial encounter between the Maghreb and the Occident. By this I do not solely refer to French colonialism but also to the Islamic conquest of the Iberian Peninsula which triggered the animosity of the Christian world against the Muslim Maghreb, and from then on the encounter between the Occident and the Maghreb, as the Occident's Orient, was shaped by war central to which is a conflict between Christianity and Islam, all the way through to the French occupation of Algeria in 1830 followed by that of Tunisia and Morocco in 1881 and 1912 respectively.

Historians have not failed to document these occurrences. However, to their historical accounts of facts and events literature has added people's feelings, reactions and interpretations of such events as lived and experienced by various strata of society. If we see literature as the mirror of its time, sidelining the literature of any period in history would be a means of shattering that mirror and therefore losing sight of the human story that recorded that specific historical period.

Through their novels, which were written with the Occidental reader in mind, these authors never failed to express their gratitude for all the civilising efforts made by France. They constantly acknowledged her mission to turn the Maghreb into a civilised location after it existed as a set of warring tribes and a notorious centre of piracy which spread havoc in the Mediterranean Sea.

Furthermore, although they described their society as divided into two separate and unequal worlds: one inhabited by the Europeans and the other by the natives, they never blamed the Occident for such inequalities but severely condemned their own people's stubborn resistance to western civilisation. However, although they did not criticise the Occident as a uniform monolith, they often pointed the finger towards the European non-French settlers whose origins they highlighted as dubious. In this way, while the Occident orientalised the Orient as one homogenous mass of uncivilised people these authors did not Occidentalise the Occident but saw different Europeans as being different people with different characteristics. This differentiation allowed them to keep their ties with the idealised Occident as they continued to believe in its abilities to save the Orientals from their barbarity.

Although these early novels could be seen as isolated and under-read letters to the Occident, this first generation of native intellectuals resorted to direct action by addressing open letters to political leaders both in the colony and in the Metropole. These letters, along with the novels studied above, depict the encounter with the Occident as one of both love and fascination. Yet with this there is also a plea to the Occident to genuinely extend its civilisation to all factions of society and not just to the French-educated elite.

This made great sense, as one cannot enjoy the bounties of civilisation while one's own people live in the darkness of ignorance.

Most famous of all such addresses to the Occident is the letter sent by Ferhat Abbas to the French President, Maréchal Pétain, bearing the title of *Rapport au Maréchal Pétain*, which he wrote in April 1941 in the name of the *Jeunes Algériens* whom he represents. He says:

> *Les Jeunes Algériens, en s'adressant à vous, désirent vous apporter et apporter aux représentants de la France une collaboration loyale et confiante pour l'établissement d'un ordre nouveau en Algérie . . . Ce rapport résume un bilan . . . Nous le soumettons au chef de l'état, dans l'espoir qu'il contribuera à emmener un changement en Algérie.*[2]

> By writing to you, we the Young Algerians, wish to bring to your attention and that of the representatives of France our loyal and confident collaboration with you for the establishment of a new order in Algeria . . . This report summarises the current situation . . . We present it to the President of France in the hope that he would contribute to bring about change in Algeria.

Abbas' report mainly presents its author as the mediator who, deeply immersed in French culture and fully believing in the benefits of its civilising mission, was also very concerned about the dire social and economic conditions endured by the vast majority of native Algerians, and weary of the constant sabotaging interventions of the greedy European settlers. Reaching out directly to Maréchal Pétain was Abbas' last hope to make Metropolitan France aware of the situation on the ground in the colony, without the censorship of the settlers, which in a way was an expression of his belief in the ideals of the French republic.

However, history proved that such beliefs were a mere illusion, and the Occident's civilising mission was a mere lie. The 8 May 1945 massacres resulted in the deepening of the gap, which separated the Orient from the Occident. After the promises made by de Gaulle in 1943 and the great sacrifices made by the natives while fighting in the Second World War, they became extremely indignant about France as a colonial power mired in its colonialist ideology. The literature that resulted from this turning point adopted a radically different tone from that which had preceded it, thus making it deserve its name as the genuine Algerian literature written by ordinary natives who had experienced colonial oppression firsthand.

Starting by exposing the truth about the miserable living conditions of their people who gained nothing but poverty and alienation from the French presence, the authors of these novels portrayed a people on edge ready for all action including war, to retrieve its dignity. This action was soon to concretise in the war of national liberation, which engulfed all tendencies and ideologies and channelled all efforts towards the liberation of the nation without which the emancipation of the individual could not concretise. This new truth drowned any other discourse which pre-existed it vis-à-vis France's civilising mission which only proved to be chimerical: a dream which never concretised. Abbas summarised this dream in the following terms:

> [. . .] le mariage de l'Occident et de l'Orient . . . la réconciliation de la France et de l'Islam . . . la formation par la culture franco-musulmane de la France orientale, c'était le plus beau miracle des temps modernes, la synthèse des deux civilisations.[3]

The marriage between Occident and Orient . . . reconciliation between France and Islam . . . the construction of the *Oriental France* through the medium of the *Franco-Muslim culture*, this would have been the most beautiful miracle of modern times: a synthesis of the two civilisations. (My emphasis.)

Notes

Notes to Introduction
1. Edward W. Said, *Orientalism: Western Conception of the Orient* (London: Penguin Books, 2003), p. 2.
2. Ibid., p. 4.
3. Ibid.
4. Robert Irwin, *For Lust of Knowing: the Orientalists and their Enemies* (London: Penguin Books, 2007), p. 6.
5. Rasheed El-Enany, *Arab Representations of the Occident: East–West Encounters in Arabic Fiction* (London and New York: Routledge), 2006, p. 205.
6. Nicholas Thomas, 'Anthropology and Orientalism', *Anthropology Today*, 7, 1991, p. 7.
7. James G. Carrier (ed.), *Occidentalism: Images of the West* (Oxford: Clarendon Press, 2003), p. 10.
8. Jean El Mouhoub Amrouche, *Journal 1928–1962*, Présenté par Tassadit Yacine (Alger: Éditions Alpha, 2009), p. 31.
9. Étienne Dinet and Slimane Ben Brahim Baamer, *Khadra, danseuse des Ouled Nail* (Paris: Piazza, 1926).
10. Saad Ben Ali and René Pottier, *La Tente noire, roman saharien* (Paris: les œuvres représentatives, 1933).
11. Tahar Ben Jelloun, *The Sacred Night*, trans. Alan Sheridan (Baltimore and London: The Johns Hopkins University Press, 2000). First published as *La Nuit Sacrée* (Paris: Le Seuil, 1985).
12. Tahar Ben Jelloun, *The Sand Child*, trans. Alan Sheridan (Baltimore and London: The Johns Hopkins University Press, 2000). First published as *L'Enfant de Sable* (Paris: Le Seuil, 1987).
13. Augustin Berque, "Les Intellectuels Algériens', *Revue Africaine*, 1947, p. 136.

14. Lazreg, *The Eloquence of Silence: Algerian Women in Question* (New York: Routledge, 1994), p. 60.
15. Augustin Berque, 'Les Intellectuels Algériens', *Revue Africaine*, 1947, pp. 138–44.

Notes to Chapter 1

1. Abdelkebir Khatibi, *Love in two Languages*, trans. Richard Howard (Minneapolis: University of Minnesota Press, 1990), pp. 105–6. First published as *Amour bilingue* (Montpellier: Fata Morgana, 1983).
2. *The Free Dictionary*, www.thefreedictionary.com. Accessed 25 October 2016.
3. Said, *Orientalism*, p. 50.
4. Hassan Hanafi, 'From Orientalism to Occidentalism'. www.fortschritt-weltweit. de. Accessed 2 November 2011. See also: Hassan Hanafi, *Muqaddimah fī ᶜilm al-istighrāb* (Beirut: al-Mu'assassah al-Jāmiᶜiyah li al-dirāssāt wa al-nashr wa al-tawzīᶜ, 2000).
5. Hassan Hanafi, 'From Orientalism to Occidentalism', www.fortschritt-weltweit. de.
6. Sadik J. Al-Azm, 'Orientalism, Occidentalism, and Islamism', Keynote Address to Orientalism and Fundamentalism in Islamic and Judaic Critique: A Conference Honouring Sadik Al-Azm, *Comparative Studies of South Asia, Africa and the Middle East*, 30: 1, 2010, p. 6.
7. Ibid., p. 7.
8. Ibid.
9. Fernando Coronil, 'Beyond Occidentalism: Towards Post-Imperial Geohistorical Categories', in *Cultural Anthropology*, 11 (1996), pp. 51–87.
10. Bill Ashcroft, Gareth Griffiths and Helen Tiffin, *Post-Colonial Studies: The Key Concepts* (London and New York: Routledge, 2010), p. 117.
11. Homi Bhabha, *The Location of Culture* (London and New York: Routledge, 1994).
12. Abbas, Ferhat, *Le Jeune Algérien* (Paris: La Jeune Parque, 1931).
13. Abbas, Ferhat, *J'Accuse l'Europe* (Alger: Libération, 1944).
14. Abbas, Ferhat, *La Nuit coloniale* (Paris: Julliard, 1962).
15. Memmi, Albert, *Portrait du Colonisé précédé du Portrait du Colonisateur* (Paris: Buchet-Chastel, 1957). Trans. by Howard Greenfeld as *The Colonizer and the Colonized* (London: Souvenir Press, 1974).
16. Abdelkebir Khatibi, *La Mémoire tatouée* (Paris: Denoël, 1971).
17. Abdelkebir Khatibi, *Amour bilingue* (Fata Morgana, Montpellier, 1983).

18. Frantz Fanon, *Black Skin, White Masks*, trans. Charles Lam Markmann (New York: Grove Press, 1967).
19. Frantz Fanon, *The Wretched of the Earth*, trans. Constance Farrington (London: Penguin Books, 2001).
20. Coronil, 'Beyond Occidentalism,' p. 57.
21. Malek Alloula, *The Colonial Harem* (Manchester: Manchester University Press, 1986).
22. Coronil, 'Beyond Occidentalism,' p. 57.
23. Malek Alloula, *The Colonial Harem*, p. 31.
24. Ibid., p. 4.
25. Marnia Lazreg, *The Eloquence of Silence: Algerian Women in Question*, p. 39.
26. Coronil, 'Beyond Occidentalism,' p. 57.
27. Alloula, *The Colonial Harem*, p. 29.
28. Anouar Abdel-Malek, 'Orientalism in Crisis,' *Diogenes*, 44 (1963), pp. 104–12.
29. Ibid., pp. 107–8.
30. Ibid., p. 107.
31. Abdelmajid, Hannoum, 'Faut-it brûler l'Orientalisme?: On French Scholarship of North Africa', *Cultural Dynamics* 16 (2004), pp. 71–91.
32. Ibid., p. 71.
33. Ibid., p. 76.
34. Ibid., p. 75.
35. Abdel-Malek, 'Orientalism in Crisis,' p. 108.
36. ibid., p. 107.
37. Michel Foucault, *Discipline and Punish: the Birth of the Prison*, trans. Alan Sheridan (New York: Vintage Books Editions, 1977), p. 27.
38. See the work of the Islamic geographers and travellers of the likes of Ibn Abū ʿAbd Allāh Muḥammad ibn ʿAbd Allāh al-Lawātī al-Ṭanjī, 1304–69/77. Known as the greatest medieval Muslim traveller and the author of one of the most famous travel books, the *Riḥlah* (*Travels*). His great work describes his extensive travels covering some 75,000 miles (120,000 km) in trips to almost all of the Muslim countries and as far as China and Sumatra (now part of Indonesia). For further details see: https://www.britannica.com/biography/Ibn-Battutah. Accessed 16 May 2018.
39. Barthélemy d'Herbelot, de Molainville, *Bibliothèque orientale, ou dictionnaire universel contenant tout ce qui regarde la connaissance des peuples de l'Orient*, 4 vols (The Hague: Quatro, 1777–99).
40. De Lacy O'Leary, *How Greek Science Passed to the Arabs*. First published in

UK (London: Routledge & Kegan Paul, 1949) *www.aina.org/books/hgsptta.htm.* Accessed 13 October 2010.

41. ʿAbd-ar-Raḥmān Ibn Khaldūn, *The Muqaddimah: An Introduction to History*, trans. Frantz Rosenthal (Princeton and Oxford: Princeton University Press: 2005), p. 39.
42. Ibid., pp. 41, 214.
43. Ibid., p. 373.
44. *Chansons de Geste* contains an expression of the Franks' fear of Islam. For more details see: James A. Bellamy, 'Arabic Names in the Chansons de Roland: Saracen Gods, Frankish Swords, Roland's Horse, and the Oliphant', *Journal of the American Orientalist Society*, 107, 1987.
45. Said, *Orientalism*, p. 65.
46. Irwin, *For the Lust of Knowing*, p. 20.
47. William E. Watson, *Tricolor and Crescent: France and the Islamic World* (London: Praeger, 2003), pp. 2–3.
48. Ibid., p. 2.
49. See William Bedwell, *Mohammedis imposturae*, 1615, and Humphrey Prideaux, *The True Nature of Imposture Fully Displayed in the Life of Mahomet*, 1697.
50. Derek Hopwood, *Sexual Encounters in the Middle East: The British, the French, and the Arabs* (Reading: Ithaca Press, 1999).
51. Commission des sciences et arts d'Égypte, *Description de l'Égypte* (Paris: French Government publication, 1809–22).
52. Abdel Latif Tibawi, 'English-speaking Orientalists,' *Islamic Quarterly*, 8 (1964), pp. 25–45.
53. Irwin, *For Lust of Knowing*, pp. 319–20.
54. Lila Abu-Lughod, 'Zones of Theory in the Anthropology of the Arab World,' *Annual Review of Anthropology*, 18 (1989), p. 267.
55. Abdel Malek, 'Orientalism in Crisis,' p. 108.
56. Abu-Lughod, 'Zones of Theory,' p. 267.
57. Carrier, *Occidentalism: Images of the West*, p. 1.
58. Ibid., p. 26.
59. Said, *Orientalism*, p. 70.
60. Laura Nader, 'Orientalism, Occidentalism and the Control of Women', *Cultural Dynamics*, 2 (1989), pp. 323–55.
61. Ibid., p. 333.
62. Ian Buruma and Avishai Margalit, *Occidentalism: A Short History of Anti-Westernism* (London: Atlantic Books: 2004), p. 5.

63. Ibid., p. 10.
64. Ibid., pp. 10–11.
65. Ibid., p. 56.
66. Maître Gisèle Halimi defended Djamila Boubacha, an Algerian freedom fighter who was arrested and tortured in prison while she was a minor. For more details see: Simone De Beauvoir and Gisèle Halimi, *Djamila Boupacha: the story of the torture of a young Algerian girl which shocked liberal French opinion*, trans. Peter Green (London: André Deutsch Ltd and George Weidenfeld and Nicolson Ltd, 1962).
67. Maître Jacques Vergès defended Djamila Bouhired, who like Djamila Boubacha, was also a freedom fighter who was arrested and tortured in prison. She later became Vergès' wife.
68. Ibid.
69. Jean Baudrillard, *The Spirit of Terrorism* (New York and London: Verso, 2002).
70. Aziz Al-Azmeh and Effie Fokas (eds), *Islam in Europe: Diversity, Identity and Influence* (Cambridge: Cambridge University Press, 2007), p. 208.
71. Stuart Hall, 'Cultural Identity, and Diaspora,' in Patrick Williams and Chrisman, *Colonial Discourse and Post-Colonial Theory: a Reader* (London: Harvester Wheatsheaf, 1994), pp. 392–401.
72. Mernissi Fatima, *Beyond the Veil: Male-Female Dynamics in Modern Muslim Society* (Bloomington: Indiana University Press, 1975).
73. Haideh Moghissi, *Women and Islam: Critical Concepts in Sociology, Images and Realities* (London and New York: Routledge, 2005).
74. Rasheed El-Enany, *Arab Representations of the Occident*, p. 6.

Notes to Chapter 2

1. Ministère de la guerre, Cited in Ruedy, J., *Modern Algeria* (London: Bloomington, 1992). Ruedy, J., *Modern Algeria* (London: Bloomington, 1992).
2. Marnia Lazreg, *The Eloquence of Silence*, p. 36.
3. Joseph Fourier, Préface historique, vol. 1 of *Description de L'Égypte*, p. xcii, quoted in Said, *Orientalism*, p. 85.
4. For more details see Baron Barchou de Penhoen, *Mémoires d'un officier d'état-major, Expédition d'Afrique* (Paris: Charpentier, 1935).
5. Jean-Robert Henry, 'Résonances maghrébines', *Revue de l'Occident musulman et de la Méditerranée*, vol. 37, no. 37, 1984 (pp. 5–14), p. 6. My emphasis.
6. Guy de Maupassant, *Au Soleil* (Paris: Ollendorff: 1902), p. 4. First published in 1884.

7. Ibid., pp. 8–9.
8. Philipe Lucas & Claude Vatin, *L'Algérie des Anthropologues* (Paris: Maspéro, 1982), pp. 96–9.
9. Ibid.
10. Victor Hugo, quoted in Hopwood, *Sexual Encounters*, p. 89.
11. Guy de Maupassant, *Au Soleil*, p. 12.
12. Louis Bertrand, *Le Sang des races* (Paris: Albin Michel, 1899).
13. D.M. Gallup, 'The French Image of Algeria: its Origins, its Place in Colonial Ideology, its Effect on Algerian Acculturation'. PhD Thesis, University of California, 1973, p. 274.
14. *Voyage dans les états barbaresques de Maroc, Alger, Tunis et Tripoli; ou lettres d'un des captives qui viennent d'être rachetés par MM. Les Chanoines réguliers de la Sainte-Trinité, suivies d'une notice sur leur rachat et du catalogue de leurs noms.* (Paris: Guillot, 1785), pp. iii–iv. The book has been reprinted by Paris: Hachette livre-BNF, 26 March 2012.
15. Louis Bertrand, *L'Afrique Latine*, May 1922. Cited in Ferhat Abbas, *Le Jeune Algérien: De la Colonie vers la Province (1930), suivi de Rapport au Maréchal Pétain (Avril 1941)* (Alger: Livres Éditions, 2011), pp. 70–1.
16. Ibid.
17. Louis Bertrand, *Figaro*, 16 Novembre 1926. Cited in Ferhat Abbas, *Le Jeune Algérien*, p. 71.
18. Ministère de la guerre. Cited in J. Ruedy, *Modern Algeria* (London: Bloomington, 1992), pp. 50–1. My emphasis.
19. Robert Aldrich, *Greater France: A history of French Overseas Expansion* (London: Macmillan, 1996), p. 145.
20. Ibid.
21. Ferhat Abbas, *Le Jeune Algérien*, p. 98.
22. Aimable-Jean-Jacques Pélissier (1794–1864) gained notoriety for killing the entire local population of men, women and children of the Ouled Riah tribe whom he cornered in the caves of the Dahra Mountains where they sought refuge. For more details see: *Encyclopaedia Britannica* available on: https://www.britannica.com/biography/Aimable-Jean-Jacques-Pelissier-duc-de-Malakoff#ref989400. Accessed 28 May 2018. See also, Jennifer Sessions, '"Unfortunate necessities": violence and civilisation in the conquest of Algeria', in Patricia Lorcin, Daniel Brewer (eds), *France and its Spaces of War: Experience, Memory, Image* (Basingstoke: Palgrave, 2009), pp. 35–6.
23. Benjamin Stora, *Algeria 1830–2000: A Short History*, trans. Jane

Marie Todd (Ithaca and London: Cornell University Press), 2001, p. 5.
24. Marie-Cecile Thoral, 'French Colonial Counter-Insurgency: General Bugeaud and the Conquest of Algeria, 1840–47', *British Journal of Military History*, 1 (2), 2015, p. 17.
25. Ibid. See also: Martin Thomas, *The French Colonial Mind: Violence, Military Encounters, and Colonialism*, Lincoln, Nebraska, University of Nebraska Press, 2011. Also, Martin Thomas, *Violence and Colonial Order: Police, Workers, and Protest in the European Colonial Empires, 1918–1940* (Cambridge, Cambridge University Press, 2012); and William Galois, *A History of Violence in the Early Algerian Colony* (Palgrave Macmillan, 2013).
26. Aldrich, p. 28.
27. Ibid., p. 218.
28. Ibid., p. 91.
29. Watson, p. 24.
30. Edward Said, 'Zionism from the Standpoint of its Victims,' *Social Text*, Vol. 1, 1979, pp. 26–7.
31. Aldrich, p. 146.
32. *Patricia M.E. Lorcin, Imperial Identities: Stereotyping, Prejudice and Race in Colonial Algeria* (London: I. B. Tauris, 1999), p. 202.
33. Raymond F. Betts, *Assimilation and Association in French Colonial Theory, 1890–1914* (Lincoln: University of Nebraska Press, 2005), p. 12.
34. For more details see: Pélissier de Reynaud, *Annales algériennes* (Paris: Librairie Militaire, Alger: Librairie Bastide, 1854).
35. In his book *The Arab Rediscovery of Europe: A Study in Cultural Encounters* (London: Saqi books, 2011), Ibrahim Abu-Lughod includes the entire text of the Napoleonic Proclamations, pp. 29–32.
36. Cited in Betts, p. 19.
37. Mohammed Mazouz, "Algeria", in Groupe de Démographie Africaine, *Population Size in African Countries: An Evaluation*, Volume II (Paris: IOP_INEO_INSEE_MINCOOP_ORSTOM, 1988), p. 3.
38. Ibid.
39. Charles-Robert Ageron, *Histoire de l'Algérie contemporaine* (Paris: PUF, 1970), p. 19.
40. Bernard Droz and Evelyne Lever, *Histoire de la guerre d'Algérie, 1954–1962* (Paris: Seuil, 1982), p. 17.

41. Neville Barbour, 'Algeria', in Colin Legum (ed.), *Africa: A Handbook to the Continent* (New York: Praeger, 1967) (pp. 5–20), p. 5. My emphasis.
42. The royal edicts of 1635 and 1642 stated that once converted to Catholicism the natives become 'citizens and natural Frenchmen'. Cited in L. Roland and P. Lampué, *Précis de legislation coloniale* (Paris: Dalloz, 1931), p. 200.
43. Hopwood, *Sexual Encounters*, p. 89.
44. Gallup, 'The French Image of Algeria', p. 274.
45. The Romans' assimilationist attitude considered whoever did not resemble them as 'barbarians', resulting in the people of North Africa, the Imazighen, becoming the Berbers, and the North African coast Barbary.
46. Betts, pp. 10–11.
47. Ibid., p. 11.
48. Walter Rodney, *How Europe Underdeveloped Africa* (London: L'ouverture, 1972), p. 277.
49. J. P. Daughton, *An Empire Divided: Religion, Republicanism, and the Making of French Colonialism, 1880–1914* (Oxford: Oxford University Press, 2006), p. 244.
50. Ibid., My emphasis.
51. Plural of *Zāwiya*. For more details on the role of the Zawāyā in fighting colonialism and preserving Islam as a form of identity see Mohammed Raouf Kacimi El Hassani, 'Tariqah Rahmania: its roots and prospects', *Journal of Sophia Asian Studies*, no. 27, December 2009, pp. 291–307.
52. Emir ᶜAbd-el-Kader: Algerian Emir and anti-colonialist leader. He was born on 6 September 1808 near Mascara in the west of Algeria. His full name is ᶜAbd al-Qadir bin Muhieddine; he is known in the Arab East as ᶜAbdel-Kader al-Jaza'iri and in Algeria as al-Amir ᶜAbd El-Kader. His father, Muhieddine al-Hassanī, was a Sufi sheikh who followed the Qādiriyya religious order and claimed to be a Hassanī (*sharīf*) descendent of the Prophet Mohammad with family ties with the Idrīssid dynasty of Morocco. In 1832, he was elected Emir al-Muʾminīn (commander of the faithful) by his fellow tribesmen. He organised a resistance movement to fight the French occupation troops and declared *jihad* against them. Between 1832 and 1842 ᶜAbdel-Kader's troops scored many victories as well as some defeats, leading the enemy, under the command of Marshal Bugeaud, to sign the Treaty of Tafna in 1837, which delimited the territories of the two parties. This truce, however, lasted for only two years as French troops marched through Algerian-liberated territory in 1839, which broke the Treaty of Tafna and made ᶜAbdel-Kader renew his resistance and call for *jihad* in

October of the same year, attacking French strongholds. In the following year, the French launched a wide action to occupy all Algerian territory and dealt ᶜAbdel-Kader's army many defeats leaving him with no other option but to surrender in 1847 on the condition that he and his family were allowed to settle in Syria. Instead, they were imprisoned in France for five years, after which they were released to settle in Bursa (Turkey) and then move to Damascus, where he died in 1883.

53. Walter Rodney, *How Europe Underdeveloped Africa* (London: L'ouverture, 1972), p. 277.
54. Cardinal Charles Martial Allemand Lavigerie (1825–92): mostly remembered for his objective to evangelise the entire continent of Africa which he made very obvious to all. In 1868 he founded the Society of Missionaries of Africa (White Fathers) followed in 1869 by the Missionary Sisters of Our Lady of Africa (White Sisters). Cardinal Lavigerie established orphanages and schools for the child victims of successive famines in Algeria whom he converted to Catholicism and refused to return them to their parents.

> He studied at the diocesan seminary of Larressore, then went to St. Nicolas-du-Chardonnet in Paris, and finally to St. Sulpice. Ordained on 2 June, 1849, he devoted the first year of his priesthood to higher studies at the newly founded Ecole des Carmes, taking at the Sorbonne the doctorates of letters (1850), and of theology (1853), to which he added later the Roman doctorates of civil and canon law. Appointed chaplain of Sainte-Geneviève in 1853, associate professor of church history at the Sorbonne in 1854, and titular of the chair in 1857, Lavigerie did not confine his activity to his chaplaincy or chair, but took a leading part in the organization of the students' cercles catholiques, and of l'œuvre des écoles d'Orient. As director of the latter he collected large sums for the benefit of the Oriental Christians persecuted by the Druses, and even went to Syria to superintend personally the distribution of the funds (1860).
>
> His brilliant services were rewarded by rapid promotion, first in 1861 to the Roman Rota, and two years later to the See of Nancy. From the beginning of his episcopate he displayed that genius of organization which is the characteristic of his life. The foundation of colleges at Vic, Blamont, and Lunéville; the establishment at Nancy of a higher institute for clerics and of a Maison d'étudiants for law students; the organization of the episcopal curia; the publication of the 'Recueil des Ordonnances épiscopales statuts et règlements du diocèse de Nancy', were but the first fruits of a

promising episcopate, when he was transferred to Algiers on 27 March, 1867.

W. G. Kofron, *New Advent*, http://www.newadvent.org/cathen/ 09050d.htm. Accessed October 2016.

For more details see: François Renault, *Le Cardinal Lavigerie* (Paris: Fayard, 1992); John O'Donohue, *Cardinal Lavigerie* (London: Athlone Press, 1994).

55. White Fathers' Missions of Africa, 'Le Cardinal Lavigerie,' 1925, trans. Penelope Royall, published in *The Muslim World*, vol. 16, issue 2, p. 176. My emphasis.
56. For more details on the work and life of Saint Augustine see: Henry Chadwick, *Augustine of Hippo: a life* (Oxford: Oxford University Press, 2009); Brian Stock, *Augustine the Reader: Meditation, Self-Knowledge, and the Ethics of Interpretation* (Cambridge, MA: Harvard University Press, 1996); and Peter Brown, *La Vie du Saint Augustin* (Paris: Le Seuil, 2001).
57. Dirèche-Slimani Karima, *Chrétiens de Kabylie 1873–1954. Une action missionnaire dans l'Algérie coloniale* (Paris: Éditions Bouchène, 2004).
58. Algerian born French author Albert Camus wrote extensively about the recurrent famines that hit Algerian populations. See for example: *Chroniques algériennes, 1939–1958, Actuelles III* (Paris: Éditions Gallimard, Collection Folio essais, 1958), and *Misère de la Kabylie* (Bejaïa: Éditions Zirem, 2005).
59. For more details on the Kabyle myth, see: *Patricia M. E. Lorcin, Imperial Identities: Stereotyping, Prejudice and Race in Colonial Algeria* (London: I. B. Tauris, 1995); Charles-Robert Ageron, *Les Algériens Musulmans et la France (1871–1919)*, vol. 1 (Paris: PUF, 1968), pp. 267–85.
60. Djurdjura Mountains: A mountain range of the Tell Atlas, located in Kabylie, Algeria.
61. For more details on the role of the white sisters in penetrating Algerian society see: Frantz Fanon, *L'An V de la révolution algérienne* (Paris: La Découverte, 2001).
62. Dirèche-Slimani, *Chrétiens de Kabylie 1873–1954*, p. 73.
63. Fadhma Amrouche, *My Life Story*, trans. Dorothy Blair (London: The Women's Press, 1988), p. xii.
64. Jean-El Mouhoub Amrouche, *Journal 1928–1962* (Alger: Éditions Alpha, 2009), p. 15.
65. Mouloud Feraoun, *Les Chemins qui mentent* (Paris: le Seuil, 1955).
66. Ibid., p. 26.
67. For more details see Dirèche-Slimani, p. 74.
68. Ibid.

69. For more details see Zahia Smail Salhi, *Politics, Poetics and the Algerian Novel* (Lampeter: The Edwin Mellen Press, 1999), pp. 7–9.
70. Mahfoud Bennoune, *The Making of Contemporary Algeria, 1830–1987* (Cambridge: Cambridge University Press), 1988, p. 60.
71. Fanny Colonna, *Instituteurs algériens 1883–1939* (Paris: Presses de la Fondation Nationale des Sciences Politiques, 1975), p. 20.
72. Mahfoud Smati, *Les Jeunes Algériens: Correspondances et Rapports 1837–1918* (Alger: Thala Éditions, 2011), p. 17.
73. A stimulating debate on the Algerian problem, often referred to as 'le problème algérien', took place on 1 July 1946 between Jean Amrouche, Ferhat Abbas, Albert Camus, and many other French intellectuals. It highlighted that the basis of this problem is essentially the huge percentage of illiteracy which was to be blamed on the colonial education policy and attitudes towards the native population. For more details see: Réjane le Baut, *Camus Amrouche: des Chemins qui s'écartent* (Alger: Casbah Éditions), 2014, pp. 105–16.
74. Mahfoud Bennoune, *The Making of Contemporary Algeria*, pp. 67–8.
75. Marnia Lazreg, *The Eloquence of Silence*, p. 62.
76. Jules Ferry, 'Le gouvernement de l'Algérie', Rapport au nom de la commission sénatoriale, 1891. Cited in Françoise Lorcerie, 'L'islam comme contre-identification française : trois moments', *L'Année du Maghreb, Dossier: Femmes, famille et droit* (Paris: CNRS Éditions), 2005–6, pp. 509–36. http://anneemaghreb.revues.org/161?lang=ar, Accessed 26 August 2013.
77. Quoted in, Spencer D. Segalla, *The Moroccan Soul: French Education, Colonial Ethnology, and Muslim Resistance, 1912–1956* (Lincoln: University of Nebraska Press, 2009), p. 1.
78. For more details see: William A. Hoisington, *Lyautey and the French conquest of Morocco* (New York: St Martin's Press, 1995).
79. Segalla, *The Moroccan Soul*, p. 12.
80. William Hoisington, *Lyautey and the French Conquest of Morocco*, p. 52.
81. Segalla, *The Moroccan Soul*, p. 7.
82. Ibid., p. 8.
83. Jeunes Tunisiens (Young Tunisians): They were a group of young French-educated Tunisian intellectuals who, in 1907, formed a political party headed by Ali Bash Hamba and Bashir Sfar. Known for their liberal views and for their adoption of French ways, they soon turned into a nationalist party that opposed the French protectorate established in 1883 and demanded total Tunisian control of the government and administration of the country and full citizenship

rights for both Tunisians and the French. Their protests against French occupation of Tripolitania among other things resulted in severe repression of their party members and the exiling of their leaders, including Ali Bash Hamba in 1912. They remerged in 1920 and reorganised themselves as the *Destour Party*, which led Tunisia to its independence.
84. Mahfoud Smati, *Les Jeunes Algériens*, p. 180.
85. Ibid, p. 181. My emphasis.
86. Ibid, p. 157.
87. Ferhat Abbas, *L'Entente franco-musulmane*, Février, 1936.
88. Algerian nationalists spoke of 45,000 victims, while the French general Tubert spoke of 15,000. On the European side, 103 were listed as killed and 110 as wounded. Benjamin Stora, *Algeria 1830–2000*, p. 22.
89. Ibid.
90. Ibid., p. 102.
91. Ibid., p. 110.

Notes to Chapter 3

1. Jabra Ibrahim Jabra, 'Modern Arabic Literature and the West', *Journal of Arabic Literature*, Vol. 2, 1971 (pp. 76–91), p. 76.
2. Albion Small, quoted in Oliver Cox, *The Foundations of Capitalism* (New York: Philosophy Library, 1959), p. 21.
3. H. V. Canter, 'Roman Civilization in North Africa', *The Classical Journal*, Vol. 35, No. 4 (Jan., 1940), pp. 197–208. Available at: http://www.jstor.org/stable/3291373. Accessed 20 March 2017.
4. William E. Watson, *Tricolor and Crescent*, p. 2.
5. For further details see: Mgr Alexandre Pons, La nouvelle Église d'Afrique ou le catholicisme en Algérie, en Tunisie et au Maroc depuis 1830 (Tunis: Édition Librairie Louis Namura, 1930).
6. Clissold in Watson, *Tricolor and Crescent*, p. 17.
7. For more details on the bombardment of Algiers see: Abdeljelil Temimi, 'Documents Turcs inédits sur le bombardement d'Alger en 1816', *Revue de l'Occident Musulman et de la Méditerranée*, Vol. 5, No. 5, 1968, pp. 111–13.
8. Several accounts of slavery and captivity at the hands of the Barbary Corsairs have been written by the captives. See for example: William Okeley; Eben-Ezer; or, *A Small Monument of Great Mercy, Appearing in the Miraculous Deliverance of William Okeley . . . from the Miserable Slavery of Algiers* (1676). See also: Adam Elliot, 'A Narrative of my Travails, Captivity, and Escape from Salle, in the

Kingdom of Fez,' in *A Modest Vindication of Titus Oates the Salamanca-Doctor from Perjury* (1682); Thomas Phelps, *A True Account of the Captivity of Thomas Phelps, at Machaness* [Meknes] *in Barbary* (1685); Francis Brooks, *Barbarian Cruelty. Being a True History of the Distressed Condition of the Christian Captives under the Tyranny of Mully Ishmael Emperor of Morocco, and King of Fez and Macqueness in Barbary* (1693). For more details see Nabil Matar, *Turks, Moors, and Englishmen in the Age of Discovery* (New York: Columbia University Press, 1999), pp. 181–3.

9. Watson, p. 18.
10. For more details see: Moshe Gershovich, *French Military Rule in Morocco: colonialism and its consequences* (London: Frank Cass, 2000).
11. For a detailed account on the occupation of Morocco, see Moshe Gershovich, *French Military Rule in Morocco*.
12. Ira M. Lapidus, *A History of Islamic Societies* (Cambridge: Cambridge University Press, 2002). pp. 315–16.
13. Rifāʿa Rāfiʿ al-Ṭahṭāwī (1801–73) was in Paris between 1826 and 1831. For more details see Rasheed El-Enany, *Arab Representations of the Occident: East-West encounters in Arabic fiction* (London and New York: Routledge, 2006), p. 33.
14. Rifāʿa Rāfiʿ al-Ṭahṭāwī, *Takhlīs al-Ibrīz fī Talkhīs Bārīz* (The extraction of Gold in the Summary of Paris) (Cairo: Al-Hayʾa al-Misriyya al-ʿĀmma lil-Kitāb, 1974). It was first printed in Cairo, 1834. It was reprinted in 1848, 1905, and 1958.
15. Ahmad Fāris Al-Shidyāq, *Al-Sāq ʿala al-Sāq fī mā huwa al-Fariyāq (La vie et les aventures de Fariac)* (Paris, 1855. Reprinted in Cairo in 1919 and 1920. Beirut: Dār Maktabat al-Hayāt, 1966).
16. Rasheed El-Enany, *Arab Representations of the Occident*, p. 33.
17. Julia A. Clancy-Smith, *Rebel and Saint: Muslim Notables, Populist Protest, Colonial Encounters (Algeria and Tunisia, 1800–1904)* (Berkeley: University of California Press, 1994), pp. 44–5.
18. Mahfoud Smati, *Les Jeunes Algériens*, p. 107.
19. Ibid. See also: Eugène Daumas, *La vie arabe et la société musulmane* (Paris: Michel Lévy Frères, 1869), pp. 459–64.
20. For more details see: Raphael Danziger, *Abd al-Qadir and the Algerians: Resistance to the French and Internal Consolidation.* (New York: Holmes & Meier, 1977), and Ahmed Bouyerdene, *Emir Abd el-Kader: Hero and Saint of Islam*, trans. Gustavo Polit (Bloomington: World Wisdom, 2012).

21. For a detailed account on popular uprisings and revolts see: Julia A. Clancy-Smith, *Rebel and Saint: Muslim Notables, Populist Protest, Colonial Encounters (Algeria and Tunisia, 1800–1904)* (Berkeley: University of California Press, 1994).
22. In terms of grievances, the French Prime minister refers to the flywhisk incident of 1827. The Dey of Algiers asked the French consul about the repayment of a long overdue loan and the latter answered him that the French King would not enter into correspondence with him on a question such as debt. The Dey took offence and hit the consul with his flywhisk and ordered him to leave the hall.
23. Guillaume Berthier De Sauvigny, *Bourbon Restoration*, trans. Lynn M. Case (Philadelphia: University of Philadelphia Press, 1966), pp. 435–6.
24. For more details see Gershovich, *French Military Rule in Morocco*.
25. Mohammed Ould Cheikh was born on 23 February 1906 in Bechar. He belonged to a noble family from the well-known Ouled Sidi Cheikh tribe in Southern Algeria. His father was Agha Cheikh Ben Abdallah who worked for the French authorities and was keen to bridge the gap between them and the people of his region. Mohammed Ould Cheikh attended French primary school in his hometown and High school at the Oran Lycée. He died following a long illness in 1938.
26. Mohammed Ould Cheikh, *Myriem dans les Palmes* (Oran: Éditions Plaza, 1936), p. 164.
27. Ibid.
28. Ibid., p. 163.
29. Ibid., p. 221.
30. Ibid., p. 164.
31. Mahfoud Smati, *Les Jeunes Algériens*, p. 109.
32. This is because Islam was the only ideological fixture that held the country together. Algeria as a political nation was rarely mentioned in the literature of the nineteenth century and its existence only occurred with the birth of Algerian nationalism in the twentieth century. It is in fact this reality that made Ferhat Abbas deny the existence of an Algerian nation in 1931 and argue for the status of the 'Français Musulman'. Although Abdulhamid Ibn Badis, the founder of the association of the Algerian ʿUlama, disagreed with Abbas, by insisting that the Algerian nation always existed, he too did not believe in a political Algerian nation. Like Abbas he militated for the integration of the Muslim Algerians into the French Polity.
33. Pierre Bourdieu, *Sociologie de l'Algérie* (Paris: Presses Universitaires de France, 1958), p. 10.

34. Frantz Fanon, *The Wretched of the Earth*, trans. Constance Farrington (London: Penguin Books, 2001), p. 171.
35. Ibid., p. 169.
36. Joseph Leriche, 'Les algériens parmi nous', *Cahiers Nord-Africains*, No. 70, December 1958, p. 215.
37. Daniel Panzac, *Les Corsaires barbaresques*, p. 5.
38. Tafilalt, or Tafilalet is a region and also the most important oasis of the Moroccan part of the Sahara Desert.
39. Quoted in Aldrich, p. 98. My emphasis.
40. *Myriem dans les Palmes,* p. i.
41. Chukri Khodja, *El-Euldj: Captif des Barbaresques*, first published by (Arras: I.N.S.A.P., 1923). The edition used in this chapter is reprinted by Algiers: Office des Publications Universitaires, 1992.
42. Shukri Khodja is the Pseudonym of Hassen Khodja Hamdane. He was born on 11 February 1891 in the Casbah of Algiers. His maternal grandfather was the president of the tribunal of Algiers and also an author. He pursued his Primary education at the école d'indigènes in Soustara, Algiers. At age 16, he lost his father and worked as an accountant. A year later he resumed his education at the *Madrasa* of Algiers to graduate with a Diplome Supérieur (High school diploma) in 1922. He then became a legal interpreter and retired in 1960. He was profoundly affected by the outbreak of the Algerian War of Independence, which signalled the end of everything in which he believed. A few years before his death in 1967 he became severely depressed and destroyed all his manuscripts.
43. See *El-Euldj: Captif des Barbaresques*, p. 5, and p. 8.
44. Famines: the first recorded famines experienced by the people of Algeria took place under French colonial rule. One of the policies of French colonialism was to starve the indigenous populations by depriving them of their main source of livelihood in the form of their best arable agricultural land and imposing oppressive land laws. By the time of the centenary of the French occupation of Algeria poverty had resulted in thousands of roaming beggars and day workers who left their villages in search of work in the cities. *La Dépêche algérienne* published several articles on this subject in the 1930s :

> 'Nous avons longé de misérables mechtas, vu d'innombrables mendiants. Les indigènes sont miséreux [. . .] La dureté des uns et l'aveuglement des autres ont apporté la famine aux indigènes d'Algérie, une famine sur laquelle nous n'avons guère besoin de nous étendre'

We passed impoverished settlements, encountered innumerable beggars. The natives are destitute [. . .] The harshness of some and the blindness of others have brought famine to Algeria's natives, a famine on which we do not need to expatiate.

André Noushi, *Enquête sur le niveau de vie des populations rurales constantinoises de la conquête jusqu'en 1919* (Paris: PUF, 1961), p. 49, quoted in Peter Dunwoodie, *Francophone Writing in Transition: Algeria 1900–1945* (Peter Lang, 2005), p. 33.

See also: Albert Camus, *Chroniques algériennes, 1939–1958*, and *Misère de la Kabylie*.
45. *El-Euldj: Cptif des Barbaresques*, p. 17 and p. 19.
46. Ibid., p. 18.
47. Ibid., pp. 28–9.
48. Ibid., p. 2.
49. Ibid., pp. 46–9.
50. Ibid., p. 58.
51. See Ibid., p. 64.
52. Ibid., p. 33.
53. Ibid., p. 63.
54. Frantz Fanon, *The Wretched of the Earth*, p. 169.
55. See *El-Euldj: Captif des Barbaresques*, pp. 96–7, and p. 102.
56. Abdelkader Djeghloul, 'Un Romancier de l'identité perturbée et de l'assimilation impossible Chukri Khodja', *Revue de l'Occident musulman et de la Méditerranée*, vol. 37, No. 37, 1984, pp. 81–96.
57. Abdelkader Djeghloul, 'Un Romancier de l'identité perturbée et de l'assimilation impossible Chukri Khodja', p. 90.
58. In their book, *Les Chrétiens d'Allah: L'histoire extraordinaire des renégats, XVIe et XVIIe siècles* (Paris: Perrin, 1989), Bartolomé and Lucile Bennassar bring to light the trajectory of the Christian captives who converted to Islam after being held in captivity by the Barbary corsairs in the sixteenth and seventeenth century.
59. Omar Lediouse' is his Muslim name, possibly to connote 'Le Dieu'.
60. *El-Euldj: Captif des Barbaresques*, p. 133.
61. Ibid.
62. Ibid., p. 116.
63. Ibid., pp. 114–15.

Notes to Chapter 4

1. Ferhat Abbas, 'En Marge du Nationalisme: La France, c'est moi', *L'Entente franco-musulmane*, No. 24, 27 February 1936.
2. Chukri Khodja, *Mamoun: L'Ébauche d'un idéal*, first published in 1928 by Alger: Éditions Radot. Current copy is a new edition by (Alger: Office des Publications Universitaires, 1992), p. 180 & pp. 106–7.
3. Bill Ashcroft, Gareth Griffiths, and Helen Tiffin, *The Empire writes Back: Theory and Practice in Post-Colonial Literatures* (London and New York: Routledge, 2002), p. 5.
4. Homi Bhabha, 'Of Mimicry and Man: The Ambivalence of Colonial Discourse', *October*, Vol. 28, Discipleship: A Special Issue on Psychoanalysis, Spring, 1984 (pp. 125–33), p. 126. Bhabha's emphasis.
5. Preface to Mohammed El Azziz Kessous, *La Vérité sur le malaise algérien* (Bône: Imprimerie Rapide, 1935).
6. Abdelkader Djeghloul, 'La Formation des Intellectuels Algériens Modernes 1880–1930', in Omar Carlier et al., *Lettres, Intellectuels et Militants en Algérie, 1880–1959* (Alger: OPU, 1988) (pp. 3–29), p. 15.
7. Abdelkader Hadj Hamou, *Zohra la femme du mineur* (Alger: Éditions Associés), 1925. Many consider this novel to be the first Francophone Maghrebi and Algerian novel.
8. Abdelkader Hadj Hamou (1891–1953), was born in the city of Méliana in West Algeria. He was son of a *Cadi* (Judge in Muslim Jurisdiction) who was appointed by the French authorities as the honorary Judge of his city. His son Abdelkader Hadj Hamou received a French education and was naturalised to become a Français Musulman. He worked closely with the Algérianist literary movement and was elected vice-president of the Association des Écrivains Algériens. According to Jean Déjeux, Robert Randau, keen to encourage a Francophone literature written by native Algerians, edited the manuscript of *Zohra la femme du mineur* going as far as correcting spelling and grammatical errors. For more details see: Jean Déjeux, 'La Littérature algérienne d'expression Française', *Cahiers Nord-africains*, No. 61, 1957, p. 17. See also, Zahia Smail Salhi, *Politics, Poetics and the Algerian Novel* (Lampeter: The Edwin Mellen Press, 1999).
9. *Zohra la femme du mineur*, p. 70.
10. Ibid., p. 193.
11. Ibid., p. 20.

12. Caïd and Agha: are titles of the local aristocracy. The majority of this class opted for becoming collaborators with French authorities to safeguard their property and status. They were often used as intermediaries between the French authorities and their people while generally seen by the latter as traitors.
13. *Zohra la femme du mineur,* p. 103.
14. Ibid., p. 174.
15. Ibid., pp. 23–4.
16. Ibid., p. 23.
17. Fanon, *The Wretched of the Earth,* p. 191.
18. Abdelkader Fikri et Robert Randau, *Les Compagnons du jardin* (Paris: Donat Montchrestien, 1933), p. 99.
19. Albert Memmi, *The Colonizer and the Colonized* (Boston: Beacon Press, 1991), p. 90.
20. *Zohra la femme du mineur,* p. 68.
21. Bicôt: meaning 'kid', is the most common racist appellation given to native Maghrebis, which continues to be used even in the post-colonial era in France. The equivalent of 'bicôt' in English would be 'wog'.
22. Youpin: racially offensive ethnic slur to designate the Jews. The English equivalent would be Yid, or Kike.
23. Gaouri/Gawri: Plural Gouar/Gwar, is an identifying name used in the Maghreb for Europeans. It is derived from Ottoman Turkish gâvur, which means: one outside the Islamic faith. From the Maghreb this word found its way into the Spanish language. It entered the *Diccionario de la lengua española de la Real Academia Española* in 1925. According to Juan Goytisolo, *guiri* is a neologism, which derives from the Moroccan and Algerian Arabic *gaouri,* a word with a similar meaning applying to white Europeans.
24. *Zohra la femme du mineur,* p. 96.
25. Memmi, *The Colonizer and the Colonized,* p. 85.
26. Ibid., p. 4.
27. Ibid.
28. Ibid., p 3.
29. See Ferhat Abbas, *Le Jeune Algérien,* 2011, pp. 99–100.
30. See Fanon, *The Wretched of the Earth,* p. 179.
31. Chukri Khodja (1891–1967): His full name is Hassan Khodja Hamdan Chukri. He was born in Algiers. He trained as an accountant and then as a legal interpreter. He believed deeply in France's civilising mission and in Algeria as a French province. Chukri lived through the years of the Algerian revolution and

into post-colonial Algeria. Before his death in 1967 he went through a nervous breakdown and set alight all his works.
32. *Mamoun: L'Ébauche d'un idéal*, p. 24.
33. Ibid., pp. 16–17.
34. The Earl of Cromer, *Modern Egypt*, p. 164, quoted in Edward Said, *Orientalism*, p. 39.
35. Said, *Orientalism*, p. 49.
36. *Mamoun: L'Ébauche d'un idéal*, p. 54.
37. Ibid., pp. 18–19.
38. Fanon, *The Wretched of the Earth*, p. 190.
39. Charles Issawi (Editor and Translator), *An Arab Philosophy of History: Selections from the Prolegomena of Ibn Khaldun of Tunis*, (London: John Murray, 1950), pp. 51–2.
40. *Mamoun: L'Ébauche d'un idéal*, p. 77.
41. Ibid., p. 32.
42. Ibid., p. 34.
43. Ibid., p. 100.
44. Fanon, *Black Skin, White Masks*, p. 63.
45. *Mamoun: L'Ébauche d'un idéal*, p. 101 and p. 102.
46. Ibid., pp. 106–7.
47. *Mamoun: L'Ébauche d'un idéal*, p. 120.
48. Arab intellectuals of the twenties and thirties in the Middle East and North Africa donned a fez in addition to their European attire as a token of Muslim identity, which in a way is also an image of the French Muslim who mixes a European costume with a Muslim headgear. This appearance has become typical of the Arab nationalist elite who became their people's leaders who launched the Arab nationalist movements. See *Mamoun: L'Ébauche d'un idéal*, p. 121.
49. *Mamoun: L'Ébauche d'un idéal*, p. 121.
50. Ibid.
51. Marie-Paule Ha, 'From "Nos Ancêtres, les Gaulois" to "Leur Culture Ancestrale": Symbolic violence and the Politics of Colonial Schooling in Indo-china', *French Colonial History*, vol. 3, 2003 (101–17), p. 102.
52. Segalla, *The Moroccan Soul*, p. 10.
53. See *Mamoun: L'Ébauche d'un idéal*, pp. 70–7.
54. Ibid., pp. 77–8.
55. Frantz Fanon, *The Wretched of the Earth*, p. 178.
56. *Mamoun: L'Ébauche d'un idéal*, p. 168.

57. Ibid..
58. Ibid., p. 17.
59. Ibid., p. 183.
60. *Myriem dans les Palmes*, p. i.
61. Ibid., p. iii.
62. Ibid., p. 19.
63. Ibid.
64. Ibid., p. 21.
65. Ibid., p. 26.
66. Ibid., p. 18.
67. Ibid., p. 25.
68. Ibid., p. 28.
69. Ibid., p. iii.
70. *Mamoun: L'Ébauche d'un idéal*, p. 168.

Notes to Chapter 5

1. Hubertine Auclert, *Arab Women in Algeria*, edited and translated by Jacqueline Grenez Brovender (Warsaw and Berlin: De Gruyter Open Ltd, 2014), p. 21. My own emphasis. This book was first published as *Les Femmes arabes en Algérie* in 1900, many years after it was written. It was reedited in 2009 in Paris by Éditions L'Harmatan as part of the *Autrement Mêmes* book series, with an introduction by French-Algerian author Denis Brahimi.
2. For more details on this aspect see Zahia Smail Salhi, 'Colonial Visual Representations of the "Femmes d'Alger"', in *The Middle East Journal of Culture and Communications*, vol. 1, issue 1, 2008, pp. 80–93.
3. Malek Alloula, *The Oriental Harem*, p. 5.
4. See for example the work of the French historian of the conquest, V. A. Dieuzaide, *Histoire de l'Algérie 1830–1878* (Tome I, Oran: Imprimerie de l'association ouvrière – Heintz, Chazeau et Cie, 1880).
5. Hubertine Auclert (1848–1914), French feminist, well known for militating for women's rights in France from the mid-1870s. In 1876 she founded the Société le droit des femmes (The Rights of Women) through which she militated for French women's suffrage. In 1883 the organisation changed its name to better reflect its mission and became the Société le Suffrage des femmes (Women's Suffrage Society). Auclert is also known for introducing the term *feminisme* in the 1880s in her journal, *La Citoyenne*, as a feminist platform to criticise male domination and to make claims for women's rights and emancipation promised

by the French Revolution. She lived in Algeria from 1888 to 1892 with her husband Antonin Lévrier. After his death she returned to France.
6. Fadhma Ait Mansour Amrouche, *Histoire de ma vie,* first published by Librairie François Maspero, Paris, 1968. Translated into English by Dorothy Blair as *My Life Story*, and was published by The Women's Press in 1988.
7. Auclert, *Arab Women in Algeria*, p. 13.
8. Ibid., p. 1.
9. Ibid.
10. Ibid., p. 8.
11. Ibid.
12. Ibid.
13. Harazeli: a nomadic tribe in southern Algeria, known for their loyalty to the Emir Abd-el-Kader, who led a resistance against the French invaders from 1832 to 1847.
14. Assia Djebar, *Women of Algiers in their Apartment,* trans. Marjolijn de Jager (Charlottesville and London: University Press of Virginia, 1992), p. 143.
15. Ibid. See also, Zahia Smail Salhi, 'Between the Languages of Silence and the Woman's Word: Gender and Language in the Work of Assia Djebar', *International Journal of the Sociology of Language*, Special Issue on 'Language and Gender in the Mediterranean Region', vol. 190, 2008, pp. 79–101.
16. Le Général Dumas, *La Grande Kabylie, Etudes historiques,* Paris: Hachette, 1847, cited in Mostefa Lachraf, *L'Algérie, Nation et société* (Paris: Maspero, 1965), pp. 101–2.
17. Capitaine Carette, 'Algérie', In *L'Univers Pittoresques, Histoire et Description de tous les Peuples, de leurs Religions, Mœurs, Coutumes, Industrie* (Paris: Firmin Didot, 1850), pp. 30–1.
18. Baron Barchou de Penhoen, *Mémoires d'un officier d'état-major*.
19. Auclert, *Arab Women in Algeria*, p. 1.
20. E. Perret, *Récits algériens 1848–1886* (Paris: Bloud et Barral, n.d.), vol. 2, pp. 14–15.
21. Lalla Fatma Nsoumer (1830–63): Known in Algeria as Lalla Fatma and Lalla Fadhma Nsoumer (Fadhma is the Kabyle equivalent of the Arabic name Fatima), she was born on 10 July 1830 in the village of Werja in Kabylie. She is the daughter of Sidi Ahmed Mohammed, a notable Marabout who headed the Zawiya of Sidi Ahmed ou Mezyan in the nearby village of Soumer. From early childhood Fadhma was attracted to the study of the Qur'an which she memorised and taught to other children, notably after the death of her father

whom she succeeded along with her brother Si Mohand Tayeb in the running of the Zawiya, both as a centre of religious learning and as a spiritual Sufi sanctuary. Being devoted to such activities, Fatma soon earned her title of Lalla, meaning a Marabout woman who possessed spiritual powers. Choosing to devote her life to learning and religious piety, she ended her marital relationship with her maternal cousin Yahia nath Iboukhoulef, whom she married at age sixteen.

This was happening at a time when the Kabylie region, which was till then not reached by the French armies, became their target and started a massive offensive to pacify its inhabitants who fought relentlessly to oppose the occupation. Taken by the urgency of the moment Fatma Nsoumer decided to launch the call for *jihad* from her religious position. She rallied to her cause all the mosques and Zawayas of the region and organised as well as led an army of men and women in a well-structured rebellion against the occupants, causing the French armies under General Randon several defeats.

The Kabyle resistance was consolidated by the arrival of Mohamed ben Abdullah, known as Bou Baghla (meaning the owner of the mule, which he took with him wherever he went), in 1849. This mysterious man was said to be an officer in the army of the Emir Abdel Kader whose resistance was defeated in 1847. Refusing to surrender to the French, bou Baghla fled to Kabylie and joined the Kabyle fighters who soon discovered in him a very pious man and a relentless fighter. His arrival in the region had a great impact on Lalla Fatma who found in him a great companion in battle, a spiritual companion as well as a soulmate; the two heroes shared many traits. It is said that he too found in her an exemplary woman and that a strong friendship grew between the two combatants. It is also reported that although bou Baghla was also coming out of a marriage relationship after divorcing his wife, Fatma could not marry him as her ex-husband would not release her despite her refusal to live with him and despite many interventions by notable intermediaries to settle the divorce between them.

Fatma Nsoumer and Bou Baghla remained as good companions who often declared their platonic love for each other and continued to fight the occupiers side by side until the martyrdom of Bou Baghla on 26 December 1854. More determined than ever Fatma Nsoumer continued to strengthen the ranks of her followers and gave the French troops under General Randon (1795–1871) several defeats, mainly in the battle of Tachkirt, which took place on 18 July 1854. Three years later, General Randon returned to Kabylie with 45,000 troops with the aim of 'pacifying the region', which had remained the last bastion in the whole of Algeria to be subdued to French rule. The offensive was launched on the Eid al-Fitr day on the 24 May 1857 as a tactic to surprise the Kabyles. Under the shock Larb'a Nath Irathen fell in one day and in the place of its famous souk, Larb'a, a fortress named after Napoleon III, was erected as Fort Napoleon and later named as Fort National, as a symbol of the defeat of the resistance and the triumph of the French armies.

Lalla Fatma Nsoumer was arrested and sent to a detention camp at the Zawiya of Beni Slimane in Tablat, under the control of a *Bachagha* (local authority) loyal to the French. Six years later, she died at the age of 33 years.

In post-independence Algeria Fatma Nsoumer is remembered as a symbol of Algerian women's heroism and is praised for her wisdom, bravery and strong character. Algerian women remember her as a symbol of feminist agency and a role model for younger generations of women in their struggle for gender equality. An Algerian feminist association takes its name 'Tharwa Nfatma Nsoumer' meaning *Daughters of Fatma Nsoumer* from Lalla Fatma, both as a way to remember her martyrdom and as an example of a steadfast and fearless woman to be emulated by today's Algerian women in their struggle against patriarchy. For more details see: Boukhalfa Bitam, *Fadhma N'Soumer: Une autre lecture du combat de l'illustre fille de Werja* (Tizi Ouzou: Aurassi, 2000); Emile Carrey, *Récits de Kabylie: La Campagne de 1857* (Alger: G. A. L., 2004); Tahar Oussedik, *Lalla Fadhma n'Summer* (Alger: Laphomic, 1983); Zahia Smail Salhi, 'The Algerian Feminist Movement between Nationalism, Patriarchy and Islamism,' *Women's Studies International Forum*, Vol. 33, No. 2, March–April 2010, pp. 113–24.

22. E. Perret, *Récits algériens 1848–1886*, pp. 132–8. See also, Camille Lacoste-Dujardin, *La Vaillance des Femmes: Les Relations entre Femmes et Hommes Berbères de Kabylie* (Alger: Barzakh, 2010), pp. 105–12.
23. Louis Massignon, *Parole donnée* (Paris: Le Seuil, 1983), p. 144.
24. Jean Déjeux *Femmes D'Algérie: Légendes, Traditions, Histoire, Littérature* (Paris: La Boîte à Documents, 1987), pp. 73–119; see also by the same author, ' La Kahina: de l'histoire a la fiction littéraire. Mythes et Épopées', *Studi Magrebini* (Naples) vol. XV, 1983, pp. 1–42.
25. Jean Déjeux *Femmes D'Algérie*, pp. 151–97.
26. E. Perret, *Récits algériens 1848–1886*, pp. 14–15.
27. Dieuzaide, *Histoire de l'Algérie 1830–1878*, p. 387.
28. Ibid., p. 164.

29. Cited in Mahfoud Bennoune, *Les Algériennes Victimes de la Société Néopatriarchale* (Alger: Éditions Marinoor, 1999), p. 46.
30. Ibid.
31. Ibid., pp. 46–7.
32. Auclert, *Arab Women in Algeria*, p. 14.
33. Ibid., p. 8.
34. Ibid.
35. Ibid., p. 10
36. Ibid. My emphasis.
37. ʿAbd al-Rahman al-Jabarti, *Tarikh Muddat al-Firansi bi Misr*, ed. S. Moreh (Leiden: E. J. Brill, 1975), cited in Derek Hopwood, *Sexual Encounters*.
38. Auclert, *Arab Women in Algeria*, p. 16.
39. Ibid., p. 21.
40. Ibid.
41. Ibid., p. 23.
42. Lila Abu Lughod, 'Do Muslim Women Really Need Saving? Anthropological Reflections on Cultural Relativism and Its Others', *American Anthropologist*, Vol. 104, No. 3, September 2002, pp. 783–90.
43. Auclert, *Arab Women in Algeria*, p. 37.
44. Ibid., p. 16.
45. Lazreg, *The Eloquence of Silence*, p. 50.
46. Julia Clancy-Smith, 'Le regard colonial: Islam, genre et identités dans la fabrication de l'Algérie Française, 1830–1962', *Nouvelles Questions Féministes*, vol. 25: 1, 2006, pp. 25–40. Translated into English as 'The Colonial Gaze: Islam, Gender, and Identities in the Making of French Algeria'. Available at: https://arizona.pure.elsevier.com/en/publications/the-colonial-gaze-islam-gender-and-identities-in-the-making-of-fr.Accessed 10 October 2017.
47. Auclert, *Arab Women in Algeria*, p. 41.
48. Lazreg, *The Eloquence of Silence*, p. 63.
49. Ibid., p. 64.
50. Rebecca Rogers, *A Frenchwoman's Imperial Story: Madame Luce in Nineteenth-Century Algeria* (Stanford: Stanford University Press, 2013), p. 120.
51. Ibid., p. 64.
52. Lazreg, *The Eloquence of Silence*, p. 65.
53. Ibid., p. 65.
54. Rebecca Rogers, *A Frenchwoman's Imperial Story*, p. 145.
55. Auclert, *Arab Women in Algeria*, p. 39.

56. Ibid.
57. Rebecca Rogers, *A Frenchwoman's Imperial Story*, p. 173.
58. Mouloud Feraoun, *Les Chemins qui mentent* (Paris: Le Seuil, 1957), p. 145.
59. Fadhma Amrouche, *My Life Story*, p. 18. Although written in 1946, it was first published in French as *Histoire de ma vie*, in 1968.
60. Mouloud Feraoun, *Lettres à ses amis* (Alger: Bouchène, 1991).
61. Clement Lambing, *The French in Algiers*, trans. Lady Duff Gordon (New York: Wiley and Putnam, 1845), p. 6.
62. Fadhma Amrouche, *My Life Story*, p. 5.
63. Ibid., p. 6.
64. Ibid., p. 9.
65. Ibid., p. 8.
66. Ibid., p. 7.
67. Auclert, *Arab Women in Algeria*, pp. 41–2.
68. Fadhma Amrouche, *My Life Story*, pp. 10–11. This excerpt resonates with Tayeb Salih's *Season of Migration to the North*, where the protagonist recounts his experience having been one of those children picked from the street and taken to a colonial school.
69. Fadhma Amrouche, *My Life Story*, p.12.
70. Ibid.
71. Lazreg, *The Eloquence of Silence*, p. 49.
72. Fadhma Amrouche, *My Life Story*, p. 18. My emphasis.
73. Ibid., p. 19.
74. Ibid., p. 18.
75. Ibid., p. 28.
76. Ibid., p. 30.
77. Ibid., p. 29.
78. Ibid., p. 46.
79. Ibid., p. xii.

Notes to Chapter 6

1. Djamila Débêche, *Leila, Jeune fille d'Algérie* (Alger: Charras, 1947), p. 163.
2. Lazreg, *The Eloquence of Silence*, p. 98.
3. Imperial Feminism, also known as colonial feminism, is based on the appropriation of women's rights in the service of empire. It has been widely utilised by colonialist women during the nineteen and twentieth century in the Middle

East and North Africa to justify colonial aggression in the name of civilising or rescuing native women from the barbarity of their own people. Interestingly, this trope continues to be used at the present and became endemic during the US invasion of Afghanistan and Iraq.
4. Carolyn J. Eichner, 'La citoyenne in the World: Hubertine Auclert and Feminist Imperialism', *French Historical Studies*, Vol. 32, No. 1, Winter 2009, p. 72.
5. Yvonne Turin, *Affrontements culturels dans l'Algérie colonial: Ecoles, médicine, religion, 1830–1880* (Alger: Entreprise Nationale du Livre, 1983), p. 54. Cited in Lazreg, *The Eloquence of Silence*, p. 64. My emphasis
6. BGR, de Lens to Mme Réveillaud, 2 October 1922, cited in Ellen Amster '"The Harem Revealed" and the Islamic-French Family: Aline de Lens and a French Woman's Orient in Lyautey's Morocco', *French Historical Studies*, Vol. 32, No. 2, Spring 2009, p. 299.
7. Fadhma Amrouche, *My Life Story*, p. xii.
8. Jennifer Anne Boittin, 'Feminist Mediations of the Exotic: French Algeria, Morocco and Tunisia, 1921–39', *Gender & History*, Vol. 22, No. 1, April 2010, p. 137.
9. Ibid., p. 136.
10. Ibid., p. 137.
11. Neil MacMaster 'The Colonial "Emancipation" of Algerian Women, the Marriage Law of 1959 and the Failure of Legislation on Women's Rights in the Post-Independence Era', Stichproben. Wiener Zeitschrift für kritische Afrikastudien Nr. 12/2007, 7. Jg., p. 98.
12. For a detailed account of native women's work during the War of Independence see: Fédération de France du FLN, *La Femme Algérienne dans la Révolution: Documents et Témoignages Inédits* (Alger: ENAG Éditions, 2006); Monique Gadant, *Le Nationalisme Algérien et les Femmes* (Paris: Éditions L'Harmattan, 1995), and Diane Sambron, *Les Femmes Algériennes pendant la Colonisation* (Alger: Éditions Casbah), 2013.
13. Fanon, *L'An V de la révolution algérienne* p. 19.
14. Zahia Smail Salhi, 'The Algerian Feminist Movement between Nationalism, Patriarchy and Islamism', p. 115.
15. For more details see Zahia Smail Salhi, 'The Algerian Feminist Movement between Nationalism, Patriarchy and Islamism'.
16. Lazreg, *The Eloquence of Silence*, p. 135.
17. Ibid.
18. Fanon, *A Dying Colonialism* (New York: Grove Press, 1967), p. 64.

19. Fadila Ahmed, 'Les deux geoliers de la femme', *Al-Manār*, 24 July 1953, cited in Neil MacMaster 'The Colonial "Emancipation" of Algerian Women", p. 98.
20. Djamila Débêche, *Leila, Jeune fille d'Algérie* (Alger: Charras, 1947).
21. Djamila Débêche was born in Sétif, on the Eastern side of the Atlas Mountains in Algeria, in 1926. She remains a lesser-known author despite her major contributions to early Algerian Francophone literature on the one hand and the beginnings of the Algerian feminist movement in the 1940s on the other. In 1947 she launched *L'Action*, a feminist review in which she published most of her feminist writings. She also published *Les Musulmans algériens et la scolarisation* (Algerian Muslim and Education) in 1950 and *L'Enseignement de la langue arabe en Algérie et le droit de vote aux femmes algériennes* (The Teaching of Arabic in Algeria and Women's Suffrage Right) in 1951, two volumes of essays on the importance of education for native Algerian women and on suffrage and other political rights.
22. *Leila, Jeune fille d'Algérie*, p. 9.
23. Ibid.
24. Ibid.
25. Ibid., pp. 44–6.
26. Auclert, *Arab Women in Algeria*, p. 41.
27. *Leila, Jeune fille d'Algérie*, p. 77.
28. Lazreg, *The Eloquence of Silence*, pp. 62–3.
29. *Leila, Jeune fille d'Algérie*, pp. 18–19.
30. Ibid., p. 36.
31. Ibid., pp. 55–6.
32. Ibid., p. 99.
33. Ibid., p. 136.
34. Ibid., p. 130.
35. Ibid., p. 77.
36. Ibid., p. 157.
37. Ibid., pp. 95–6.
38. Ibid., p. 99.
39. Ibid., p. 153.
40. Mahfoud Smati, *Les Jeunes Algériens*, p. 141.
41. Ibid., p. 157.
42. Ibid., p. 161.
43. Other such reports include: Mohammed Aziz Kessous, *La Vérité sur le Malaise*

Algérien (Bône: Imprimerie Rapide, 1935); Rabah Zenati, *Le Problème Algérien vue par un indigène* (Paris: Comité de l'Afrique Française, 1938), and Mohammed Lechani's, *Le Malaise Algérien* (Alger: Imprimeries Pfeiffer et Assant, 1939). All of these reports were written in the pre-WWII period.
44. *Leila, Jeune fille d'Algérie*, p. 161.
45. Djamila Débêche, *Aziza* (Alger: Imprimerie Imbert), 1955, p. 9.
46. *Aziza*, p. 9.
47. Memmi, *The Colonizer and the Colonized*, p. 124.
48. Ibid.
49. Ibid., p. 125.
50. *Aziza*, p. 9.
51. Ibid. p. 38.
52. Ibid., p. 113.
53. Ibid., p. 123.
54. Memmi, *The Colonizer and the Colonized*, p. 121.
55. For more details see Claude Liauzu, *Passeurs de Rives: Changements d'identité dans le Maghreb Colonial* (Paris: L'Harmattan, 2000), pp. 26–30.
56. Jacques Vergès obituary (5 March 1925–15 August 2013), *The Guardian*, 16 August 2013. https://www.theguardian.com/world/2013/aug/16/jacques-verges. Accessed 11 September 2018.
57. *Aziza*, p. 14.
58. Ibid., p. 124.
59. Ibid., p. 135.
60. Ibid., p. 140.
61. *Leila, Jeune fille d'Algérie*, pp. 150–6.
62. Ibid., p. 153.
63. *Aziza*, p. 124.
64. Ibid., p. 30.
65. Y. Isaac, *Le Thème de L'Aliénation dans le Roman Maghrébin d'Expression Française: 1952–1956* (Sherbrooke: CELEF, 1972), p. 138.

Notes to Chapter 7

1. Jean Amrouche, 'Quelques raisons de la révolte algérienne', p. 113.
2. This is the figure given by the PPA. James McDougall estimates the figure to be between 6,000 and 8,000. James McDougall, *A History of Algeria* (Cambridge: Cambridge University Press, 2017), p. 180. According to Benjamin Stora, 'The French general Tubbert spoke of 15,000 killed among the Muslim population.

Algerian nationalists put forward the figure of 45,000 dead', *A Short History of Algeria: 1830–2000*, p. 22.

3. For a detailed account of the causes and effects of 8 May 1945 see James McDougall, *A History of Algeria*, pp. 179–94.
4. Stora, *A Short History of Algeria: 1830–2000*, p. 22.
5. Ibid.
6. Memmi, *The Colonizer and the Colonized*, p. 86.
7. Ibid.
8. Jean Amrouche, 'La France d'Europe et la France d'Afrique', *Le Figaro*, 1945.
9. Albert Camus, *L'Étranger* (Paris: Gallimard, 1942).
10. For more details see Rejane Le Baut, *Camus, Amrouche: Des Chemins qui s'écartent*.
11. James McDougall, *History and the Culture of Nationalism in Algeria*. My Emphasis,
12. Memmi, *The Colonizer and the Colonized*, p. 121.
13. Rejane Le Baut, *Camus, Amrouche*, p. 28.
14. Ibid., p. 29.
15. Memmi, *The Colonizer and the Colonized*, pp. 88–9.
16. Jean Amrouche, 'Quelques raisons de la révolte algérienne', *Économie et Humanisme*, March–April 1956. Cited in Alain Romey, 'Jean El Mouhoub Amrouche, ou le dilemme d'une solidarité controversée (1945–1961)', p. 112.
17. Ibid., p. 114.
18. Memmi, *The Colonizer and the Colonized*, p. 141.
19. Jean Amrouche, 'Quelques raisons de la révolte algérienne', p. 113.
20. Ferhat Abbas, *Le Jeune Algérien*, p. 99.
21. Mouloud Feraoun, *Le Fils du Pauvre* (Alger: ENAL, 1986). The novel was rejected by Les Éditions Latines who wanted to impose a preface by a French author whom Feraoun did not know. He then took the manuscript to Les Cahiers du Nouvel Humanisme who published it at the authors' cost in 1950. The first edition of one thousand copies sold out very quickly. A second edition followed in 1954 but did not contain the last two parts of the first edition which, on the advice on Feraoun's friend Emmanuel Robles, were saved for a sequel novel to *Le Fils du Pauvre*.
22. Mouloud Feraoun, *Lettres à ses amis*, p. 205.
23. Mohammed Dib, *La Grande maison* (Paris: Le Seuil, 1952), p. 7.
24. Mouloud Mammeri, *La Colline Oubliée* (Paris: Plon, 1952).
25. Mouloud Feraoun, *Lettres à ses amis*, p. 158.

26. Wadi Bouzar and Andrea Page, 'The French-Language Algerian Novel', *Research in African Literatures*, Vol. 23, No. 2, Summer, 1992 (pp. 51–9), p. 52.
27. Jean Amrouche, 'La France d'Europe et la France d'Afrique', *Le Figaro*, 1945.
28. Mouloud Mammeri, *La Colline Oubliée,* p. 32.
29. Mouloud Mammeri, *Le Sommeil du Juste,* p.128.
30. Jean Amrouche, 'Quelques raisons de la révolte algérienne', *Économie et Humanisme*, March–April, 1956.
31. Mouloud Mammeri, *Le Sommeil du Juste,* p. 139.
32. Mouloud Mammeri, *Le Sommeil du Juste,* p. 145. In Kabyle culture the act of urinating on witchcraft, or charms and amulets is the known remedy to annul their effect.
33. Frantz Fanon, *The Wretched of the Earth*, p. 175.
34. Mouloud Mammeri, *L'Opium et le bâton* (Paris: Plon, 1965).
35. Frantz Fanon, *The Wretched of the Earth*, p. 175.
36. Simone De Beauvoir and Giséle Halimi, *Djamila Boubacha: the story of torture of a young Algerian girl which shocked liberal French opinion,* p. 9.
37. Memmi, *The Colonizer and the Colonized*, p. 147.
38. Ibid., p. 147.
39. Rejane Le Baut, *Camus, Amrouche,* p. 120. My emphasis.
40. Marie-Aimée Helie Lucas, 'Women, Nationalism and Religion in the Algerian Liberation Struggle' in Margot Badran and Miriam Cooke (eds), *Opening the Gates: A Century of Arab Feminist Writing* (Virago, 1992) (pp. 105–14), p.109.
41. Arabisation was supported by Ahmed Ben Bella who headed the new state from 1963 to 1965, by Houari Boumédienne who ruled from 1965 to 1978, and by Chadli Bendjedid until his demise in 1991. Even in the midst of the war against Islamic terrorism the Arabisation project was not forgotten; Liamine Zéroual declared that total Arabisation was going to be definitively implemented by 5 July 1998, the anniversary of independence. Under President Bouteflika things took a decisive turn; His declaration that Berber would never become a national language, was followed by riots in the Berber region resulting in many deaths. Finally, in 2002 President Bouteflika declared Berber a national language, and in 2016 it won the status of an official language.
42. Fatima Sadiqi, *Women, Gender and Language in Morocco* (Leiden and Boston: Brill, 2003), p.49.
43. Anne Emmanuelle Berger (ed.), *Algeria in Others' Languages* (Ithaca and London: Cornell University Press, 2002), p. 2.
44. President Chadli Benjedid could barely decipher the written content of his first

speech. Breaking with this tradition, the late President Mohammed Boudiaf was the first Algerian president to have addressed the people in colloquial Arabic in 1992.

45. Malek Haddad, *La Dernière impression* (Paris: Julliard, 1958); *Je t'offrirai une gazelle* (Paris: Julliard, 1959); *L'Élève et la leçon* (Paris; Julliard, 1960); *Le Quai aux fleurs ne répond plus* (Paris: Julliard, 1962).
46. Malek Haddad, *Écoute et je t'appelle-poemes, précédé* de *Les Zéros tournent en rond*-Essai (Paris: Maspéro, 1961).
47. Ibid., p. 9.
48. Rachid Boudjedra, *Le Démantèlement* (Paris: Denoël, 1982*).*
49. Hafid Gafaiti, 'The Monotheism of the Other: Language and De/Construction of National Identity in Postcolonial Algeria', in Anne Emmanuelle Berger (ed.), *Algeria in Others' Languages* (Ithaca and London: Cornell University Press, 2002), p. 27.
50. Assia Djebar, *Les Enfants du nouveau monde* (Paris: Julliard, 1962).
51. Assia Djebar, *Les Allouettes naïves* (Paris: Julliard, 1967).
52. Assia Djebar, *Women of Algiers in their Apartment,* trans. Marjolijn de Jager (Charlottesville and London: University Press of Virginia, 1992), p. 176.
53. Assia Djebar, 'Du Français comme butin', *La quinzaine littéraire* 436, March 16–31, 1985, p. 25.
54. Interview with Kateb Yacine by Geneviève Serreau, 'Situation de l'écrivain Algerien', *Les Lettres Modernes* (July–August, 1956), p. 108.
55. Assia Djebar, *Women of Algiers in their Apartment,* p. 184.
56. Ibid., p. 196.
57. Marsaud, Olivia, 'Les écrivains Algériens a l'honneur'. http://forum.dzfoot.com. Accessed 7 June 2006. See also; Assia, Djebar, 'Du Français comme butin', p. 25.
58. Leïla Sebbar, *La Seine était rouge* (Paris: Thierry Magnier, 1999).
59. Julia Clancy Smith, 'North Africa and France: Imperialism, Colonialism, and Women, 1830–1962'. Author's interviews with Dorra Bouzid, La Marsa, Tunisia, June–July 2009. http://africanhistory.oxfordre.com/view/10.1093/acrefore/9780190277734.001.0001/acrefore-9780190277734–e-97. Accessed 12 September 2018.
60. Ferhat Abbas, *La Nuit coloniale*, p. 233.

Notes to Afterword

1. Michel Foucault, 'Truth and Power', in C. Gordon (ed.): *Power/knowledge. Selected Interviews & Other Writings by Michel Foucault, 1972–1977* (Brighton: Harvester, 1980), p. 131.
2. Ferhat Abbas, *De la Colonie vers la Province,* p. 139.
3. Ibid., p. 99.

Bibliography

Abbas, Ferhat, *Le Jeune Algérien* (Paris: La Jeune Parque, 1931).
Abbas, Ferhat, *L'Entente franco-musulmane* (Février, 1936).
Abbas, Ferhat, *J'accuse l'Europe* (Alger: Libération, 1944).
Abbas, Ferhat, *La Nuit coloniale* (Paris: Julliard, 1962).
Abbas, Ferhat, *Le Jeune Algérien: De la Colonie vers la Province (1930), suivi de Rapport au Maréchal Pétain (Avril 1941)* (Alger: Livres Éditions, 2011).
Abdeljelil Temimi, 'Documents Turcs inédits sur le bombardement d'Alger en 1816', *Revue de l'Occident Musulman et de la Méditerranée*, Vol. 5, No. 5, 1968, pp. 111–33.
Abdel-Malek, Anouar, 'Orientalism in Crisis,' *Diogenes*, 44, 1963, pp. 104–12.
Abu-Lughod, Ibrahim, *The Arab Rediscovery of Europe: A Study in Cultural Encounters* (London: Saqi Books, 2011).
Abu-Lughod, Lila, 'Zones of Theory in the Anthropology of the Arab World,' *Annual Review of Anthropology*, Vol. 18, 1989, pp. 267–306.
Abu Lughod, Lila, 'Do Muslim Women Really Need Saving? Anthropological Reflections on Cultural Relativism and Its Others', *American Anthropologist*, Vol. 104, No. 3, September 2002, pp. 783–90.
Ageron, Charles-Robert, *Histoire de l'Algérie contemporaine* (Paris: Presses Universitaires de France, 1970).
Ageron, Charles-Robert, *Les Algériens Musulmans et la France (1871–1919)*, Vol. 1 (Paris: Presses Universitaires de France, 1968).
Ahmed, Fadila, 'Les deux geoliers de la femme', *Al-Manār*, 24 July 1953.
Al-Azm, Sadik J. 'Orientalism, Occidentalism, and Islamism', Keynote Address to 'Orientalism and Fundamentalism in Islamic and Judaic Critique: A Conference Honouring Sadik Al-Azm', *Comparative Studies of South Asia, Africa and the Middle East*, Vol. 30, No.1, 2010, pp. 6–13.

Al-Azmeh, Aziz and Effie Fokas (eds), *Islam in Europe: Diversity, Identity and Influence* (Cambridge: Cambridge University Press, 2007).
Aldrich, Robert, *Greater France: A History of French Overseas Expansion* (London: Macmillan Press, 1996).
Al-Jabarti, ᶜAbd al-Rahman, *Tārikh Muddat al-Firansī bi Misr*, ed. S. Moreh (Leiden: E. J. Brill, 1975).
Alloula, Malek, *The Colonial Harem* (Manchester: Manchester University Press, 1986).
Al-Shidyāq, Ahmad Fāris, *Al-Sāq ᶜala al-sāq fī mā huwa al-fariyāq* (*La vie et les aventures de Fariac*) (Paris: B. Duprat, 1855).
Al-Ṭahṭāwī, Rifāᶜa Rāfiᶜ, *Takhlīs al-ibrīz fī talkhīs bārīz* (The extraction of Gold in the Summary of Paris) (Cairo: Al-Hay'a al-Misriyya al-ᶜĀmma lil-Kitāb (1834) 1974).
Amrouche, Fadhma Aït Mansour, *Histoire de ma vie* (Paris: Librairie François Maspèro, 1968).
Amrouche, Fadhma, *My Life Story*, trans. Dorothy Blair (London: The Women's Press, 1988).
Amrouche, Jean El Mouhoub, *Journal 1928–1962*, Présenté par Tassadit Yacine (Alger: Éditions Alpha, 2009).
Amrouche, Jean, 'La France d'Europe et la France d'Afrique', *Le Figaro*, 1945.
Amrouche, Jean, 'Quelques raisons de la révolte algérienne, *Économie et Humanisme*, Mars-Avril, 1956.
Amster, Ellen, '"The Harem Revealed" and the Islamic-French Family: Aline de Lens and a French Woman's Orient in Lyautey's Morocco', *French Historical Studies*, Vol. 32, No. 2, Spring 2009, pp. 279–312.
Ashcroft, Bill, Gareth Griffiths, and Helen Tiffin, *The Empire Writes Back: Theory and Practice in Post-Colonial Literatures* (London and New York: Routledge, 2002).
Ashcroft, Bill, Gareth Griffiths, and Helen Tiffin, *Post-Colonial Studies: The Key Concepts* (London and New York: Routledge, 2010).
Auclert, Hubertine, *Arab Women in Algeria*, edited and translated by Jacqueline Grenez Brovender (Warsaw and Berlin: De Gruyter Open Ltd, 2014).
Barbour, Neville, 'Algeria', in Colin Legum, ed., *Africa: A Handbook to the Continent* (New York: Praeger, 1967), pp. 5–20.
Barthélemy d'Herbelot, de Molainville, *Bibliothèque orientale, ou dictionnaire universel contenant tout ce qui regarde la connaissance des peuples de l'Orient*, 4 vols (The Hague: Quatro, 1777–99).
Baudrillard, Jean, *The Spirit of Terrorism* (New York and London: Verso, 2002).

Bedwell, William, *Mohammedis imposturae*, 1615, and Humphrey Prideaux, *The True Nature of Imposture Fully Displayed in the Life of Mahomet*, 1697.
Bellamy, James A., 'Arabic Names in the Chansons de Roland: Saracen Gods, Frankish Swords, Roland's Horse, and the Oliphant', *Journal of the American Orientalist Society*, 107, 1987.
Ben Ali, Saad and René Pottier, *La tente noire, roman saharien* (Paris: les œuvres représentatives, 1933).
Ben Jelloun, Tahar, *La Nuit Sacrée* (Paris: Le Seuil, 1985).
Ben Jelloun, Tahar, *L'Enfant de Sable* (Paris: Le Seuil, 1987).
Ben Jelloun, Tahar, *The Sacred Night*, trans. Alan Sheridan (Baltimore and London: The Johns Hopkins University Press, 2000).
Ben Jelloun, Tahar, *The Sand Child*, trans. Alan Sheridan (Baltimore and London: The Johns Hopkins University Press, 2000).
Bennassar, Bartolomé and Lucile Bennassar, *Les Chrétiens d'Allah: L'histoire extraordinaire des renégats, XVIe et XVIIe siècles* (Paris: Perrin, 1989).
Bennoune, Mahfoud, *Les Algériennes Victimes de la Société Néopatriarchale* (Alger: Éditions Marinoor, 1999).
Bennoune, Mahfoud, *The Making of Contemporary Algeria, 1830–1987* (Cambridge: Cambridge University Press, 1988).
Berger, Anne Emmanuelle (ed.), *Algeria in Others' Languages* (Ithaca and London: Cornell University Press, 2002).
Berque, Augustin, "Les Intellectuels Algériens', *Revue Africaine*, 1947, pp. 136–48.
Bertrand, Louis, *Le Sang des races* (Paris: Albin Michel, 1899).
Betts, Raymond F., *Assimilation and Association in French Colonial Theory, 1890–1914* (Lincoln: University of Nebraska Press, 2005).
Bhabha, Homi, 'Of Mimicry and Man: The Ambivalence of Colonial Discourse', *October*, Vol. 28, Discipleship: A Special Issue on Psychoanalysis, Spring, 1984, pp. 125–33.
Bhabha, Homi, *The Location of Culture* (London and New York: Routledge, 1994).
Bitam, Boukhalfa, *Fadhma N'Soumer: Une autre lecture du combat de l'illustre fille de Werja* (Tizi Ouzou: Aurassi, 2000).
Boittin, Jennifer Anne, 'Feminist Mediations of the Exotic: French Algeria, Morocco and Tunisia, 1921–39', *Gender & History*, Vol. 22, No. 1, April 2010, pp. 131–50.
Bourdieu, Pierre, *Sociologie de l'Algérie* (Paris: Presses Universitaires de France, 1958).
Bouyerdene, Ahmed, *Emir Abd el-Kader: Hero and Saint of Islam*, trans. Gustavo Polit (Bloomington: World Wisdom, 2012).

Bouzar, Wadi and Andrea Page, 'The French-Language Algerian Novel', *Research in African Literatures*, Vol. 23, No. 2, Summer, 1992, pp. 51–9.
Brown, Peter, *La Vie du Saint Augustin* (Paris: Le Seuil, 2001).
Buruma, Ian and Avishai Margalit, *Occidentalism: A Short History of Anti-Westernism* (London: Atlantic Books: 2004).
Camus, Albert, *L'Étranger* (Paris: Gallimard, 1942).
Camus, Albert, *Chroniques algériennes, 1939–1958, Actuelles III* (Paris: Éditions Gallimard, Collection Folio Essais, 1958).
Camus, Albert, *Misère de la Kabylie* (Bejaïa (Algérie): Éditions Zirem, 2005).
Canter, H. V., 'Roman Civilization in North Africa', *The Classical Journal*, Vol. 35, No. 4 (January 1940), pp. 197–208. Available at: http://www.jstor.org/stable/3291373. Accessed: 20 March 2017.
Capitaine Carette, 'Algérie', in *L'Univers Pittoresque, Histoire et Description de tous les Peuples, de leurs Religions, Mœurs, Coutumes, Industrie* (Paris: Firmin Didot, 1850).
Carrey, Emile, *Récits de Kabylie: La Campagne de 1857* (Alger: G. A. L., 2004).
Carrier, James G. (ed.), *Occidentalism: Images of the West* (Oxford: Clarendon Press, 2003).
Chadwick, Henry, *Augustine of Hippo: a life* (Oxford: Oxford University Press, 2009).
Clancy-Smith, Julia A., *Rebel and Saint: Muslim Notables, Populist Protest, Colonial Encounters (Algeria and Tunisia, 1800–1904)* (Berkeley: University of California Press, 1994).
Clancy-Smith, Julia, 'Le regard colonial: Islam, genre et identités dans la fabrication de l'Algérie Française, 1830–1962 ', *Nouvelles Questions Féministes*, Vol. *25, No. 1,* 2006, pp. 25–40.
Clancy-Smith, Julia, 'The Colonial Gaze: Islam, Gender, and Identities in the Making of French Algeria', https://arizona.pure.elsevier.com/en/publicatio ns/the-colonial-gaze-islam-gender-and-identities-in-the-making-of-fr. Accessed 10 October 2017.
Clancy Smith, Julia, 'North Africa and France: Imperialism, Colonialism, and Women, 1830–1962'. Author's interviews with Dorra Bouzid, La Marsa, Tunisia, June–July 2009, http://africanhistory.oxfordre.com/view/10.1093/ acrefore/9780190277734.001.0001/acrefore-9780190277734–e-97. Accessed 12 September 2018.
Colonna, Fanny, *Instituteurs algériens 1883–1939* (Paris: Presses de la Fondation Nationale des Sciences Politiques, 1975).

Commission des sciences et arts d'Égypte, *Description de l'Égypte* (Paris: French Government publication, 1809–1822).

Coronil, Fernando, 'Beyond Occidentalism: Towards Post-Imperial Geohistorical Categories', *Cultural Anthropology*, Vol. 11, 1996, pp. 51–87.

Cox, Oliver, *The Foundations of Capitalism*, New York: Philosophy Library, 1959.

D'Herbelot, Barthélemy de Molainville, *Bibliothèque orientale, ou dictionnaire universel contenant tout ce qui regarde la connaissance des peuples de l'Orient*, 4 vols (The Hague: Quatro, 1777–99).

Daughton, J. P., *An Empire Divided: Religion, Republicanism, and the Making of French Colonialism, 1880–1914* (Oxford: Oxford University Press, 2006).

Daumas, Eugène, *La Vie arabe et la société musulmane* (Paris: Michel Lévy Frères, 1869).

Danziger, Raphael, *Abd al-Qadir and the Algerians: Resistance to the French and Internal Consolidation.* (New York: Holmes & Meier, 1977).

De Beauvoir, Simone and Gisèle Halimi, *Djamila Boupacha: the story of the torture of a young Algerian girl which shocked liberal French opinion*, trans. Peter Green (London: André Deutsch Ltd and George Weidenfeld and Nicolson Ltd, 1962).

De Maupassant, Guy, *Au Soleil* (Paris: Ollendorff, 1902).

De Molainville, Barthélemy d'Herbelot, *Bibliothèque orientale, ou dictionnaire universel contenant tout ce qui regarde la connaissance des peuples de l'Orient*, 4 vols (The Hague: Quatro, 1777–99).

De Penhoen, Baron Barchou, *Mémoires d'un officier d'état-major, Expédition d'Afrique* (Paris: Charpentier, 1935).

De Reynaud, Pélissier, *Annales algériennes*, Paris: Librairie Militaire (Alger: Librairie Bastide, 1854).

De Sauvigny, Guillaume Berthier, *Bourbon Restoration*, trans. Lynn M. Case (Philadelphia: University of Philadelphia Press, 1966).

Débêche, Djamila, *Leila, Jeune fille d'Algérie* (Alger: Charras, 1947).

Débêche, Djamila, *Les Musulmans algériens et la scolarisation* (Alger: Charras, 1950).

Débêche, Djamila, *L'enseignement de la langue arabe en Algérie et le droit de vote aux femmes algériennes* (Alger: Charras, 1951).

Débêche, Djamila, *Aziza* (Alger: Imbert, 1955).

Déjeux, Jean, 'La Kahina: de l'histoire a la fiction littéraire. Mythes et Epopée', *Studi Magrebini* (Naples) vol. XV, 1983, pp. 1–42.

Déjeux, Jean, 'La Littérature algérienne d'expression Française', *Cahiers Nord-africains*, No. 61, 1957.

Déjeux, Jean, *Femmes D'Algérie: Légendes, Traditions, Histoire, Littérature* (Paris: La Boîte à Documents, 1987).
Mohammed Dib, *La Grande maison* (Paris: Le Seuil, 1952).
Dieuzaide, V.-A., *Histoire de l'Algérie 1830–1878* (Tome I, Oran: Imprimerie de l'association ouvrière – Heintz, Chazeau et Cie, 1880.)
Dinet, Étienne and Slimane Ben Brahim Baamer, *Khadra, danseuse des Ouled Nail* (Paris: Piazza, 1926).
Dirèche-Slimani, Karima, *Chrétiens de Kabylie 1873–1954. Une action missionnaire dans l'Algérie coloniale* (Paris: Éditions Bouchène, 2004).
Djebar, Assia, *Les Enfants du nouveau monde* (Paris: Julliard, 1962).
Djebar, Assia, *Les Allouettes naïves* (Paris: Julliard, 1967).
Djebar, Assia, *Women of Algiers in their Apartment*, trans. Marjolijn de Jager (Charlottesville and London: University Press of Virginia, 1992).
Djebar, Assia, 'Du Français comme butin', *La quinzaine littéraire* 436, March 16–31, 1985, p. 25.
Djeghloul, Abdelkader, 'La Formation des Intellectuels Algériens Modernes 1880–1930', in Omar Carlier et al., *Lettres, Intellectuels et Militants en Algérie, 1880–1959* (Alger: OPU, 1988), pp. 3–29.
Djeghloul, Abdelkader, 'Un Romancier de l'identité perturbée et de l'assimilation impossible Chukri Khodja', *Revue de l'Occident musulman et de la Méditerranée*, Vol. 37, No. 37, 1984, pp. 81–96.
Droz, Bernard and Evelyne Lever, *Histoire de la guerre d'Algérie, 1954–1962* (Paris: Le Seuil, 1982).
Dumas, Le Général, *La Grande Kabylie, Etudes historiques* (Paris: Hachette, 1847).
Dunwoodie, Peter, *Francophone Writing in Transition: Algeria 1900–1945* (Oxford: Peter Lang, 2005).
Eichner, Carolyn J., 'La citoyenne in the World: Hubertine Auclert and Feminist Imperialism', *French Historical Studies*, Vol. 32, No. 1, winter 2009, pp. 64–84.
El-Enany, Rasheed, *Arab Representations of the Occident: East–West Encounters in Arabic Fiction* (London and New York: Routledge, 2006).
Fanon, Frantz, *Black Skin, White Masks*, trans. Charles Lam Markmann (New York: Grove Press, 1967).
Fanon, *A Dying Colonialism* (New York: Grove Press, 1967).
Fanon, Frantz, *L'An V de la révolution algérienne* (Paris: La Découverte, 2001).
Fanon, Frantz, *The Wretched of the Earth*, trans. Constance Farrington (London: Penguin Books, 2001).

Feraoun, Mouloud, *La Terre et le Sang* (Paris: Le Seuil, 1953).
Feraoun, Mouloud, *Les Chemins qui mentent* (Paris: Le Seuil, 1957).
Feraoun, Mouloud, *Le Fils du Pauvre* (Alger: ENAL, 1986).
Feraoun, Mouloud, *Lettres à ses amis* (Alger: Bouchène, 1991).
Fédération de France du FLN, *La Femme Algérienne dans la Révolution: Documents et Témoignages Inédits* (Alger: ENAG Éditions, 2006).
Fikri, Abdelkader, and Robert Randau, *Les Compagnons du jardin* (Paris: Donat-Montchrestien, 1933).
Foucault, Michel, *Discipline and Punishment* (London: Tavistock, 1977).
Foucault, Michel, 'Truth and Power', in C. Gordon (ed.): *Power/knowledge. Selected Interviews & Other Writings by Michel Foucault, 1972–1977* (Brighton: Harvester, 1980), pp. 109–33.
Gadant, Monique, *Le Nationalisme Algérien et les Femmes* (Paris: Éditions L'Harmattan, 1995).
Gafaiti, Hafid, 'The Monotheism of the Other: Language and De/Construction of National Identity in Postcolonial Algeria', in Anne Emmanuelle Berger (ed.), *Algeria in Others' Languages* (Ithaca and London: Cornell University Press, 2002), pp. 19–43.
Gallup, D. M., 'The French Image of Algeria: its Origins, its Place in Colonial Ideology, its Effect on Algerian Acculturation'. Unpublished PhD Thesis, University of California, 1973.
Galois, William, *A History of Violence in the Early Algerian Colony* (London: Palgrave Macmillan, 2013).
Gershovich, Moshe, *French Military Rule in Morocco: Colonialism and its Consequences*. (London: Frank Cass, 2000).
Ha, Marie-Paule, 'From "Nos Ancêtres, les Gaulois" to "Leur Culture Ancestrale": Symbolic Violence and the Politics of Colonial Schooling in Indo-china', *French Colonial History*, vol. 3, 2003, pp. 101–17.
Haddad, Malek, *La Dernière impression* (Paris: Julliard, 1958).
Haddad, Malek, *Je t'offrirai une gazelle* (Paris: Julliard, 1959).
Haddad, Malek, *L'Élève et la leçon* (Paris; Julliard, 1960).
Haddad, Malek, *Écoute et je t'appelle* (Poèmes), précédé de *Les Zéros tournent en rond*. (Essai) (Paris: Maspéro, 1961).
Haddad, Malek, *Le Quai aux fleurs ne répond plus* (Paris: Julliard, 1962).
Hadj Hamou, Abdelkader, *Zohra la femme du mineur* (Alger: Éditions Associés, 1925).
Hall, Stuart, 'Cultural Identity, and Diaspora,' in Patrick Williams and Chrisman,

Colonial Discourse and Post-Colonial Theory: a Reader (London: Harvester Wheatsheaf, 1994), pp. 392–401.
Hanafi, Hassan, 'From Orientalism to Occidentalism', www.fortschritt-weltweit.de. Accessed 2 November 2011.
Hanafi, Hassan, *Muqaddimah fī 'ilm al-istighrāb* (Beirut: al-Mu'assassah al-Jāmi'iyah li al-dirāssāt wa al-nashr wa al-tawzī', 2000).
Hannoum, Abdelmajid, 'Faut-it brûler l'Orientalisme? On French Scholarship of North Africa', *Cultural Dynamics* 16 (2004), pp. 71–91.
Hélie Lucas, Marie-Aimée, 'Women, Nationalism and Religion in the Algerian Liberation Struggle', in Margot Badran and Miriam Cooke (eds), *Opening the Gates: A Century of Arab Feminist Writing* (London: Virago, 1992), pp. 105–14.
Henry, Jean-Robert, 'Résonances maghrébines', *Revue de l'Occident musulman et de la Méditerranée*, Vol. 37, No. 37, 1984, pp. 5–14.
Hoisington, William A., *Lyautey and the French conquest of Morocco* (New York: St Martin's Press, 1995).
Hopwood, Derek, *Sexual Encounters in the Middle East: The British, the French, and the Arabs* (Reading: Ithaca Press, 1999).
Ibn Khaldūn, ʿAbd-ar-Raḥmān, *The Muqaddimah: An Introduction to History*, trans. Frantz Rosenthal (Princeton and Oxford: Princeton University Press: 2005).
Irwin, Robert, *For Lust of Knowing: the Orientalists and their Enemies* (London: Penguin Books, 2007).
Isaac, Y. *Le Thème de L'Aliénation dans le Roman Maghrébin d'Expression Française: 1952–1956* (Sherbrooke: CELEF, 1972).
Issawi, Charles, *An Arab Philosophy of History: Selections from the Prolegomena of Ibn Khaldun of Tunis* (London: John Murray, 1950).
Jabra Ibrahim Jabra, 'Modern Arabic Literature and the West', *Journal of Arabic Literature*, Vol. 2, 1971, pp. 76–91.
Kacimi, Mohammed Raouf El Hassani, 'Tariqah Rahmania: its roots and prospects', *Journal of Sophia Asian Studies*, no. 27, December 2009, pp. 291–307.
Kessous, Mohammed Aziz, *La Vérité sur le Malaise Algérien* (Bône: Imprimerie Rapide, 1935).
Khatibi, Abdelkebir, *La Mémoire tatouée* (Paris: Denoël, 1971).
Khatibi, Abdelkebir, Amour *bilingue* (Montpellier: Fata Morgana, 1983).
Khatibi, Abdelkebir, *Love in two Languages*, trans. Richard Howard (Minneapolis: University of Minnesota Press, 1990).
Khodja, Chukri, *Mamoun: L'Ébauche d'un idéal* (1928) (Alger: Office des Publications Universitaires, 1992).

Khodja, Chukri, *El-Euldj: Captif des Barbaresques* (1923) (Alger: Office des Publications Universitaires, 1992).

Kofron, W.G., *New Advent*, http://www.newadvent.org/cathen/09050d.htm. Accessed 12 October 2016.

Lacheraf, Mostefa, *L'Algérie, Nation et société* (Paris: Maspero, 1965).

Lacoste-Dujardin, Camille, *La Vaillance des Femmes: Les Relations entre Femmes et Hommes Berbères de Kabylie* (Alger: Barzakh, 2010).

Lapidus, Ira M., *A History of Islamic Societies* (Cambridge: Cambridge University Press, 2002).

Lambing, Clement, *The French in Algiers*, trans. Lady Duff Gordon (New York: Wiley and Putnam, 1845).

Lazreg, Marnia, *The Eloquence of Silence: Algerian Women in Question* (New York: Routledge, 1994).

Le Baut, Réjane, *Camus Amrouche: des Chemins qui s'écartent* (Alger: Casbah Éditions, 2014).

Lechani, Mohammed, *Le Malaise Algérien* (Alger: Imprimeries Pfeiffer et Assant, 1939).

Leriche, Joseph, 'Les algériens parmi nous', *Cahiers Nord-Africains*, No. 70, December 1958, Special Issue.

Liauzu, Claude, *Passeurs de Rives: Changements d'identité dans le Maghreb Colonial* (Paris: L'Harmattan, 2000).

Lorcerie, Françoise, 'L'islam comme contre-identification française: trois moments', *L'Année du Maghreb, Dossier: Femmes, famille et droit* (Paris: CNRS Éditions, 2005–6), pp. 509–36. http://anneemaghreb.revues.org/161?lang=ar, Accessed 26 August 2013.

Lorcin, Patricia M.E., *Imperial Identities: Stereotyping, Prejudice and Race in Colonial Algeria* (London: I. B. Tauris, 1999).

Lorcin, Patricia and Daniel Brewer (eds), *France and its Spaces of War: Experience, Memory, Image* (Basingstoke: Palgrave, 2009).

Lucas, Philipe and Claude Vatin, *L'Algérie des Anthropologues* (Paris: Maspéro, 1982).

MacMaster, Neil, 'The Colonial "Emancipation" of Algerian Women, the Marriage Law of 1959 and the Failure of Legislation on Women's Rights in the Post-Independence Era', *Stichproben. Wiener Zeitschrift für kritische Afrikastudien*, Nr. 12, 2007, 7. Jg., pp. 91–116.

Mammeri, Mouloud, *La Colline Oubliée* (Paris: Plon, 1952).

Mammeri, Mouloud, *Le Sommeil du juste*. (Paris: Plon, 1955).

Mammeri, Mouloud, *L'Opium et le bâton* (Paris: Plon, 1965).

Marsaud, Olivia, 'Les écrivains Algériens a l'honneur', http://forum.dzfoot.com. Accessed 7 June 2006.
Massignon, Louis, *Parole donnée* (Paris: Le Seuil, 1983).
Matar, Nabil, *Turks, Moors, and Englishmen in the Age of Discovery* (New York: Columbia University Press, 1999).
Mazouz, Mohammed, 'Algeria', in *Groupe de Démographie Africaine, Population Size in African Countries: An Evaluation*, Volume II (Paris: IOP_INEO_INSEE_MINCOOP_ORSTOM, 1988).
McDougall, James, *History and the Culture of Nationalism in Algeria* (Cambridge: Cambridge University Press, 2006).
McDougall, James, *A History of Algeria* (Cambridge: Cambridge University Press, 2017).
Memmi, Albert, *Portrait du Colonisé précédé du Portrait du Colonisateur* (Paris: Buchet-Chastel, 1957). Trans. Howard Greenfeld as *The Colonizer and the Colonized* (London: Souvenir Press, 1974).
Memmi, Albert, *The Colonizer and the Colonized* (Boston: Beacon Press, 1991).
Mernissi, Fatima, *Beyond the Veil: Male-Female Dynamics in Modern Muslim Society* (Bloomington: Indiana University Press, 1975).
Moghissi, Haideh, *Women and Islam: Critical Concepts in Sociology, Images and Realities* (London and New York: Routledge, 2005).
Nader, Laura, 'Orientalism, Occidentalism and the Control of Women', *Cultural Dynamics*, Vol. 2, 1989, pp. 323–55.
Noushi, André, *Enquête sur le niveau de vie des populations rurales constantinoises de la conquête jusqu'en 1919* (Paris: Presses Universitaires de France, 1961).
O'Donohue, John, *Cardinal Lavigerie* (London: Athlone Press, 1994).
O'Leary, De Lacy, *How Greek Science Passed to the Arabs* (London: Routledge & Kegan Paul, 1949). www.aina.org/books/hgsptta.htm. Accessed 13 October 2010.
Ould Cheikh, Mohammed, *Myriem dans les Palmes* (Oran: Éditions Plaza, 1936).
Oussedik, Tahar, *Lalla Fadhma n'Summer* (Alger: Laphomic, 1983).
Panzac, Daniel, *Les Corsaires barbaresques: la fin d'une épopée, 1800–1820* (Paris: CNRS Éditions, 1999).
Perret, E., *Récits algériens 1848–1886* (Paris: Bloud et Barral, n.d.), vol. 2.
Pons, Mgr Alexandre, La nouvelle Église d'Afrique ou le catholicisme en Algérie, en Tunisie et au Maroc depuis 1830. (Tunis: Édition Librairie Louis Namura, 1930).
Renault, François, *Le Cardinal Lavigerie* (Paris: Fayard, 1992).

Rodney, Walter, How *Europe Underdeveloped Africa* (London: L'ouverture, 1972).
Rebecca Rogers, *A Frenchwoman's Imperial Story: Madame Luce in Nineteenth-Century Algeria* (Stanford: Stanford University Press, 2013).
Roland L. and P. Lampué, *Précis de legislation coloniale* (Paris: Dalloz, 1931).
Romey, Alain, 'Jean El Mouhoub Amrouche, ou le dilemme d'une solidarité controversée (1945–1961)', *Cahiers de la Méditerranée*, Vol. 63, 2001, pp. 113–12.
Ruedy, J., *Modern Algeria* (London: Bloomington, 1992).
Sadiqi, Fatima, *Women, Gender and Language in Morocco* (Leiden and Boston: Brill, 2003).
Said, Edward, 'Zionism from the Standpoint of its Victims', *Social Text*, Vol. 1, 1979, pp. 7–58.
Said, W. Edward, *Orientalism: Western Conceptions of the Orient* (London: Penguin Books, 2003).
Salhi, Zahia Smail, 'Colonial Visual Representations of the "Femmes d'Alger"', *The Middle East Journal of Culture and Communications*, vol. 1, issue. 1, 2008, pp. 80–93.
Salhi, Zahia Smail, *Politics, Poetics and the Algerian Novel* (Lampeter: The Edwin Mellen Press, 1999).
Salhi, Zahia Smail 'Between the Languages of Silence and the Woman's Word: Gender and Language in the Work of Assia Djebar', *International Journal of the Sociology of Language*, Special Issue on "Language and Gender in the Mediterranean Region", vol. 190, 2008, pp. 79–101.
Salhi, Zahia Smail, 'The Algerian Feminist Movement between Nationalism, Patriarchy and Islamism', *Women's Studies International Forum*, Vol. 33, No. 2, March–April 2010, pp. 113–24.
Sambron, Diane, *Les Femmes Algériennes pendant la Colonisation* (Alger: Éditions Casbah, 2013).
Sebbar, Leïla, *La Seine était rouge* (Paris: Thierry Magnier, 1999).
Segalla, Spencer D., *The Moroccan Soul: French Education, Colonial Ethnology, and Muslim Resistance, 1912–1956* (Lincoln: University of Nebraska Press, 2009).
Serreau, Geneviève, "Situation de l'écrivain Algerien', *Les Lettres Modernes* (July–August, 1956), p. 108.
Sessions, Jennifer, '"Unfortunate Necessities": Violence and Civilisation in the Conquest of Algeria', in Patricia Lorcin, Daniel Brewer (eds), *France and its*

Spaces of War. Experience, Memory, Image (Basingstoke: Palgrave, 2009), pp. 29–44.

Smati, Mahfoud, *Les Jeunes Algériens: Correspondances et Rapports 1837–1918* (Alger: Thala Éditions, 2011).

Stock, Brian, *Augustine the Reader: Meditation, Self-Knowledge, and the Ethics of Interpretation* (Cambridge, MA: Harvard University Press, 1996).

Stora, Benjamin, *Algeria 1830–2000: A Short History*, trans. Jane Marie Todd (Ithaca and London: Cornell University Press, 2001).

Temimi, Abdeljelil, 'Documents Turcs inédits sur le bombardement d'Alger en 1816', *Revue de l'Occident Musulman et de la Méditerranée*, Vol. 5, No. 5, 1968, pp. 111–33.

Thomas, Martin, *The French Colonial Mind: Violence, Military Encounters, and Colonialism* (Lincoln, Nebraska, University of Nebraska Press, 2011).

Thomas, Martin, *Violence and Colonial Order: Police, Workers, and Protest in the European Colonial Empires, 1918–1940* (Cambridge: Cambridge University Press, 2012).

Thomas, Nicholas, 'Anthropology and Orientalism', *Anthropology Today*, 7, 1991, pp. 4–7.

Thoral, Marie-Cecile, 'French Colonial Counter-Insurgency: General Bugeaud and the Conquest of Algeria, 1840–47', *British Journal of Military History*, 1 (2), 2015, pp. 8–27.

Tibawi, Abdel Latif, 'English-speaking Orientalists,' *Islamic Quarterly*, 8, 1964, pp. 25–45.

Turin, Yvonne, *Affrontements culturels dans l'Algérie colonial: Ecoles, médicine, religion, 1830–1880* (Alger: Entreprise Nationale du Livre, 1983).

Vergès, Jacques (5 March 1925 – 15 August 2013), 'Obituary', *The Guardian*, 16 August 2013. https://www.theguardian.com/world/2013/aug/16/jacques-verges. Accessed 11 September 2018.

Voyage dans les états barbaresques de Maroc, Alger, Tunis et Tripoli; ou lettres d'un des captives qui viennent d'être rachetés par MM. Les Chanoines réguliers de la Sainte-Trinité, suivies d'une notice sur leur rachat et du catalogue de leurs noms. (Paris: Guillot, 1785).

Walter, Rodney, *How Europe Underdeveloped Africa* (London: L'ouverture, 1972).

Watson, William E., *Tricolor and Crescent: France and the Islamic World* (London: Praeger, 2003).

White Fathers' Missions of Africa, 'Le Cardinal Lavigerie,' 1925, trans. Penelope Royall, *The Muslim World*, Vol. 16, No. 2, p. 176.

Yetiv, *Isaac, Le Thème de L'Aliénation dans le Roman Maghrébin d'Expression Française: 1952–1956* (Sherbrooke: CELEF, 1972).

Zenati, Rabah, *Le Problème Algérien vue par un indigène* (Paris: Comité de l'Afrique Française, 1938).

Index

Abbas, Ferhat, 181, 193–4, 202, 205, 214–15
  as Algerian nationalist, 197
  on Algerian nationhood, 233n32
  assimilationist ideals, 66–8, 193
  Le Jeune Algérien, 45
  La Nuit Coloniale, 206
  as representative of the Young Algerians, 218, 219
Abdel Kader, Emir, 54, 78, 227–8n52
Abdel-Malek, Anouar, 18, 19–20, 25
Abu-Lughod, Lila, 26–7, 138–9
Afghanistan, US intervention in, 138
Ahmed, Fadhila, 165
Al-Andalus, 21, 23, 24, 72, 73, 91
Al-Azm, Sadik Jalal, 12
Aldrich, Robert, 44–5, 46, 48
Algeria
  8 May 1945 massacres and aftermath, 68, 189, 191–7, 213, 218, 247–8n2
  European population in, 46, 62
  French conquest/colonisation of, 19, 30, 40–8, 74
  and the language question, 207–8
  and nationhood, 233n32
  Ottomans in, 73, 83
  popular resistance in, 78
  poverty in, 234–5n44
  Roman relics in, 72
  Spanish occupation of, 83
  see also Arabisation; colonial schools; *Évolués* (indigenous elite)
Algerian Communist Party, 163
Algerian War of Independence (1954–62), 160, 165, 197, 204–5, 206–7
  events leading to, 68
  representations of women in, 211
Les Algérianistes *see* Francophone literature/novelists

Algiers, 72–3
  Battle of (1956–7), 164
  fall of, representations of, 75–8
alienation, 179, 186, 202
al-Jabarti, ʿAbd al-Rahman, 136
al-Khattabi, Abdel Karim, 78
Alloula, Malek, 15–18, 126
Al-Shidyāq, Ahmad Fāris, 76
al-Ṭahṭāwī, Rifāʿa Rāfiʿ, 75–6
Amazigh culture *see* Berbers
Amrouche, Fadhma Aït Mansour, 57, 144–51, 159, 244n68
Amrouche, Jean, 4, 57–8, 68, 82, 195, 200–1, 230n73
  on the natives' sacrifices for the *mère-patrie*, 189–90
  on racism of the French Algeria, 190–1, 202–3
  on 'stagnation', 196
anthropology, European, 26–7
Arab Bureau, 19–20
Arabic language
  classical, 78, 79, 80, 92
  colloquial/vernacular, 76–9, 80, 92, 208, 209, 250n44
Arabisation, 21, 207–11, 249n41
Arabophone novelists, 209–11
Arab-Orientals, stereotype of, 105; *see also* Orientalism
aristocracy, indigenous, 128–9, 237n12
Aristotle, 22, 75
Ashcroft, Bill, 14, 94
assimilation, 8–9, 81
  and acculturation, 161
  changing names, 178–9
  as a fiction/fallacy, 89, 112–13, 178
  idealisation of the Occident, 111, 113, 115–17

assimilation (*cont.*)
  new model of, 90
  see also cultural assimilation
Auclert, Hubertine, 156–8, 159, 239–40n5, 239n1
  critique of, 140
  on girls' education, 143, 168
  on the heroism of Algerian women, 130, 131–2
  Les Femmes arabes en Algérie, 127–30, 139
  on the victimisation of Algerian women, 129–30, 131, 134–9
autobiography, Maghrebi, 57, 144–51
Al-Azmeh, Aziz, 32

barbarism, colonial education on, 81–2
Barbary Corsairs, 72–3, 87; *see also* Ottoman Empire/Ottomans
Battle of Algiers (1956–7), 164
Battle of Tours-Poitiers, 72
Beauvoir, Simone de, 30, 204
ben Abdullah, Mohamed (Bou Baghla), 241n21
Ben Jelloun, Tahar
  The Sacred Night, 6
  The Sand Child, 6
Ben Khalfat, Mejdoub, 65–6, 175
Benhadouga, Abdelhamid, 209–10
Berbers (Amazigh), 21, 207, 208, 213, 227n45, 249n41
Berger, Anne-Emmanuelle, 208
Berque, Augustin, 8
Berque, Jacques, 20
Bertrand, Louis, 42–4, 47–8, 62, 68
  Le Sang des races, 42
Betts, Raymond F., 52
Bhabha, Homi, 14, 94–5
binaries, 105
Bonaparte, Napoleon, 25, 38
Bottini-Houot, Jeanne, 159
Bou Baghla, 241n21
Boubacha, Djamila, 224n66
Boudjedra, Rachid
  The Dismantling, 210
  La Répudiation, 210
  Les 1001 Années de la Nostalgie, 210
  L'Escargot entêté, 210
Bouhired, Djamila, 182, 224n67
Bourdieu, Pierre, 81
Bouzar, Wadi, 200
Brunschvicg, Cécile, 159

Bugeaud, Marshal, 44, 46
Buruma, Ian, 29–31

Camus, Albert, 68, 192, 194–5, 230n73
  La Peste, 198–9
Carrier, James, 4, 27
Catholicism
  conversion to, 49, 144, 227n42, 228n54
  see also Christianity
child marriage, 125, 137
Christianity
  conversion to, 49, 50–9, 66, 111, 144
  stigmatisation of converts, 57–8
citizenship, 46, 64–5
  denial of, 189–90
  political options, 67–8
La citoyenne (journal), 157
civil service, 60
civilisation(s)
  Christianity and, 52–4
  and knowledge, 22
Clancy-Smith, Julia, 76, 140, 214
class system, colonial, 109
classical Arabic, literature, 78, 79, 80, 92
  and Arabisation, 209–10
collaborative novels, 4
colloquial Arabic *see under* Arabic language
colonial mimicry, 8, 94–5
colonial schools, 88, 244n68
  assimilationist project, 59–63, 82–3
  elitism of, 108–9
  girls', 147–50, 168–9
  and idealisation of the Occident, 117
  Oriental intellectuals at, 8–9, 13
  and the teacher role, 105, 114–15
  see also literacy/illiteracy
colonialism
  colonial violence, 41, 45–6, 48, 80, 134, 204, 225n22
  and domination, 11–12
  French authors on, 41–8
  ideology, 59, 61, 81–2, 88, 195
  Maghrebi authors on, 66–8, 70
  see also land appropriation/expropriation; Orientalism
conversion *see under* Catholicism; Christianity; Islam
Coronil, Fernando, 12–13, 15
critics, French/Maghrebi, on the Algérianistes, 5
Cromer, Earl of, 105
crusades, 23, 65–6, 72–3

cultural assimilation, 67, 68–9, 107–8
  of indigenous women, 130
cultural nationalism, 207
cultural resistance, women's, 161

Dagher, Youssef Asaad, 18
Daughton, J. P., 52–3
de Lens, Aline Réveillaud, 158–9
De Sacy, 19, 21
Débêche, Djamila, 246n21
  Aziza, 156, 165–83, 185–7
  Leila, Jeune fille d'Algérie, 155–6, 165–76, 183–5
decolonisation, 9, 206–8
  and the post-colonial Algerian novel, 208–14
Dejeux, Jean, 132–3
Dib, Mohammed, *La Grande Maison*, 199, 201
Dieuzaide, V. A., 133–4
Dihya (al-Kahina), Berber warrior Queen, 132
Direche-Slimani, Karima, 55–7
direct action, Maghrebi *see* letters, to the Occident/political leaders
Djebar, Assia
  Les Allouettes naïve, 211
  Les Enfants du nouveau monde, 211
  La Nouba, 211
  stylistic signature of, 212
Djeghloul, Abdelkader, 89
dress/clothing, 95, 111–12, 123, 162, 238n48
  recreating 'Oriental', 5–6
  see also under women/girls

education
  closure of *madrasas* and Qur'anic schools, 105, 108
  see also colonial schools
Egypt
  Bonaparte expedition to, 25, 38, 72, 76, 136
  British occupation of, 74
Eichner, Carolyn J., 157
El-Enany, Rasheed, 35, 76
English language, Maghrebi Diaspora use of, 32
essentialism, 18, 25–8, 31, 35, 113; *see also* Orientalism
ethnic cleansing, 45, 48
European settlers *see* settlers, European

Europeanisation, 90–1
Évolués (indigenous elite), 59–60, 94–6, 114–16, 117, 122–3, 169
  as mediators, 63–4
  representations of, 202
  see also names of individual *Évolués*; Young Algerians

family law, 159–60
famines, 55–6, 84, 234–5n44
Fanon, Frantz, 99–100, 160–1, 181, 203, 204
  Black Skin, White Masks, 110, 178
  on the evolution of the colonised intellectual, 115–16
  on precolonial history, devaluing of, 88
  The Wretched of the Earth, 81–2, 107
fashion, Maghrebi *see* dress/clothing
feminism, Algerian, 162–5, 183, 239–40n5, 242n21, 246n21
feminism, French
  and education, 140–3
  and imperialism, 156–61, 173–4, 244–5n3
  see also Auclert, Hubertine; Débêche, Djamila
Femmes d'Algérie (journal), 163
Feraoun, Mouloud, 58, 197–9, 200
  Le Fils du pauvre, 197–8, 212
  Les Chemins qui montent, 144
  Lettres à ses amis, 145, 198
Ferry, Jules, 51, 59, 61, 83–4, 149
fez, the, 112, 162, 238n48
Fez, treaty of, 75
Le Figaro (newspaper), 44, 190–1, 200–1
FLN (National Liberation Front), 206–7
Foucault, Michel, 20, 216
Fourier, Joseph, 38
Français Musulman, status as, 64–5, 112, 123
La Française (newspaper), 159, 160
France
  assimilationist project, 8–9, 49–63, 81, 88, 196
  colonialist discourse, 37–8, 83–4, 167, 175
  Metropole, ideals of, 60–2, 69
  Orientalising the Maghreb, 38–48
  see also assimilation; crusades; Paris
Francophone literature/novelists, 79–80, 81, 84, 92, 94–124, 208–13, 246n21; *see also* Occidentophilia

French language
    and colonial mimicry, 95
    as a liberating tool, 211–12
    relegated to backstage, 207, 208–9
French Orientalism *see* Orientalism

Galland, Antoine, 24
Gaulle, Charles de, 188, 190, 218
genocide, 45–6, 80

Haddad, Malek, 208–9
Hadj Hamou, Abdelkader, 236n8
    Les Compagnons du jardin, 100–1
    Zohra la femme du mineur, 97–104, 124, 236n8
Halimi, Gisèle, 30, 224n66
Hall, Stuart, 33
Hanafi, Hassan, 11–12
Hannoum, Abdelmajid, 18–19, 20
Harazeli women, 130
harems, 126, 139, 158–9
Hélie-Lucas, Marie-Aimée, 207
Henry, J.-R., 39–40
Herbelot, Barthélemy d', 21, 23–4
Hopwood, Derek, 25
hostage taking, 73, 121, 134
Hugo, Victor, 41

Iberian Peninsula, 21, 72, 73, 216
Ibn Badis, Abdul Hamid, Sheikh, 233n32
Ibn Khaldun, 107
    The Muqaddimah, 22–3
ibn Ziyād, Tariq, 72
imitation, of the coloniser by the colonised, 107, 109
imperialism, and French feminism, 156–61
indigenous elite *see Évolués* (indigenous elite)
Irwin, Robert, 2, 24
Islam, 233n32
    and anti-Islamic media, 23–4
    conversion to, 86, 235n58
    French feminism on, 159
    French identity and, 64–5, 123
    and identity formation, 33–4
    representations of in Francophone literature, 99
    and resistance to colonial forces, 53
Islamic science/philosophy, 75
Islamisation, 21, 55
istishrāq, 12

Jews, expulsion from Spain, 73
jihad, 54, 78, 241n21

Kabyles, Kabylie region, 55–8, 131, 144–5, 147–51, 241–2n21
    Kabyle myth, 163
    women's dress codes, 165
Khatibi, Abdelkebir, 6, 10
Khodja, Chukri, 93, 234n42, 237–8n30
    El-Euldj, 84–92
    Mamoun: L'Ébauche d'un idéal, 104–17, 119, 124, 168
Khodja, Louis, 64–5
knowledge, and power/civilisations, 20–3, 27

land appropriation/expropriation, 44, 46–8, 51, 69, 78, 103–4
languages, North African, 72; *see also* Arabic language
Lapidus, Ira M., 75
Latin translations, 75
Lavigerie, Charles Martial Allemand, 54–6, 59, 228–9n54
Lazreg, Marnia, 17, 38, 60, 140, 141–2, 148, 155, 164, 168
letters, to the Occident/political leaders, 63–4, 137, 174–6, 198, 217–18
Liauzu, Claude, 182
Libya, 73, 74
liminality, and hybridity, 14
literacy/illiteracy, 60, 155, 209, 211, 230n73
Lorcin, Patricia, 48
Louis IX, King of France, 73
Luce, Eugénie Allix, 141–3, 157
Lyautey, Louis-Hubert, 61–3

MacMaster, Neil, 159–60
madrasas, 105, 108, 155
Maghreb, the, as space of crossing over, 6
Maghrebi *Évolués see Évolués* (indigenous elite)
Mammeri, Mouloud
    La Colline Oubliée, 199
    L'Opium et le bâton, 203–4
    Le Sommeil du juste, 202
al-Maʾmūn, Caliph, 22
Margalit, Avishai, 29–31
marriage
    child marriage, 125, 137
    colonial legislation on, 159–60

forced, 139
mixed, 67, 118–20, 124, 148, 181–2, 193
polygamy, 137
Massignon, Louis, 132
Maupassant, Guy de, 40, 41–2
Mazouz, Mohammed, 49
Memmi, Albert, 3, 177–8, 195, 196, 204–5
Mernissi, Fatima, 33
missionaries, 52–9, 69, 127, 144, 145, 228n54
Mohammed the Prophet, 23–4, 185
Morocco, 3
French colonial schools in, 61–3
as French/Spanish protectorate, 74–5
harems, 158–9
popular resistance in, 78
Spanish in, 73, 83
MTLD (the Movement for the Triumph of Democratic Freedoms), 162
Muslim(s)
expulsion from Spain, 73
family law, 159–60
see also Islam

Nader, Laura, 28
Napoleon Bonaparte, Egyptian expedition, 25, 38
Napoleon III, Emperor of France, 49–50, 61
national liberation movements, 20
nationalism/nationalists
Algerian, 30, 158, 179–80, 207
French, 74
Tunisian, 230–1n83
and the 'woman question', 162–6
native intellectuals see Évolués (indigenous elite)
naturalisation, French, 57, 69
Nsoumer, Lalla Fatma, 132–3, 240–2n21

Occidentalism/Occidentalist
defined, 34–5
versus Orientalism, 10–18
as post-colonial discourse, 31–4
see also Occidentophilia
Occidentology (ʿilm al-istighrāb), 11–12
Occidentophilia, 111, 175–6, 183–4, 217
writers, 76, 93–124, 191, 217
see also Francophone literature/novelists
Orientalism
academic scholarship, 18–20

Bonaparte Expedition, accounts of, 25
and colonialism, 19–20
crisis of, 18–31
critiques of, 25–7
and the crusades, 23
versus Occidentalism, 10–18
Orientalist art/literature, 4–6, 15–18, 125–6, 158
the Other
and colonial mimicry, 95
see also essentialism; Orientalism
Ottoman Empire/Ottomans, 73–4, 83
Ould Cheikh, Mohammed, 79, 84, 124, 233n25
Myriem dans les Palmes, 117–22

Page, Andrea, 200
Paris
massacre of Algerian immigrants (1961), 213
religious-based discrimination, post-9/11, 33–4
patriarchy, 28, 164, 210
PCA (Parti Communiste Algérien), 163
Pélissier, Aimable-Jean-Jacques, 49, 225n22
Perret, E., 132, 133
Persian culture, 22
Pétain, Maréchal, 218
Peter the Venerable, 23–4
photographs, colonial/Orientalist, Maghrebi women, 15–18, 126
pied noir see settlers, European
piracy, 49, 73–4, 78, 87, 217
poetry, Maghrebi, 72, 77–8, 80, 92
Polignac, French Prime Minister, 78
polygamy, 137
post-colonial Algerian novels, 208–14
PPA (the Party of the Algerian People), 162

Qur'an, 23, 64

Randau, Robert, 100–1, 236n8
rape, 134
Raynal, Pierre, 41
religious identifiers, suppression of, 112
Rodney, Walter, 52, 54
Rogers, Rebecca, 141–2
Romans, Roman Empire, 123
assimilationist attitude, 227n45
decline of, 52
and Latinisation, 52
occupation of the Maghreb, 71–2

Sabatier, Camille, 148
Said, Edward, 1–3, 11, 21, 26–8, 47
Sari, Mohamed, 210
schools *see* colonial schools
science/philosophy, Islamic, 75
Sebbar, Leïla, *La Seine était rouge*, 213
secularism, French
   and the Maghrebis, 59
   and religious identifiers, 112
   see also colonial schools
Segalla, Spencer, 62, 63, 113–14
self-Orientalism, and Occidentalism, 4–6
settlers, European, 46, 69–70, 217
   colonialist ideology of, 60–2, 161–2, 195–6
   representations of, 102–4, 109, 128, 171–3, 179
   see also land appropriation/expropriation
Shari'a laws, 138
slaves, slavery, 49, 52, 74, 78, 84–6, 134, 231n8
Smati, Mahfoud, 175
smoke-outs, 45–6, 225n22
social sciences, and Orientalism, 20
Spain
   occupation of the Maghreb, 83
   Reconquista (1492), 73, 91
   see also Al-Andalus
Stora, Benjamin, 45, 68, 189
subaltern, literature of the, 197–201, 211
suffrage (French women's), 160, 239n5
Syria, Umayyad dynasty, 21

tattoos, 148
teachers, 105, 114–15, 141–3
Le Tell (settler's journal), 44
terror/terrorism, 31, 32, 33–4, 78, 194, 207–8; *see also* smoke-outs
The Thousand and One Nights (1704–17), 24–5
theatrical performance, 209
Thoral, Marie-Cecile, 45–6
Tibawi, Abdel Latif, 25–6
tourism, and self-Orientalism, 5–6
Tours-Poitiers, Battle of, 24
transcultural space, 14

Tunisia, 230–1n83
   assimilationist project, 55
   Évolués (indigenous elite), 63
   French conquest/colonisation of, 73, 74
   Ottomans in, 73
   popular resistance in, 78
   Roman relics in, 72

UFA (Union des Femmes d'Algérie), 163
Umayyad dynasty, 21
universal values, 113, 114

Vergès, Jacques, 30, 182, 224n67
vernacular Arabic literature, 72, 76–9, 80, 92

Watson, William E., 47, 74
Wattar, Tahar, 209–10
White Fathers, 55, 59, 228n54
White Sisters, 55, 56, 144, 146, 228n54
women/girls
   Algerian feminist movement, 162–5
   alienation, 181, 183
   as cultural custodians, 100–1, 120, 139–40, 180
   education of, 140–3
   essentialist representations of, 28
   French, suffrage, 160, 239n5
   heroism/resistance of, 130, 131–2, 145–6, 161, 240–2n21
   literacy, 60, 155
   Oriental, representations of, 15–18, 28, 41, 121, 125–7
   public unveiling of, 164–5
   as subaltern, 129
   testimonies on the Algerian War of Independence, 211
   veiling/seclusion of, 130, 135, 136, 161, 164–5
   violence/persecution against, 126–7, 129–30, 131, 134–9
   whiteness as ideal, 110

Yacine, Kateb, 209, 211–12
Young Algerians, 63, 92, 155, 162, 175–6, 184–5 191; *see also Évolués*

Zawāyā, 53–4

EU representative:
Easy Access System Europe
Mustamäe tee 50, 10621 Tallinn, Estonia
Gpsr.requests@easproject.com

www.ingramcontent.com/pod-product-compliance
Lightning Source LLC
Chambersburg PA
CBHW050212240426
43671CB00013B/2304